The Other Shore

The Other Shore

ESSAYS ON WRITERS AND WRITING

Michael Jackson

UNIVERSITY OF CALIFORNIA PRESS

BERKELEY LOS ANGELES LONDON

University of California Press, one of the most distinguished university presses in the United States, enriches lives around the world by advancing scholarship in the humanities, social sciences, and natural sciences. Its activities are supported by the UC Press Foundation and by philanthropic contributions from individuals and institutions. For more information, visit www.ucpress.edu.

University of California Press
Berkeley and Los Angeles, California

University of California Press, Ltd.
London, England

Library of Congress Cataloging-in-Publication Data

Jackson, Michael, 1940-

  The other shore : essays on writers and writing / Michael Jackson.
     p.   cm.
  Includes bibliographical references.
  ISBN 978-0-520-27524-9 (cloth : acid-free paper)
  ISBN 978-0-520-27526-3 (pbk. : acid-free paper)
  1. American fiction—20th century—History and criticism. 2. English literature—History and criticism. 3. English language—Writing.
4. Authorship. I. Title.
  PS379.J23   2012
  813'.509—dc23   2012030150

22   21   20   19   18   17   16   15   14   13
10   9   8   7   6   5   4   3   2   1

Man is that which is incomplete, although he may be complete in his very incompletion; and therefore he makes poems, images in which he realizes and completes himself without ever completing himself completely.

OCTAVIO PAZ
The Bow and the Lyre

To be alive and to be a "writer" is enough.

KATHERINE MANSFIELD
Journal

Even in a personal sense, after all, art is an intensified life.

THOMAS MANN
Death in Venice

All that we do
Is touched with ocean, yet we remain
On the shore of what we know.

RICHARD WILBUR
"For Dudley"

CONTENTS

PREFACE

I considered myself a writer long before I completed a volume of poetry, wrote a novel, or published an anthropological monograph. Writing, for me, was a way of life. As for the origins of this calling, I suspect that it was a longing to connect with places, people, and periods of history that lay beyond the provincial town in which I came of age. Fascinated by exotic worlds, I saw writing as my means of transport and escape. Writing, I came to realize, was a *techné*,[1] like prayer or ritual, for bridging the gulf that lay between myself and others. In this sense, writing resembles religion, which also works at the limits of what can be said, known, or borne, entering penumbral fields of experience where the absent is made present, the distant becomes near, the inanimate appears animate, and the singular subsumes the plural.[2]

In the half century since my first book appeared,[3] I have witnessed—and adjusted to—mind-boggling transformations in communication technologies. I have switched from fountain pen to typewriter to word processor. In the early '60s I worked as a letterpress machinist before the offset press made me redundant. Nowadays, books are published online and read on electronic tablets.[4] But while many claim that these new technologies are "disruptive," undermining and transforming the way we work and live, I see them as "sustaining" what we have always sought to do[5]—bearing witness to what we learn of life, struggling to express it adequately, and comparing our findings with the findings of others.

Yet ours is, undeniably, an information society. We move about with our heads in clouds of data. E-mail, Skype, Facebook, and LinkedIn keep us in touch with scattered friends, family, colleagues, and collaborators. We cross streets with cell phones pressed to our ears, or stand on the sidewalk using earphones and microphone to talk unselfconsciously to an invisible other, oblivious to those around us. Though ethereally elsewhere, we can always be located. No one has to guess where we are, where we have come from, or where we are going; the details are relentlessly tweeted, twittered, blogged or e-mailed. We pass the time playing *interactive* games *alone*, unsurprised by this apparent contradiction in terms. Our most banal opinions can be accessed by all and sundry. Our perverse yearnings, romantic longings, and wild imaginings are disseminated without a moment's thought. Hardly a month passes without some new App or device promising still faster and more fantastic means of making connections. The safe storage of personal files is no longer entrusted to memory, which is fallible, but to cryptic facilities with multiple backups. Our computers are not simply extensions of our brains, they have minds of their own, and dictate the terms on which we comprehend our own psychology. As books morph into e-books, read on iPads, Nooks, and Kindles rather than printed pages, machines translate our spoken words into visible signs. In *The Idea of the Holy*, Rudolph Otto used the phrase *mysterium tremendum* to capture the awe, humility, and fascination we feel in the overpowering presence of "the wholly other."[6] Technology now inspires the mixture of rapture and dread once associated with the divine. The critical tension in our lives is no longer between the sacred and the secular, but between the divine and the digital. When Nicholas Negroponte, cofounder of the MIT Media Lab, retired in May 2011, he spoke of the "digital revolution" that had occurred during the previous 25 years, as "a revolution that is now over. We are a digital culture."[7] But perhaps our infatuation with the new blinds us to our continuities with the old. To what extent are we dealing with "digital affordances"[8]—new ways of doing old things? Which among the new technologies (biogenetic, prosthetic, robotic) can be said to *utterly* transform our sense of who we are and what life means? This question has always been asked about novel technologies, from the knotted cord to the hieroglyph, from the manuscript to movable type, from the typewriter to the word processor, from the telephone to the cell phone. There is a long tradition in scholarship of seeing oral and literate technologies of communication as betokening essentially different sensibilities and essentially different ontologies. It is argued that the transition from orality to literacy entails a dramatic transformation in consciousness in which words cease to sing,[9] intellectuality becomes divorced from feeling, the arts of memory atrophy, vision is privileged over all other senses, thought becomes independent of conventional wisdom, and the reader is alienated from his or her community.[10] These arguments are often informed by a romantic view that oral cultures enshrine a more ecologically balanced and socially attuned mode of existence in which the life of the community takes precedence over the life of the mind—as in Walter Benjamin's lament that modernity prefers information processing to storytelling, data to wisdom,[11] an echo of Socrates' conviction that writing is a phantom, undermining memory, poisoning/drugging the mind, and leading us astray.[12]

The shock of the new leads us to confuse means and ends. We assume that a technology of communication actually determines the character of what is communicated. The medium is the message. Yet, before the digital revolution there was always more than met the eye—subliminal signals, nonverbal nuances, ambiguities, unspoken intentions. There was always a cloud of unknowing in the ether that surrounded us and obscured the space between us. There was always a gap between a speaker and his or her interlocutor. The monk hesitated over his manuscript as the student now panics at the sight of a blank page. Some small betrayal was implicated in every attempt to speak one's mind, recount an event, or faithfully pass on a piece of news. Convinced that history is marked by radical discontinuities, one worldview giving ground to another, we fall into thinking that every new invention *fundamentally* alters our lives when, in fact, it may simply enable old goals to be met in new ways. Is a story written with a quill pen basically different from a story written on a typewriter or word processor? Is the life of a reader so very different from the life of someone listening to an oral tale? Did literacy bring about the atrophy of face-to-face social life? Does text messaging diminish the quality of a teenager's life? In this book, I am interested in the rite in writing. My argument is that writing is like any other technology of self-expression and social communication, and that in exploring the lifeworlds of writing and writers we discover the same existential imperatives that have always preoccupied human beings, regardless of their cultural or historical circumstances—the need to belong to lifeworlds wider than their own, to feel that they can act on the world rather than merely suffer its actions upon them, and to express what seems peculiar and problematic about their own experiences in ways that resonate with the experiences of others.

ONE

The Other Shore[1]

WALTER BENJAMIN ONCE OBSERVED THAT our human gift for
seeing resemblances "is nothing other than a rudiment of the powerful
compulsion . . . to become and behave like someone else."[2] But our capacity
for recognizing what we have in common with others, let alone connecting
with them, appears to be as limited as our capacity for putting experience
into words. The blank page confronts the writer like the face of a stranger.
Though we cling to the belief that we can read one another's minds or mimic
reality in art, the gaps between us, like the gaps between words and the world,
can never be closed. "Always it is not what I say but something else."[3] "All is
not as it seems."[4] Anyone who lectures for a living will recognize this experience. No matter how painstakingly one prepares a talk, it will draw comments that bear no relationship to what one thought one was saying and
attract questions that preclude any response.

But lecture halls and classrooms aren't the only places where we pass each
other like ships in the night, and should an alien anthropologist visit earth
he or she would undoubtedly be struck by our extraordinary capacity for
talking past each other and not catching each other's drift. At the same time,
our imaginary anthropologist would surely be baffled by the different meanings that attach to the same gestures in different cultures—a nod signaling
negation in Greece but affirmation in England, direct eye contact convey-
ing sincerity of interest in America but antagonism in Polynesia and Africa,
touching taken as an unwanted invasion of a person's private space in some
societies but in others communicating empathy. Not only would our alien
anthropologist wonder at the mutual misunderstanding and downright misery that spring from the inherent ambiguity of everything human beings say
and do in the presence of one another, he or she would also be astonished by

the energy devoted to reducing this ambiguity and dealing with the fallout from never knowing exactly what others are feeling, thinking, or intending.

If our alien strayed into a university, he or she might be amazed at the industry generated by the passion for rational, systematic, unambiguous knowledge of others and of ourselves, and he or she might wonder how human beings have managed to succeed in the Darwinian struggle for survival, given their Babel of mutually incomprehensible languages, dialectics, and argots, not to mention their capacity for misreading one another's gestures and minds. But our visiting ethnographer might ask a more fundamental question: Why would well-educated earthlings set such store by the idea of knowing the other, or knowing themselves, when social existence is manifestly not predicated upon theoretical understanding, any more than meaningful speech is predicated upon a formal knowledge of grammar. Indeed, theories, like prejudices, would seem to be one of the principal causes of misrecognition, since they tend to make the other an object whose only value is to confirm our suspicions or prove our point of view. As long as mutually congenial outcomes occur, our alien anthropologist might argue, it does not matter whether one begins, or ends, with a clear understanding of what one is doing, an empathic understanding of the other, or even knowledge of oneself.

Is writing also a matter of working in the dark? Of trying to cross the wide Sargasso Sea that separates us from what we call the wider world? One thing is sure: regardless of *what* we write, the very act of writing signifies a refusal to be bound by the conceptual categories, social norms, political orders, linguistic limits, historical divides, cultural bias, identity thinking ,and conventional wisdom that circumscribe our everyday lives.[5] In a Nigerian prison cell, Wole Soyinka scribbles fragments of plays, poems, and a memoir between the lines of books smuggled to him from the outside. "In spite of the most rigorous security measures ever taken against any prisoner in the history of Nigerian prisons, measures taken both to contain and destroy my mind in prison, contact was made."[6] In a novel decreed obscene when first published in 1856, Gustave Flaubert writes Emma Bovary into existence, famously declaring, "Madame Bovary, c'est moi." For thirty-one years, Marcel Proust commutes in his imagination to Illiers-Combray, and the year he dies (1922) James Joyce publishes *Ulysses,* his epic return through lost time to the Dublin of his youth.

After many years of searching for the opening sentence of the book he wanted to write, Gabriel Garcia Márquez realizes "in a flash" while driving to Acapulco with his wife and children, that he would "tell the story the way [his] grandmother used to tell hers,"[7] and so emerged the figure of José Arcadio Buendía, who dreams and then builds a luminous city of mirrors surrounded by water.[8] Coincidentally, the story of Macondo, which is also the story of Columbia, recalls a story by Jorge Luis Borges in which a stranger disembarks one night from a bamboo canoe on an island in a river, wanting "to dream a man with minute integrity and insert him in reality."[9] This "magical project" exhausts his soul, and leaves him wondering whether reality is brought into existence by our dreams or we the dreamers are the dreamt.

In the act of writing, as in spirit possession, sexual ecstasy, or spiritual bliss, we are momentarily out of our minds. We shape-shift. We transgress the constancies of space, time, and personhood. We stretch the limits of what is humanly possible. And we overcome the loneliness of being separated from the other, the stranger in whose shadowy presence we dwell. "Again and again, writes Octavio Paz, "we try to lay hold upon him. Again and again he eludes us. He has no face or name, but he is always there, hiding. Each night for a few hours he fuses with us again. Each morning he breaks away. Are we his hollow, the trace of his absence?"[10]

These boundless waters into which writers, like fishermen, cast their lines or, like shipwrecked mariners, consign their bottled messages, are the haunts of lost soul mates, remote societies, other epochs, myriad divinities, half-forgotten events, and unconscious processes. But in every case, what moves us to write (and read what others have written) is an impulse to broaden our horizons, to reincarnate ourselves, and "satisfy our perpetual longing to be another."[11]

Although Maurice Blanchot wrote of the impossibility of literature[12] and Walter Ong dismissed the writer's audience as "always a fiction,"[13] the passion and paradox of writing lies in its attempt to achieve the impossible[14]—a leap of faith that bears comparison with the mystic's dark night of the soul, unrequited love, nostalgic or utopian longing, or an ethnographer's attempt to know the world from the standpoint of others, to put himself or herself in their place. For every writer—whether of ethnography or fiction—presumes that his or her own experiences echo the experiences of others, and that despite the need for isolation and silence his or her work consummates a relationship with them.

For Orhan Pamuk, a writer "is a person who shuts himself up in a room, sits down at a table and alone turns inward; amid its shadows, he builds a new world with words." But no sooner have we shut ourselves away, Pamuk says, than we "discover that we are not as alone as we thought." We are in the company of others who have shared our experiences. "My confidence comes from the belief that all human beings resemble each other, that others carry wounds like mine—that they will therefore understand. All true literature rises from this childish, hopeful certainty that all people resemble each other. When a writer shuts himself up in a room for years on end, with this gesture he suggests a single humanity, a world without a centre."[15] Asked whether solitude was essential to a writer, Paul Auster answered in a similar vein. "What is so startling to me, finally, is that you don't begin to understand your connection to others until you are alone. And the more intensely you are alone, the more deeply you plunge into a state of solitude, the more deeply you feel that connection."[16]

D. H. Lawrence pursues a similar train of thought in a letter to his friend the barrister Gordon Campbell in March 1915.

> I wish I could express myself—this feeling that one is not only a little individual living a little individual life, but that one is in oneself the whole of mankind, and one's fate is the fate of the whole of mankind, and one's charge is the charge of the whole of mankind. Not me—the little, vain, personal D. H. Lawrence—but that unnameable me which is not vain nor personal.[17]

In the same letter, Lawrence says, "each of us is in himself humanity," an opinion shared by some anthropologists,[18] myself among them.

But the gap between particularizing and universalizing perspectives is notoriously difficult to close. How can we be sure that the connections and continuities we posit between ourselves and others are not projections of our own limited view of the world? And how can we overcome the suspicion that often stays a writer's hand, that the words and ideas he or she deploys with such artistry constitute a sleight of hand that creates the appearance of connectedness where there is none?

> The knowledge imposes a pattern, and falsifies,
> For the pattern is new in every moment
> And every moment is a new and shocking
> Valuation of all we have been.[19]

TWO

The Red Road

I WAS NOT THE FIRST ADOLESCENT POET, nor will I be the last, to adopt Arthur Rimbaud as an alter ego. In Rimbaud's resolve to be other than he was, I found legitimacy for my own revolt against bourgeois values. Often drunk and confrontational, and possessed by a perverse desire to be different, I cultivated an uncouth and anarchic persona, yet all the while unclear as to what kind of metamorphosis I wished for myself.

It is not possible, of course, to simply walk out on yourself, discarding your first identity as a snake sloughs off its skin. You do not know the secrets for changing your life; all you can do is search for them.[1] What governs you is a craving for "new affections, new noises",[2] and you are aware that this work you do on yourself is more fundamental than any work of art. Indeed, Rimbaud's writing may be read as a commentary on this *oeuvre vie,* in which poetry will be written only for as long as it takes for the *personal* change to be effected, whereupon the work of language will come to an end.

For several years you are in limbo. Breaking free, hitting the road, living rough, only to return to the place you set out from to lick your wounds and prepare for another journey into the unknown. But you are stricken by the realization that no matter how far you travel from home, the old self goes with you, refusing to be shaken off by the trick of changing your environs. As Horace put it, 'Those who chase across the sea change their skies but not their souls.'[3] And so you resemble one of Joseph Conrad's restive characters, drifting from one remote island or port to another, no sooner arrived than departed—whether in flight from or in search of something, no one knows.

At twenty-four, Rimbaud is working as an overseer in a quarry on Cyprus. "The heat is oppressive," he writes in a letter to his family, and the work is hard—dynamiting rocks, loading stones onto barges, living miles away from the nearest village, tormented by mosquitoes, sleeping in the open by the sea. His life is like a rehearsal for Africa.[4]

At twenty-four, and without the benefit of any rehearsal, I went to Africa as a volunteer with the United Nations Operation in the Congo. I had expected some kind of conversion. Watching the lurid sunsets from the Stanley Memorial high above the Congo River or hearing alarmist reports of insurgencies in the interior, my imagination took fire. But my thoughts turned constantly to home. When the rains came, I retreated to the Palace Hotel overlooking the Congo River and wrote a novel as much to prove myself capable of the sustained and lonely labor demanded of any writer as to unburden myself of recurring dreams of my grandparents' early married life after their migration from England to New Zealand in 1906. I imagined that in abandoning what they called "the old country," they were oppressed by nostalgia as well as unsettled by the backwater town in which they now had to make their home. In their separation trauma I wrote about my own, for was I not both enthralled and intimidated by the vast hinterland out of which the great river flowed? And were not my dreams of New Zealand daily reminders of how deeply I resisted the ordeal of passing from the life I had known into this new but unknown life that I associated with Africa? Day after day I wrote in my hotel room as islands of hyacinth slipped past in the swift-flowing river and refugees gathered at a landing stage shaded by mango trees, waiting for the rusty ferry that would return them, by order of the Congolese government, to Brazzaville, whose white colonial buildings were barely discernible through the haze.

When you are starting out as a writer, you tend to write about the inner turmoil and difficulty of expressing yourself, even when appearing to be writing on some entirely objective topic. This was certainly true of my early piece called *The Livingstone Falls* that conjures the thunderous and unnavigable stretch of water between the Stanley Pool and the lower reaches of the Congo.

I cross a fragile and swaying bridge between two islands, buffeted by spray. I greet two women who are gathering driftwood, their babies asleep on their backs, their voices drowned by the noise of the river. I find myself in a disused quarry and wonder if I have stumbled on that "vast artificial hole" that Conrad describes in *Heart of Darkness*,[5] whose purpose was "impossible to divine," but whose remorseless excavation had cost the lives of countless Congolese, chained together in forced labor and in death. A dead Mamba lies on the trail, an embodiment of that old injustice. I drive back to the city and a café on the Boulevard du Trente Juin. Peddlers show me ivory ornaments, carved tusks from elephants slaughtered near Lac Leopold II, bone ornaments blackened with shoe polish, hand-painted postcards, black market cheese, canned fruit, and cigarettes.

One weekend, a Dutch friend and amateur lepidopterist asked me to accompany him to Pic Mensi, a forested uplands in the Bas-Congo. Hank laid out his baits in a forest clearing—fermented mangoes mixed with his own feces. We watched and waited as rare blues, every bit as brilliant as the ultramarine windows in Chartres Cathedral, fluttered and drifted through shafts of sunlight before settling nervously to feed.

Hank netted several, and showed me how to handle them, gently squeezing the life out of their bodies before transferring them to a collection box. Each one, he explained, was worth a small fortune on the European market. But this was not why he collected them. He was enthralled by their beauty and fascinated that such beauty had evolved simply to attract a mate, so that in a lifetime of no more than a few days, these creatures were driven by little else than the exigencies of reproduction. Their own life had no other meaning than to create another life, to perpetuate their kind.

We camped that evening on a grassy plain. As night fell, a young man passed up the track, holding a *mbira* on his head and playing a melody that seemed to mingle with the stars. A warm wind murmured in the long grass.

In the middle of the night I woke to hear an animal splashing across a stream, crashing into the forest beyond. Unable to sleep, I walked out into the grassland and lay on my back, looking up at the stars. I was ecstatically happy. And yet, when I contemplated the conditions that had made that moment possible (Hank's passion for butterflies, the fruit pulp and fecal matter that he carefully prepared to capture them) and the sheer contingency of things (the swallowtails that survived his net because they were far more common than the brilliant blues, the lives of insects, sustained only for as long as it took to breed, and the countless ants gutting the fallen bodies, tearing the veiled wings, filing away with them along the forest trail), all this conspired to suggest that my happiness had been won at someone else's expense, and that simply by being in the Congo I was participating in, and perhaps perpetuating, a history of terrible wrongs. And I remember the longing I felt, as we drove past the village of Bibwe and onto the main road to Léopoldville—to live in such a village, to get to know its people, to give up trying to change the Congo for the better and suffer the transfiguration of myself.

Not long after my excursion to Pic Mensi, a dusk to dawn curfew was imposed in Léopoldville. At ONUC[6] headquarters, several "nonessential" personnel packed up and flew back to Geneva or New York. Travel outside the city was banned. Some of the Haitian girls at Le Royal responded to the curfew by throwing all-night parties. It was fun for a while. A welcome distraction. I would drive my jeep home at dawn. Women would be walking along the side of the road with basins of manioc, firewood lashed with lianas, and bundles of clothing balanced on their heads. I felt like driving out of the city and into the interior, as far as I could go.

I had a companion for a while. A girl I met in a nightclub called Le Carousel—*une fille de joie*. We would spend the evenings drinking and dancing in the hotel bar, and the nights at cross-purposes. I tried to persuade Sophie to take me on a visit to her home, but her life was off limits, like her real name.

> Lips caked with lipstick
> and the smell of booze
> you dance with the man with 10,000 francs
> until the music moves him to
> take you to the room where the rite will be.
>
> Preferring him not
> to put out the light
> you remove a bonnet of dead women's hair
> beneath which you jealously preserve
> stiff braids of an African coiffure.
>
> Down to your silken underthings
> and his own undoing scarcely seen
> you are the cur under midnight heat
> of a mad dog doing it
> for what in Europe would have been love.

Then I met Dominique at one of the Haitian parties, and I thought I was in love with her. But love was as tantalizing and elusive as the villages I romanticized, the lifeworlds I longed to enter, the rites I wanted to see, the masks I wanted to try on, the drums I wanted to hear.

She was French, and married to an entrepreneur. They had an apartment in Parcembise—a suburb inhabited, in colonial times, by Léopoldville's élite. Its streets were shaded by jacarandas. Villas were enclosed by high walls, topped with broken glass and barbed wire. Behind wrought-iron gates, guard dogs salivated, bared their fangs, and barked at Congolese passing up and down the street. The air was scented with frangipani and bougainvillea.

I was oppressed by the contradictions. The beauty and order that accompanied such entrenched inequality. The civilizing mission that masked racism, violence, and delirium. I thought of the rare blues in the forests of Pic Mensi, lured to their death by a white man's feces.

How could I be in love with someone whose lifestyle seemed like a studied insult to the servants who made it possible? How could I attend the cocktail parties at Dominique's when the man who served us drinks had to support his family on the pittance he was paid? How could I stand in the same room as the gangly Australian complaining about the roadblocks, telling us that the Congolese had been in the trees so long that they all wanted to be branch managers? How could I give friendly pats to the dog that had been trained to fly at the throat of any and every black man? And how could Dom respect a husband who was doing everything in his power to obstruct her brother's marriage to his Rwandan fiancée?

Though I had been admitted to this social circle on account of my color and my work, I nonetheless tried to stand apart from it. Like Sophie, I suppose, keeping from me her thoughts, her family, her village, her name.

It was about this time that the Congolese Prime Minister, Moïse Tshombe, hired an Irish-born mercenary, "Mad" Mike Hoare, to lead a group of 300 South African mercenaries against the rebel Simbas in the eastern Congo. The rebellion was momentarily and violently suppressed, but it took a terrible toll. As the mercenary columns drove along potholed roads between tall brakes of elephant grass and through remote villages, they made no attempt to discriminate between friend and foe. An African was a savage: stupid, ungovernable, and untrustworthy. And so the mercenaries opened fire on whoever hindered their progress or was seen as a potential threat or simply happened to be in the wrong place at the wrong time.

With Kasai "pacified," I was dispatched to the region on a reconnaissance tour, to see whether any ONUC projects had survived the war.

I remember the stench of death. Outside Albertville, there were corpses on the roadsides. Emaciated dogs fought over the bloated bodies, snarling and scavenging. In the main street, not a building remained unscathed: windows had been smashed, interiors looted, buildings torched. The town was deserted, save for groups of gun-toting boys in ill-fitting fatigues, half-crazy on hemp, who mimed what they would do when they got their hands on anyone who had consorted with the rebels.

One afternoon, I went down to the lake. Though the dead had now been buried, the sand hills were still littered with shell cases and scraps of clothing.

A small boy approached me with cupped hands. He was indistinguishable from all the other orphans that begged or hung about us as we worked, except he was alone like me, in a place where no one now set foot, and he held out his hands in fatalistic submission. I said I had nothing, but if he accompanied me back to town I would find him some food. I asked, as one did through habit, the pointless question, Where is your family? And he told me, as if I needed to know, that they were all dead.

That night he slept outside my billet, and for the next two days he dogged my heels, until it was time for me to leave.

He wanted to come with me. "That isn't possible," I said. "I have to go far away. I cannot take you."

As I crossed the tarmac to the UN C-130, he clawed at my sleeve, imploring me not to desert him.

On an airplane, high above the Katangan plateau, looking down at the deceptively peaceful manioc gardens, red roads, and thatched villages, I told myself that he was better off in that place where he had a life, than in any mission or orphanage where I might have taken him. But he followed me just the same—his spectral presence weighing on my mind—because he had offered me my only opportunity for redemption in that dark time, my one chance to make a difference. And every time I thought of him, I experienced my appalling passivity and impotence, like a dead albatross around my neck.

Like Rimbaud, I finally found my second self in Africa, though I remained haunted by the impossibility of ever really losing myself in that so-called dark continent, shucking off my first life like a suit of ill-fitting clothes. Strange, therefore, that one of my first Congo poems should use the same image that appears in Rimbaud's enigmatic line, "You follow the red road to arrive at the empty inn."[7]

The Red Road

The red road led to nowhere I could go
Nowhere was a village I would never know
For days I drove companionless along it
The forest had no horizon
I wore a mask of red dirt
The wheel steered me
My body ached

At night I lay awake in terror at the night
People everywhere
Saw to me with the same indifference
They shared their food
I passed through country
Only on a map
And came back along the same road
Nothing in particular fulfilled
The red road led to nowhere I could go
Nowhere was a village I would never know.

It is often overlooked by those who mourn or are mystified by Rimbaud's contemptuous dismissal of poetry that the man who spent much of the last ten years of his life as a trader in the interior of Abyssinia became as well versed in local custom as any ethnographer—acquiring fluency in local languages, "orientalizing himself," and becoming respected for his knowledge of the Qu'ran and Islamic philosophy.[8]

As I would discover in the Congo, the red road did not necessarily go nowhere. But to find those unmapped destinations I would have to abandon the purposes that first drove me down that road, and learn to ask directions from those who lived along it.

———

THREE

Kindred Spirits

HANK KLOOSTERMAN PICKED ME UP at Léopoldville airport when I first arrived in the Congo, and he dropped me off there ten months later. The same hot wind that gently battered me on that first journey into the city still flowed over the grasslands as if nothing under the sun had changed. But I had changed, or been changed, in ways I could not yet fully understand, though an unexpected encounter in the airport departure lounge on the day I left for France gave me a glimmering of what I now know.

Only a week before, I had been summoned to a conference in Le Royal—the large apartment building that the UN had commandeered as a center of operations. The newly appointed Head of ONUC's Département des Affaires Sociales was clearly irked by reports he'd heard of my lackadaisical attitude toward the aid and development projects to which I had been assigned. He gave me a choice between "buckling down and justifying my existence" or returning to England. In the preceding months, I had become increasingly disenchanted with the hidden agenda of the UN mission, regarding it as a continuation of colonial policies, but had not had the courage to quit. Gifford's ultimatum relieved me of the burden of choice. Moreover, I could always blame him for throwing me out, and absolve myself of my indifference to the humanitarian ideals to which my UN colleagues paid lip service.

I was surprised, therefore, to meet Mrs. Gifford at the airport, and learn that she too was on her way back to England. Her children were in a boarding school there, and she was going to visit them.

I had met her briefly at a cocktail party when she and her husband arrived. She appeared to be sympathetic to my desire to live closer to Congolese people and not impose Western values on them, and she seemed to have a genuine, if maternal, interest in my welfare. Now, with a long wait for our Sabena flight to depart, we fell into conversation.

I was curious to know why her husband was not there to see her off, but did not broach the matter. But she was well aware of the circumstances that had led up to my abrupt departure, and apologized for her husband's insensitive handling of my situation.

"What will you do now?" she asked.

"I have no idea. I would like to return to Africa in some different capacity. Not go prying into places where I have no business of being."[1]

It was soon evident, as we talked on, that Mrs. Gifford shared my misgivings about the kind of work to which her husband had dedicated himself. My first thought was that Mrs. Gifford was, like me, skeptical about the good that comes of foreign interventions in the affairs of poor nations, or the manner in which Euro-American and Soviet interests had turned Africa into a cold war zone. But her criticism was more personal, and I was taken aback that she should confide to a twenty-four year old stranger her disillusionment.

Before their posting to the Congo, the Giffords had spent several years in Cyprus, also with the United Nations. During this time, their two older children were in an English boarding school. But the two younger children, aged four and six, had been with them in Cyprus.

"We are both Christians," she said. "In fact we met at a church social. But I am afraid we differ in what our faith requires of us. For my husband, it demands unconditional devotion to the well-being of others, even to the extent of taking refugee children into our own home, regardless of the health risks to our own children. It may be that I have never fully understood Christ's call or example. But there is a limit, especially for a mother, to what she can give others without compromising her own children. Even sending our two daughters to boarding school was, for me, an act of abandonment. Our sensitive, vulnerable, seven and eight year old girls, packed off to England filled me with such guilt. But my husband was, and remains, adamant. It will do them no harm. He left home at the same age. It toughened him. It prepared him for the work he now does for the greater glory of God. But tell me, Michael, is God's glory greater than the happiness of a child, or the bond between a mother and her daughters?"

I was too young for this moral burden. The questions were beyond me.

Mrs. Gifford saw my difficulty.

"I am so sorry. What am I doing, offloading my tribulations onto you? You have enough to worry about. How selfish of me."

We were sitting on an upholstered bench. A dying aspidistra, an unswept parquet floor, and a slow-moving ceiling fan provided a tawdry backdrop. Gathering around us, silent, unobtrusive and shell-shocked, were thirty or more nuns recently rescued by Belgian paratroopers from the rebel-held city of Stanleyville.

Also distracted, Mrs. Gifford looked at the refugees and felt ashamed.

"What *they* must have been through," she said.

I envied them. I had only glimpsed the war. And I too felt ashamed that I was leaving the Congo unscathed, that I had avoided my baptism of fire. *Et j'étais déjà si mauvais poète/Que je ne savais pas aller jusqu'au bout....* [2]

I told Mrs. Gifford of my journeys to the interior. I cannot remember how she responded, though I think I know why I confided in her. My experiences echoed her own. It was my clumsy, makeshift way of telling her I understood her dilemma—torn between protecting those closest to her and offering succor to strangers with contagious diseases. Had I known, at this time, of Orwell's essay on Gandhi, I might have cited it.

> For the seeker after goodness there must be no close friendships and no exclusive loves. Close friendships, Gandhi says, are dangerous, because "friends react on one another" and through loyalty to a friend one can be led into wrong-doing. This is unquestionably true. Moreover, if one is to love God, or to love humanity as a whole, one cannot give one's preference to any individual person. This again is true, and it marks the point at which the humanistic and the religious attitude cease to be reconcilable.[3]

We did not board the aircraft together, or sit together, or seek each other out at Le Bourget to say goodbye and exchange addresses. I remember the throng of reporters and cameramen trying to interview or photograph the nuns and priests who had been rescued from Stanleyville. I remember the sudden cold, my regret at having left the Congo, and the long taxi ride to my old hotel at 8 rue de la Harpe in the cinquième.

I sat in the back seat, dog-tired, reluctant to talk. The driver, recognizing this, or thinking I did not speak French, kept his thoughts to himself, though I could see he wanted to talk.

His right arm was missing. He held the wheel with his left hand, and steadied it with the two stainless steel fingers that were his right.

I wondered whether he'd lost his arm in the war, and how he'd managed to get a license. Though the Citroën had automatic shift.

Our eyes met in the rear view mirror. He had a Gauloise stuck in the corner of his mouth, and his face was screwed up in a permanent squint against the smoke. He looked like a man with a sense of humor and a lot of goodwill. I felt myself relaxing into the seat as we drove along the river toward the old quarter.

Notre Dame was floodlit. In its dark moat, the Seine was slicked with oily light.

It was raining now. Quai des Grands-Augustins. Rue Saint-Jacques.

At the corner of the Boul'Mich, we stopped for a red light. A group of students hurried across the intersection, bundled in coats.

They were laughing, and their faces were wet with the rain.

The driver half turned to me, and made a small gesture with his steel hand. "Les jeunes s'amusent!"

That morning, I bought a Spirax notebook and wrote of that solitary boy under the bruised rainy season skies over Lake Kivu—asking myself why I had forsaken him, who had no one dependent on me, unless it was my own undeveloped self crying out to be mentored, toughened and matured, so that it could come into its own. And with masochistic nostalgia I recalled the opening lines of A. R. D. Fairburn's "Rhyme of the Dead Self."

> Tonight I have taken all that I was
> and strangled him that pale lily-white lad
> I have choked him with these my hands these claws
> Catching him as he lay a-dreaming in his bed.

FOUR

Writing under the Influence

ITALO CALVINO OBSERVES THAT WHEN WE READ, "we measure our-selves against something else that is not present, something . . . that is . . . past, lost, unattainable, in the land of the dead."[1] This was certainly the case for me in Paris. I plunged into reading Blaise Cendrars as if my life depended on it. Feverishly, I sketched a work of fiction about an imaginary figure that I had glimpsed in the pages of Cendrars' *Moravagine,* Gide's *Voyage au Congo,* and Conrad's *Heart of Darkness.* And there were moments, late at night, when I felt as if I was co-authoring Cendrars' posthumous work, channeling him, a custodian of his afterlife.

The story of *Moravagine* echoes its author's biography, which in turn kalei-doscopically reminds one of Arthur Rimbaud. Rimbaud died a few months after the amputation of his right leg; the narrator of *Moravagine* loses his left leg in the war, and in a Cannes hospital he encounters the writer Blaise Cendrars who has had his right arm amputated.

Born Frédéric-Louis Sauser in the small watch-making city of La Chaux-de-Fonds (its two other famous sons were Le Corbusier and Chevrolet), Cendrars spent much of his childhood on the move. When the family returned to La Chaux-de-Fonds in 1901 and Freddy's father enrolled him in a trade school, the fifteen-year old rebelled. Truant and restive, he ran up bills at local wine shops and kiosks, subscribed to dirty magazines, screwed around, and yearned for the exotic elsewhere he had glimpsed in Alexandria, Genoa, Naples, Brindisi, London, and Paris. Locked in his room one night by his anguished father, Freddy stole out of the house "like a sleepwalker," sick in his stomach at the thought that he might never return. He boarded the first train out of Neuchâtel and ended up in Basel. From there he picked up a train to Berlin. After traveling aimlessly around Germany for several weeks, he arrived in Pforzheim and fell in with a Warsaw Jew and jewelry merchant called Rogovine. Together they headed east toward Russia and the first tremors of the revolution.

Cendrars' Russian journeys would become immortalized in his epic of the open road, *The Prose of the Trans-Siberian:*

> Back then I was still an adolescent
> Barely sixteen though my childhood was already half forgotten
> Sixteen thousand leagues from my birthplace
> In Moscow, city of the thousand and three bell towers and
>   the seven stations
> And I couldn't get enough of those seven stations and the
>   thousand and three towers
> My adolescence so ardent and crazy
> That my heart burned, by turns, like the temple at Ephesus
>   and Moscow's Red Square at sundown
> My eyes reconnoitering ancient roads
> Though I was such a lousy poet
> I did not know how to push myself to the limit, to go as far
>   as I had to go.

In Paris a few years later, Cendrars declared the Hôtel des Étrangers his true birthplace and called for the complete erasure of his past. Since fire and ash are universal images of rebirth, and one's previous life must be reduced to ashes if the phoenix is to rise, the young poet coined his name for its associations of embers, cinders and auto-da-fé. With Nietztsche's smoldering lines in the back of his mind—*Und alles wird mir nur zur Asche/Was ich liebe, was ich fasse* (And everything of mine turns to ashes/What I love and what I do)'—Cendrars was also aware that Blaise and braise were near homonyms, and that the sobriquet Cendrars ironically merged ashes (*cendres*) and art (*ars* in Latin, as in arson).

Moravagine was first published in 1926. Raymond, the narrator, is a psychiatrist, recently transferred from Paris to the luxurious Waldensee Sanatorium near Berne in Switzerland. Rather than dismiss disease as essentially morbid, Raymond believes that what we classify as pathological conditions, and seek to combat or cure, are transitory, intermediary, and potential states of health. As such, they should be allowed to run their course. Conversely, "What is conventionally called health is nothing more or less than a temporary aspect of a morbid condition, frozen into an abstraction."

One of the patients confined in the Sanatorium is a certain Moravagine, allegedly the sole surviving heir of the last King of Hungary. Moravagine was admitted after murdering the prepubescent princess to whom he had been betrothed. Though Moravagine's appearance is pitiful, even imbecilic, his voice is seductive. "It possessed me completely. I felt an immediate and irresistible liking for this tragic and singular little effigy who dragged himself along within his iridescent voice like a caterpillar in its own skin." Moravagine becomes the means whereby Raymond will realize his views on the nature of disease. He will liberate this monster and accompany him out into the world. "At last I would live on intimate terms with a great human fauve, watching over, sharing in, accompanying, his life. Steeped in it. Participating in it . . . studying it." And so, for several years, this improbable pair travel the length and breadth of Europe, much as Cendrars did in the company of Rogovine, getting caught up in the Russian Revolution, traveling through America, and winding up in the Orinoco before returning to Paris and the maelstrom of the First World War.

It did not take me long to see that the book I planned to write had already been written. What would endure, however, was a fascination with what it means to be possessed by another, by the shadow side of oneself, and how one might understand the connection between the characters that take over a writer's life and the personae he or she might take on. *Africa* was, finally, my simile for these neglected or nocturnal aspects of myself [3]—the stillborn or unrealized aspects of my own personality that I wanted to explore, steep myself in, participate in, and study,

But even this search for myself in an Other had been anticipated by Cendrars. In his endnotes to *Moravagine* he writes:

> I don't believe there are any literary subjects, or rather that there is only one: man.
>
> But which man? The man who writes, of course. There is no other subject possible.
>
> Who is he? In any event it's not me, it is the Other. *"I am the Other,"* Gérard de Nerval writes under one of the very rare photographs of himself.
>
> But who is this other?
>
> It doesn't much matter. You meet someone by chance and never see him again. One fine day this guy resurfaces in your consciousness and screws you about for ten years. It's not always someone memorable; he can be colorless and without character.

This is what happened to me with Mister X—Moravagine. I wanted to start writing. He had taken my place. He was there, installed deep down in me, as in an armchair. I shook him, struggled with him, he didn't want to trade places.

He seemed to say, "I'm here and here I stay!" It was terrible. I began to notice that this Other was appropriating everything that had happened in my life, assuming character traits I thought of as mine. My thoughts, my favorite studies, my tastes, everything converged on him, belonged to him, nourished him. At great cost to myself, I fed and reared a parasite. In the end I no longer knew which of us was copying the other. He took trips in my place. He made love instead of me. But he never possessed any real identity, for each of us was himself, me and the Other. Tragic *tête-à-tête*.

Which is why one can write but one book, or the same book again and again. It's why all good books are alike.

They are all autobiographical. It's why there is only one literary subject: man.

It's why there is only one literature: that of this man, this Other, the one who writes.

FIVE

A Typewriter Collecting Dust

I CAME BACK TO NEW ZEALAND FROM the Congo in the same frame of mind in which my literary heroes returned from their excursions to the ends of the earth—impatient to get away again. My plan was to pay my parents the money I owed them for my fare home then go to Vietnam as a war correspondent. That was before I met Pauline. At first, I was caught between the Scylla of being utterly free and the Charybdis of losing myself in love. Yet I knew from the moment I set eyes on her which imperative would win out. I recalled hitchhiking south of the Congolese border a week before Northern Rhodesia became Zambia, and the refusal of the Southern Rhodesian immigration officials to allow me to cross the Zambezi.

With my passport now bearing a stamp that gave me seven days to leave Northern Rhodesia, I began my long trek back to the Congo. For hours on end I sat in the dissembling shade of an acacia, waiting for a car to pass. The sun beat down. I was parched. Nothing moved in the stony landscape. I picked up a pebble and made it a talisman. Days later, in the last town before the border, looking for something to read, I bought a copy of Rider Haggard's *She* in a local dairy. It nourished the idea that had taken root in my mind, that I was destined to meet someone who would change my life. Despite my many moves by plane, by train, or on foot, from the Congo to France, France to England, England to Greece, I kept the pebble and the book, and showed them to Pauline a few days after we met. I don't think she believed in omens, and she was appalled that I should identify her with the mysterious white queen, Ayesha, the all-powerful "She who must be obeyed," but the spirit of my story held true.

I took work as a relief teacher in a Wairarapa high school, hitchhiking back to Wellington every Friday to spend the weekend with Pauline. In my free time during the week, I tried to write. Poems about the Congo.[1] An essay on the Congolese painter, Albert Nkusu. An occasional piece of journalism, or a translation of something by Blaise Cendrars.[2] But I could make nothing substantial of these fragments, and confessed my frustration to my old mentor, Herman Gladwin.

Herman immediately threw three questions at me. "What is your aim in writing? Have you anything to say? Do you want to build or destroy?"

Feebly, I asked what he meant by "destroy." "Masturbating," he said. "Feeling sorry for yourself. Wishing you were somewhere else, or someone else."

I recalled the fin-de-siècle Viennese poet Hugo Von Hofmannsthal whose "Letter to Lord Chandos" describes the despair of a writer who has become so disenchanted with language that he can longer write. In the late 1960s, something akin to Von Hofmannsthal's "inexplicable condition" afflicted me. At first I suspected that my inability to write stemmed from a disenchantment with language that would only deepen in the years to come—a doubt that words could ever capture or convey a sense of the life one lived or the world one lived in but would only gesture pathetically and longingly toward experiences that remained forever beyond one's grasp. Most writers are all too familiar with the sense of disillusionment and disgust that overwhelms them when they return to passages that they believed to have captured the vitality of an event only to find no trace of what had been so vividly in mind during the act of writing. Some, like T. S. Eliot, have likened the poet's "intolerable wrestle with words and meanings"[3] to the existential plight of humanity, waiting for God to reveal Himself, to illuminate the dark cold and the empty desolation[4] of life on earth. The fictitious Lord Chandos, whose "inner stagnation" imposed on him "a life of barely believable vacuity," admits to being able to keep his despair from his wife and servants, going about his business as if nothing untoward had occurred, "rebuilding a wing of his house" and "conversing occasionally with the architect." But I was not sure how long I could pretend that I had not lost my way in Dante's selva oscura.

That summer, I rented a house in the Wairarapa, and when Pauline had finished her exams in Wellington, she came to live with me.

The paddocks were dry, divided by dark green shelterbelts. The heat shimmered above the road, distorting the landscape as if it were behind molten glass.

Late one afternoon, we drove to the Tauherenikau River in a borrowed car. After swimming, we threw ourselves down in the long grass. Fantails flickered in the manuka. Red commas of flax flowers punctuated the bush.

I confessed that I could not live with the thought that I could not write. Pauline consoled me with the words of Trollope. "They are most happy who have no story to tell." She reminded me of the stories we don't have a hand in making. How they affect us more deeply than the stories we tell ourselves.

I was not consoled. It would take me years to realize that writing must be allowed to come to us, like life itself, and not be hassled into answering our summons. And yet an immense happiness flooded through me in that arid landscape, dusk already falling on the ranges, the river out of earshot and the moon rising. I was in love. The past had no hold on me. There was nothing outside that moment.

When we returned to the car, the dark green world of night birds and foliage was tinged with the spilled milk of the moon. Pauline said she would like to walk into the night, to sleep under the stars, bathed by the moon.

"Bitten by mosquitoes," I added.

I drove slowly along the darkened road. Once, our headlights startled a rabbit that bolted ahead before swerving suddenly into the grass.

I knew now that if I were to become a writer I would need something real to write about. My essay on Nkusu failed because I had known him only in passing. Like my other Congolese sketches, it went nowhere because the experiences that inspired it were fugitive and fragmentary.

I became convinced that ethnography would provide the depth of engagement that I had sought, but not found, in the Congo. Ethnography would give me a pretext for returning to Africa. It would give me the raw material with which to write. My "spoils," as Conrad put it. In the meantime, I would turn to translation. I would attach myself to Blaise Cendrars as he had attached himself to Moravagine. "—Hypocrite lecteur,—mon semblable,—mon frère!"[5] And I would begin by writing about not being able to write and the reasons why a writer might voluntarily desist from writing and prefer silence.

In the summer of 1938, Cendrars was planning to circumnavigate the world in a four-masted sailing ship when war intervened. Following the fall of France in May 1940, he retired to Aix-en-Provence and three "agonizing years of silence."[6]

In Aix, he lived alone. In the kitchen of his small apartment, a portable Remington collected dust. His books remained unopened, though he immersed himself in the life of Joseph of Cupertino, the patron saint of aviators—probably because his two sons, Odilon and Rémy, were fliers. In his garden he grew some salad greens and medicinal herbs. Though editors and journalists implored him to write, he wrote nothing.

There are certain events and experiences of which we choose not to speak. Not because they hold us in thrall, stilling the tongue. Nor because we fear they might reveal our flaws or frailty. Still less because we feel our words can never do them justice. Silence is sometimes the only way we can honor the ineffability and privacy of certain experiences. And so, in silence, we dwell upon, rather than seek to override or alter, the way things are. This, said Miriam Cendrars, was why her father could never write his book on the life of Mary Magdalene.

Cendrars would always refer to this work as his "secret book." Entitled *La Carissima,* it was a fictional life of Mary Magdalene, "the lover of Jesus Christ, the only woman who made our savior weep."[7] Though the book was never written, Cendrars considered it "the most beautiful love story and the greatest love that have ever been lived on earth." But the same experiences that compelled Cendrars to write this book also demanded silence. "His silence was its truth," writes Miriam Cendrars. "Had he written it, it would have been, for him, a negation of this truth. Its truth is preserved in his silence."[8] One thinks of Wittgenstein, who fought in the same war as Cendrars, though on the other side. "Whereof one cannot speak thereof one must be silent. . . ."[9]

On August 21, 1943, Edouard Peisson, a friend ("une main amie") and fellow writer, dropped in on a regular visit. The men chatted about mundane things, then fell to reminiscing about the war. It was the spark that touched off a fire, for that same day Cendrars dusted off his Remington and began the first of his three great autobiographical novels.

I read *L'Homme Foudroyé*[10] in a Livre de Poche edition when I was living in the Congo in 1964. The novel begins with a letter to Edouard Peisson, who was also living in Aix. This letter, which explains how a visit from Peisson inspired Cendrars' return to writing, would become a text to which I would return many times in the years ahead, for it was a touchstone, a luminous example—in its tone, phrasing, and evocations—of how I wanted to write. Translating it into English and mindful of how much of its beauty is tarnished and betrayed in this process, I am no longer in the Wairarapa but back in Elizabethville, recalling the spellbinding impression these paragraphs made on me when I first encountered them.

> My dear Edouard Peisson—this morning, you told me that the German officer who has been billeted at your place in the country came looking for you in your kitchen last night so that you might observe a perfect eclipse of the

moon, only to leave you lying flat on your back while he went up to his room with an unlikely-looking whore he'd picked up in Marseilles . . . and you had remained there, alone, on the terrace, long into the night, contemplating the defeat . . . and you ended by saying how outrageous it was, the night heavy with dew and silence, the moonlight, the silver and black olives, the warm air perfumed with grass and pines on the encompassing hills, this star-filled August night, so clear, so silent, so peaceful, and this guy screwing his whore in your house. What humiliation!

As soon as you left, my dear Peisson, for reasons I cannot fathom, I began mulling over what you had just told me, and moved by these nocturnal reflections I found myself recalling other nights, equally intense, that I have known in different latitudes, of which the most terrible was the one I lived through, alone, at the front in 1915.

It was also summer and a beautiful starry night, though not the translucent sky of Provence but outside Roye, on a northern plain, among fallow fields and rank grasses, untended for more than a year, from which a milky aroma arose . . . opaque, ethereal, frayed . . . with stars riddling the landscape like ink spots on a torn piece of blotting paper, and everything becoming ghostly . . . no longer a moon in the sky . . . I was chewing a blade of grass . . . and the eclipse that I observed then, as you will see, was an eclipse of my very identity, and it is a miracle that I am still alive . . . this fear, that I have never spoken of to anyone yet would have confided to you in an instant had you been still around. Indeed, I leaned out the window just as you turned the corner of the street, perched on your bicycle. But with no chance of calling you back, rather than run after you I dusted off my typewriter and impulsively began writing the present narrative for you, my dear Peisson. You will understand my feelings, knowing that since June 1940, and in spite of your warm and frequent encouragement, and the self-interested solicitations of newspaper and journal editors—not to mention the misery my inactivity caused me—I have never written a line.

My dear Peisson, because you are the unwitting cause of my return to writing, allow me not only to pay homage to you in my opening story, but to consider you from today the godfather of my future work. I very much hope that you will do me the honor of accepting this title that is neither honorary nor gratuitous since it carries so much of the responsibility.

Even though I wish you to assume this responsibility, I ask myself how your brief visit this morning could release in me such a shock wave that I set about writing without a moment's hesitation, and why I returned to writing today of all days. I have no answer to this question. But everything you recounted, of the night, the sky, the moon, the landscape, the silence, stirred in me so many memories, including echoes of the war whose presence pervaded your bitter reflections and the invasion of your privacy by a German lieutenant who not only abused your hospitality, violating your house with a common whore, but robbing you of your refuge as a writer. Then I was fired, in my solitude, for to write is to be consumed by fire.

Writing ignites a welter of ideas and throws light on chains of images before reducing everything to flickering embers and crumbling ash. But though flames set off a fire alarm, spontaneous combustion is a mysterious process. For to write is to be burned alive as well as to be reborn from the ashes.

SIX

Writing in Limbo

NOT LONG BEFORE PAULINE AND I WENT to Sierra Leone, a story broke in the English *Sunday Times* about the fate of an English yachtsman called Donald Crowhurst.[1] His trimaran ketch, *Teignmouth Electron,* had been found adrift in mid-Atlantic. The life raft was lashed in place, the helm swung freely, and the sails lay folded on the deck ready to be raised. But Crowhurst had vanished.

Three blue-bound logbooks on the chart table revealed what had befallen him.

On October 31, 1968, Crowhurst had set sail from Teignmouth, Devon, in a bid to win the Golden Globe single-handed round-the-world race. His trimaran had been built and equipped in a hurry. There had been no time for intensive sea trials, and Crowhurst had sailed late with his course unplanned. To make matters worse, hatches leaked, steering gear malfunctioned, and the electrics failed. The reasonable course would have been to abandon the voyage. But loathe to admit defeat, Crowhurst began to work out an elaborate deception in which he would calculate and radio false positions, giving the impression that he had rounded the Horn in record time and was making excellent progress across the Pacific. In fact, he was sailing in circles in the South Atlantic, well away from shipping lanes, awaiting an opportune moment to announce that he had reached the Cape of Good Hope and was again in the Atlantic on the final leg of a circumnavigation of the globe.

What brought Crowhurst to the realization that he would never be able to pull off the deception? Inconsistencies in his carefully forged logbooks? Guilt over having deceived those who loved him and had supported his enterprise? Doubt in his ability to remember every detail of his concocted story and remain consistent in everything he said on his return to a hero's welcome in England?

In the ineluctable silence and solitude of the sea, the yachtsman began to lose touch with reality. Entangled in the web of lies he had spun, he saw that his voyage was doomed. By the time he sailed into the Sargasso Sea, he had retreated into a wholly private world. Becalmed, and having lost all track of time, he began to imagine that he could leave his body at will and make himself divine. Surrounded by a debris of dirty dishes and dismantled radios, he penned one of the last entries in his log:

It is the end of my

game the truth

has been revealed

A few minutes later, he climbed the companion ladder to the deck, then stepped off the *Teignmouth Electron* into the sea.

As Pauline and I stepped from the aircraft, the hot soup–sweet African night enveloped us. My body felt swollen. My shirt stuck to my skin. Inside the airport terminal, African bodies pressed around us, pungent and cloying. It took two hours to get our passports stamped, to reclaim our baggage, and to clear Customs. We moved in a state of torpor, saying nothing, as if we were strangers to each other.

It was after midnight by the time we got away from the airport. Lightning flashed along the Bullom shore, and the humid air was heavy with the stench of decomposing vegetation and the sea.

In the taxi, the breeze through the open windows revived me. But I was beginning to rue the promise I'd made to my friend Alex Guyan in London. Alex had insisted that when we arrived in Freetown we stay at the City Hotel. Graham Greene had killed a lot of time there during the war, and Alex was an avid fan of Greene's. It amused him to think of me sitting on the same balcony where Wilson sat at the beginning of *The Heart of the Matter*, "his bald pink knees thrust against the ironwork . . . his face turned to the sea."

I asked the taxi driver if he knew the City Hotel. Sure, he knew it. He could take us there for only thirty leones. It sounded like a lot of money, but I didn't know the exchange rate and, besides, it was a bit late now to negotiate our fare.

Too tired to take anything in, we crossed the Sierra Leone River on a throbbing ferry and were driven through labyrinthine streets, lit by braziers and flickering oil lamps. By the time our taxi set us down outside the City Hotel, our minds were in a fug and we had lost track of time.

In the darkness, the wind thrashed at the palms in the hotel forecourt. Thunder rolled and caromed in the peninsular hills.

We found the main entrance to the hotel barred by a metal grille, and the shuttered windows showed no signs of life. Already we were wishing we had taken the airport bus with the other whites and gone to the Paramount Hotel, even though the cost of a room there would have been prohibitive, and even though we had vowed to steer clear of tourists, to plunge straight into Africa and keep our promise to Alex.

I shouted up at the dark and decaying concrete facade. "Anybody there?"

A first-story window was wrenched open, and a woman called down to us in Krio. At the same moment the rain came bucketing out of the sky.

Pauline and I must have looked ridiculous, soaked to the skin, with our shoes awash in the floodwater sluicing down the street.

The woman at the window was joined by others. They laughed and shouted down at us.

"We don't speak Krio," Pauline shouted back.

"Wait," the first woman said, "I dae kam."

They all traipsed down, dressed in miniskirts, shrieking with laughter. They held beach umbrellas above their heads to protect their jet-black wigs from the downpour.

They wanted a dash.

I dug in my pockets and came up with some English coins. The women took them gleefully and ran around to the front of the hotel, beckoning us to follow.

The lobby was feebly lit. Off to the left was a deserted saloon bar. Ahead was a flight of wooden stairs. The prostitutes clattered up the stairs in their high heels and fishnet stockings, gales of laughter going into the darkness, the smell of cheap perfume lingering in the clammy air.

When the hotel porter emerged from the shadows, bleary-eyed from his interrupted sleep, I explained that we had come in on the London flight and wanted a room.

"Kam we go," he ordered. Dragging a bunch of ancient keys from his pocket, he started to climb the stairs, using the banister to pull himself up. Pauline and I lugged our suitcases after him.

Our room was at the end of a dingy corridor on the first floor. It was furnished with a double bed under a torn mosquito net, two chairs, and a chest of drawers. The room stank of mildew and excrement.

I went into the bathroom. The toilet hadn't been flushed, nor would it flush. When I pulled the chain, there was a noisy gurgling in the pipes and a mess of paper pulp and shit disgorged into the stained bowl.

We were too tired to care. I bolted the door and we stripped off our wet clothes, toweled ourselves dry, and crawled under the mosquito net onto the bed where we lay jarred and spent from our journey. I thought: We have done what Alex wanted us to do. I can write him tomorrow and say we have experienced Greenland in all its seediness. Then we can find somewhere else to live.

We woke at first light to the jangle and blare of hi-life music. I went to the louvered window and looked down into the street. Several Toyota and Datsun taxis were parked at an angle to the curb, and the drivers were washing their cars with buckets of sudsy water. I was reminded of the way young men in the Congo used to wash their bodies, soaping themselves until they were all but invisible for lather.

Beyond the intersection, over laterite stonework and rusty roofs, I glimpsed the sea. Far out, a sunken freighter showed only its funnel and mastheads above the surface of the ocean. It must have gone down during the war, when Atlantic convoys used to assemble in the harbor. I made a mental note to mention this in my letter to Alex.

"What are you looking at?" Pauline asked.

I told her about the taxi drivers and the sunken freighter on the sand bar. Then I asked if she felt like getting up and going downstairs, to try to find something to eat.

"Don't even talk about food," Pauline said. She was suffering from morning sickness. She felt as if she were going to throw up.

"We'll move out of here," I said.

"At least let's get a room with a toilet that flushes. I'm going to try to get some more sleep," Pauline said. "If you go out, try not to make too much noise when you come back."

I lifted the mosquito net and kissed her on the mouth.

I went out of the room thinking we should not have come to Africa. I felt sick in the stomach at the thought of Pauline pregnant and having our baby in such a place. I should have called it off, this year in Sierra Leone doing fieldwork for my Ph.D. I should have come alone or not at all.

In the downstairs dining room, some retired Krio clerks were eating breakfast. No one looked up as I walked in.

When the waiter asked if I wanted an English breakfast, I made the mistake of saying yes, and was served braised spam, glutinous eggs, and chips fried in rancid oil. The cook had been with the hotel since colonial times. Like the ex-clerks in their English serge and bowlers, his menu parodied the world that Sierra Leoneans had once been encouraged to emulate.

I had no appetite for the food in front of me and was beginning to think that my dream of returning to Africa, which had sustained me for five years, had been as absurd and anachronistic as the idea of Empire. When I tried to imagine myself in a remote village, speaking an African language, asking people to tell me about their lives, a terrible sense of despair came over me, such as Malcolm Lowry described in his story 'Through the Panama': "the inenarrable inconceivably desolate sense of having no right to be where you are."[1]

In the days that followed, I filled my notebooks with such misgivings, panicking whenever I thought of the journey I had embarked upon. And each night I was tormented by the same dream, in which I wandered disoriented in an immense building, looking for a room where I was supposed to enroll.

Pauline grew impatient with me, and recollected the series of events that had brought us to Freetown *together*—the month we had spent in Copenhagen where she did an intensive course in Danish, the modern language most akin to Old Icelandic, the weeks in Paris waiting for a sailing from Le Havre to West Africa, and finally the flight back to London when she fell ill, and where, in the course of an operation to remove an ovarian cyst, she was found to be six weeks pregnant. "I want to be here," she assured me. "I want to have our baby here, in this climate, with you!"

Vultures wheeled high above the city. In the street markets, peddlers cried, "Biscuit dae! Five five cents." We tried out our Krio, "Omus for da wan dae? Omus for dis," buying pineapples, bunches of bananas, and scoops of groundnuts wrapped in funnels of brown paper. We went to Immigration to get our visas. In the piss-soaked alley outside the Immigration Department, a sign had been posted: URINATING PROHIBITED IN THIS AREA. We found a pharmacy with the improbable name of Vulga Thera.

Beggars crowded around us. Some leaned on staves, their legs like burnt matchsticks. Paraplegics sat in little carts and shoved themselves along on their knuckles.

Pauline pressed coins into the fingerless hands of a burnt-out leper. In the street, a Toyota Coaster moved slowly through the traffic, a logo above the cab saying SWEET ARE THE USES OF ADVERSITY.

Now reconciled to remaining in our hotel, we sat on the hotel balcony in the cool of the evening, drinking tonic water and writing postcards home. The sad-eyed Swiss proprietor, who had run the hotel in Graham Greene's time, limped to and fro behind the bar.

Our waiter was a thickset man with a coarse-featured, morose face. He derived unending pleasure from prying caps off bottles of Star beer with a grand and sweeping gesture, then watching as kids scrambled around his feet, fighting for possession of the bottle tops. If there was a blue star printed under the cork inlay, you won a prize.

"Fortunes are precarious here," I wrote to Alex. "We met a deaf mute boy on the street today who thrust a scrap of paper under our noses and urged us to read what was written on it: 'Good morning I am no hable to spick and I can not find chob Please will you help me Tankyou God pless...'"

I was going to add something about the inescapability of poverty when I became aware that a boy was standing close to me, watching me write.

"Kushe," I said, and hoped he would go away.

He said his name was James. He had been attending school but could not continue because his family did not have the money to pay his fees. He begged us to help him out.

"Wusai you dae?" I asked.

James said he lived in the East End. His expression wavered between shiftiness and shame.

"Can you come and see us in the morning?" Pauline said. "If you bring your school books, I can get some idea what you've been doing."

James said he would come early. Then he announced that he was going, and disappeared into the street.

"Do you think he's on the level?" I asked.

"I've no idea. Does it really matter?" Pauline said.

A couple of days later, I was lying on the bed in our hotel room reading Melville's *Typee*. Pauline was sitting at a desk near the window, turning the pages of a cheap *cahier*, correcting James's exercises. James stood stock-still beside her, chewing his fingernails.

"Do you prefer reading books or listening to stories?" Pauline asked.

"I like to read books," James replied.

"Why?"

"Because they're true."

"Do your mother and father tell you stories?"

"Yes."

"Do they tell you stories about Conny Rabbit?"

"I know those stories."

"Aren't those stories just as interesting as the ones you read in books?"

"No, people always tell them in different ways and change them, and you never know which one is true."

"Aren't they more exciting and interesting like that—when they're different every time?"

James shook his head.

"Why not?"

"Because you never know which one is true."

"Are all books true?"

"Yes."

My ears were ringing. I was bathed in perspiration. I pushed through the crowded streets, determined to finalize the business of getting our Land Rover released from Customs. But no sooner was one obstacle overcome than another arose. Day after day, I trudged from one Port Authority office to another, collecting Customs clearance certificates, import-duty exemption authorizations, set surcharge forms, insurance schedules, shipping notes, delivery and condition reports, and certificates of importation and release. Then there were letters of affiliation to the university, residence permits, vehicle registration and insurance, a driver's license, more visits to dismal offices where clerks sat slumped over their desks and some taciturn minion would want his palm greased with a dash.

I began to think seriously of abandoning my plans to do field work. I imagined myself holed up in the City Hotel, drawing on my scholarship money to write an ethnography of an entirely fictitious society. The task did not seem too daunting. The Fourah Bay College library was well stocked with monographs from which I could glean the formulaic patterns of structural-functionalist ethnography. To invent a society, one had only to decide the nature of the economy, the mode of descent and inheritance, and the principles of legal and political life; everything else could be deduced. Since conventional ethnographies were generally so devoid of in-depth descriptions of actual individuals, I need not concern myself unduly with details of real lives. Stereotypes would suffice. And sweeping generalizations would gloss over the subtleties of lived experience and give my account an aura of objectivity. Even the language of my make-believe world could be concocted as a dialect of some actual West African language. Hadn't Jorge Luis Borges done something akin to this in his account of the world of Tlön?

The more I pondered my idea, the more it engrossed me. But when I confided my scheme to Pauline, she said I should not let myself be disheartened by the weeks we had been stuck in Freetown. It was hard not knowing where we were going or what we were going to do, but shouldn't we give ourselves time to get acclimatized and find our feet?

What brought me back to reality was a map. The map was stapled to the wall of the corridor in the Institute of African Studies at Fourah Bay College. It showed Sierra Leone divided into tribal areas. The research I had proposed at Cambridge for my Ph.D. would have meant living among the Mende in the southeast, studying the impact of literacy on village life. I had never been entirely happy with this plan—a continuation of research I had done for my M.A. on the impact of literacy in early nineteenth century Maori New Zealand—but I had not been able to come up with anything else.

The map showed a region in the north, defined by a dotted line. Across this blank space was written KURANKO.

I do not know why I responded as I did to this map. All I knew was that this remote region was where I wanted to go. I told the director of the Institute of my plans. He said that very little was known about the Kuranko. This was all I needed to make me absolutely sure of my path. A few days later, Pauline and I loaded our supplies into the Land Rover and headed north.

A warm wind flowed through the cab of the vehicle. Grasslands stretched away under an immensity of sky. For a moment I was back in the Congo. The road behind us was lost in billows of red dust.

We were going to a town called Kabala. We were enamored of the name. It invoked the Hebrew *qabbalah* and its esoteric traditions of cosmic union. But we couldn't be sure where we would end up at the end of the day. Few roads were signposted, and north of Makeni the road degenerated into a tortuous and eroded track.

We passed through towns where people were celebrating the end of Ramadan. Women danced in tight circles, resplendent in voluminous gowns and high silken kerchiefs. Men lounged in hammocks slung under the eaves of verandas.

We crossed turbid streams where butterflies danced in shafts of sunlight. In the lophira plains, the air was singed with the smell of burned elephant grass.

I reached for Pauline's hand, and we glanced at each other and smiled.

"It's hard to believe I seriously thought of staying on in Freetown and writing a fake ethnography," I said.

"The trouble with lying," Pauline said, "is that you always have to make a mental note of everything you say, so you won't be caught out in the future. If you tell the truth, you don't have to remember anything. You are free to live."

It was then that I remembered the story of Donald Crowhurst and became aware that for as long as we had been in Freetown, this story had been at the back of my mind, casting its shadow over everything I thought and did.

SEVEN

The Magical Power of Words

FOR SEVERAL WEEKS BEFORE GOING TO SIERRA LEONE, Pauline and I had camped in the Bois de Boulogne in Paris, awaiting word of a cargo sailing from Le Havre to Freetown. It was an Indian summer, and I should have been grateful for this period of idleness. But our delayed departure only intensified the anxiety that oppressed me whenever I contemplated returning to Africa as an anthropologist. I had glimpsed this future for myself in the Congo, five years before, and it had been in Paris, penurious and disoriented, that I had begun to see that ethnography might be my vocation, my way of entering into another world, and my literary path. But now, standing in the wings, I was seized by stage fright, and I had mislaid my script.

To distract myself I would take long walks to Puteaux and Suresnes, often finding myself at the old Fort Mont-Valerien, where I would sit and contemplate the haze-blurred city, only the upper level of the Eiffel Tower visible above the smog. Or I would lie in the grass outside our tent in the Bois reading of Chagall's first enraptured impressions of Paris: "I knew I could work in this light and that my dreams would take shape in it. I was overwhelmed by it all. When I saw Seurat I was dazzled. When I saw Monet I could have wept." Yet, even in these luminous recollections, Chagall cautions that it is not art that inspires great art but immersion in the world. "Theory and technique have not enabled me to advance one step. I owe everything to life."

Our indolent days in Paris ended abruptly when Pauline fell ill. After consulting a gynecologist we were advised to return to England, where she could receive free treatment under the National Health Service. Within twelve hours of flying back to London, Pauline underwent an operation in Middlesex Hospital for the removal of an ovarian cyst, and she was found to be pregnant. While she recuperated in hospital and we rethought our plans,

I imposed on the hospitality of our friends Alex and Meg, who only a few weeks before had sent us on our way, not expecting to see us again for at least a year.

One afternoon, I came back from visiting Pauline to find Alex, Meg, and several of their friends sitting in the kitchen with cans of beer and looking as though they had just received bad news. "Come on in," Alex said. "There's a problem you might help us solve."

I was introduced to Matt, Jay, and Jay's wife and child. They all shared a house in Swiss Cottage with a guy called Andy. Andy had suffered some kind of mental breakdown; they had panicked, not knowing whether to call a doctor or ambulance or simply wait for Andy to come to his senses. In the end they had driven to East Finchley to ask Alex and Meg for advice.

"Where's Andy now?" I asked.

Matt said that Andy had locked himself in his room.

I urged that we drive back to the house immediately. I was not impressed by any of them. Jay took an aggressive stance, saying they should get Andy to move out. Matt was in a daze. "We just want to make the scene again," he said. "We want him to be the real Andy again." Jay said Andy might trash the house or even kill himself. And he was concerned that if the police or paramedics were called they would find evidence of drug use in the house, and everyone would be incriminated.

As we climbed the steps to the front door, I was as nervous as anyone. The others stood behind me as I rang the doorbell. Without any explicit negotiation it had been decided that I was best equipped to handle the situation.

Andy opened the door with an inane grin on his face.

I felt like George Orwell in "Shooting an Elephant"—the expectations of Andy's friends behind me, Andy grinning roguishly in front of me, the burden of what to do falling squarely on my shoulders. I introduced myself and asked Andy if we could talk somewhere in private.

I didn't know what to expect. As Andy led the way upstairs, the others remained downstairs, talking (so Alex told me later) about the Rolling Stones, how to procure the best weed, anything but Andy's plight.

Andy sat on the edge of his bed. I took a chair nearby and listened attentively as he told me about this organization he and the other guys had got going. It was called J.A.M.—the initials of Jay, Matt, and Andy. He then explained that my name was compatible with this acronym. MIKE—the M corresponded with the M for Matt, then I, Kay, and Ego. I warily asked who Kay was. Kay was a friend of Brenda's. Brenda was a Rhodesian girlfriend who had married another guy. B for Britain, where they were lived together and were happy, R for Rhodesia, and the END of A for Andy. As he rambled on, sharing his word salad with me (Wother, for example, was a portmanteau word, combining mother and wife) I tried to get the hang of his impenetrable logic. And Andy did his best to guide me, using such cryptic phrases as "Mental guts hanging out," and "Skeleton becomes exoskeleton." I must have listened to Andy for an hour and a half before I felt confident enough to broach with him the possibility of seeking help and to assure him that I would make all the phone calls, ensure that he was treated well, and accompany him to the hospital.

I never saw Andy again. And within ten days of Pauline's discharge from hospital we were on our way to Sierra Leone, this time by air—on a dilapidated DC8 that had a plaque on one of the bulkheads that read *This Philippine Airlines DC8 flew nonstop from Tokyo, Japan, to Miami, Florida, a distance of 8705 statute miles, in 13 hours and 52 minutes, establishing a world distance record, Feb. 22, 1962.* It made me think of Andy's schizophasia, and it brought to mind the way we deploy words magically to echo events, create semblances of order in a sea of chaos, and give the impression that we actually grasp the hidden meaning of the world in which we move, ships that pass each other in the night, or aircraft climbing above the pack ice of cloud into air so cold and rarified that if we were exposed to it we would not survive. Would the language of anthropology prove any different, or would it also be little more than another form of sorcery, restating the obvious in a nebulous language, writing more and more about less and less, losing touch with reality, confusing words and things, an arcane technique for consoling lost souls that the world was indeed within their grasp?

In Sierra Leone, where only a minority of people could read or write, some of the only text you saw outside Freetown was on the cabs of trucks or the washstrakes of canoes, succinct pleas or hopeful signs that offered the Western visitor glimpses into local preoccupations. God is Great . . . Justice . . . Nar God Go Gree [God Willing] . . . Look For Me . . . Loose You Face [Cheer Up!] . . . Judgment Day Is Coming . . . No Justice for the Poor . . . Power Vision . . . Patience Is a Virtue.

I used the last of these slogans in my first essay at ethnographic writing—an exploration of the magical power of words, and of the stoicism and patience so often characteristic of those living in the world's poorest societies.

It is not unusual for anthropologists entering the field for the first time to wind up in the company of people who have been marginalized in their own communities. So it was for me. Linguistically inept, socially disoriented, anomalous in appearance, and possessed by questions the point of which no one could grasp, it was inevitable that I would end up with Mamina Yegbe.

He was at least seventy—small, spry, and always, it seemed to me, slightly bemused. Though my field assistant warned me that Mamina Yegbe had lost his marbles, and tried to dissuade me from setting too much store by what he told me, I felt at ease in the old man's company and often sought him out at the town chief's house near the Kabala market, buying him packets of tobacco in gratitude for his tolerance of my stilted Kuranko.

"The world began in Mande," Mamina Yegbe said, alluding to the great fourteenth century empire that had dominated the West Sudan. "But yesterday and today are not the same. Whatever sun shines, that is the sun in which you have to dry yourself. We are now in the period of the white man's rule."

He remembered when this period began before the Cameroon War (World War I), and recalled the names of Palmer and Captain Leigh, who built the barracks at Gbankuma before the British moved to Falaba. He also described the first barracks at Kabala, built on the site of today's town market, and told me when the frontier was fixed, and when the Court Messenger Force and the Chiefdom Police were established. And he recounted how taxes were paid to District Commissioner Warren—or Warensi, as he was known. Initially, the annual hut tax was two shillings and sixpence, but later rose to five, then to nine shillings, and finally to one pound five shillings, and one pound ten shillings per head.

"In those days, people were happy," Mamina Yegbe said. "We were happy with our government. All the chiefs had their favorite music, and whenever the chiefs assembled, the jelibas would play. Chiefs Belikoro, Konkofa, Sinkerifa—I knew them all."

At the District Officer's office one morning, I was working through a stack of intelligence diaries and daybooks from the colonial period, hoping to corroborate Mamina Yegbe's recollections of local history. Around me the clerks were busy with their own bureaucratic chores, filing memoranda, moving dog-eared files from the "out" tray of one desk to the "in" tray of another, sharpening pencils, or fetching ice-cold Coca-Colas for the D.O.

Before being allowed to inspect the records, I had been obliged to submit five copies of an application, all typed, signed, sealed in official envelopes, stamped, and countersigned. It was not long, however, before I was ruing the effort, and my eyes wandered to the whitewashed wall where two wasps were adding yet another accretion of moist red clay to their nest and beyond the barred windows of the office where the leaves of an enormous mango tree hung limply in the heat. I closed the daybook and made to go, already anticipating a few relaxed hours at home talking with Pauline over a simple lunch of bread and peanut butter.

At that instant, two clerks deserted their desks and asked for a lift to the market.

As I switched on the ignition I caught sight of Mamina Yegbe sitting on a rock under the mango tree, smoking his Bavarian pipe with the hinged metal lid.

"Do you want a lift?" I called, and gestured in the direction of the market.

Mamina Yegbe clambered up into the front seat of the Land Rover, beside the clerks. He was wearing an embroidered tunic and a blue silk cap with a tassel and sat bolt upright with an almost smug expression on his face, holding against his chest a large manila envelope marked in capital letters ON SIERRA LEONE GOVERNMENT SERVICE. The envelope was embellished with ornate signatures and sealed in several places with red wax. It resembled a Saul Steinberg drawing.

The clerks were clearly amused by the envelope.

"What's the joke?" I asked.

The first clerk winked at me, then nodded toward Mamina Yegbe who was gazing straight ahead. The other clerk dodged the question by suddenly recognizing two friends sauntering along the road.

"Mosquito!" he yelled. "Heh! Peacecorps!" And he hung his arm out the window of the Land Rover.

A thin, gangly youth who answered to the first description, and his companion, wearing faded jeans with frayed cuffs, lifted their arms to wave, but the dust in the wake of the vehicle enveloped them.

After dropping the clerks at the market, I sought to satisfy my curiosity about the envelope.

"What is it?" I asked.

The old man continued to gaze straight ahead, but raised a finger to his lips. He then got down from the Land Rover and without a word disappeared into a crowd around the kola-nut traders.

That night I drove back into Kabala from our house at "One-Mile" to buy some cold Fanta at Lansana Kamara's bar. The bar was a shabby and poky corner room that opened onto a verandah and the marketplace. It was furnished with several warped and dusty shelves, a battered deep freeze, and five armchairs with polystyrene foam bulging out through rents in the red vinyl upholstery. The jangling strains of a hi-life hit issued from a dilapidated record player at one end of the bar. "I really love you, Fati Fatiii . . ."

Lansana Kamara did not particularly like hi-life tunes, and whenever business was slack he would get out his records from Guinea and, with tears welling up in his eyes, listen to the stirring refrains of praise-songs from old Mali.

On the walls of L.K.'s bar were several fly-speckled calendars showing beaming Africans in open-necked shirts holding aloft bottles of Vimto, Fanta or Star beer. L.K. disdained such drinks.

With a lugubrious air he poured himself another large Martell brandy and a Guinness chaser.

I bought what I wanted and was about to go when I noticed Mamina Yegbe in the corner, surrounded by a dozen boisterous youths, among them the two clerks from the D.O.'s office. One of them made a remark that I could not catch, but it drew a burst of taunting laughter from the others, and the old man shrank back as if from a blow. I saw that Mamina Yegbe was still holding the big envelope, only now it had been ripped open, and bits of sealing wax littered the floor among the beer-bottle caps.

When the old man saw me he seemed to regain his composure, but before either of us could speak one of the clerks confronted me with bloodshot eyes and beery breath.

"He says it's from Seku Touré and Siaka Stevens!" the clerk roared. "That envelope! He says they've given him a big country in Guinea and a million pounds cash! He says he's coming to the D.O. tomorrow to collect it!"

Everyone broke into laughter. Then they looked at me, waiting for my reaction.

The clerk became angry. "He says he's going to be appointed to a high position, in the government!" he shouted, as if I had failed to grasp the situation. "It's all in the letter!"

I glanced at Mamina Yegbe, who raised a finger to his lips and smiled ingenuously. I appealed to L.K. for a clue as to what was going on, but L.K. simply smoothed his knitted singlet over his enormous belly, lowered his eyes, and took another sip of brandy.

The clerk, exasperated by my stupidity, lurched over to the old man, wrenched the envelope from his hands, and shook out its contents onto the bar. L.K. dolefully moved his glass to one side as his customers pawed at the sheaf of papers, spreading them out so that I could see what they were.

I recognized several old G.C.E. examination papers, some official memoranda and letters, and a page from my own field notes. I could not think how it had come into the old man's possession.

Stabbing at the papers, the clerk drew my attention to a bundle of leaflets, all advertisements for Surf washing powder.

"This is the letter from the prime minister!" the clerk hooted. "Can't you see what it is?'"

I recalled a Volkswagen Kombi that had turned up outside the market a few days before. A large display packet of soap powder had been fitted to the roof rack, and a loudspeaker blared out hi-life tunes. Four or five men in sunglasses and pale blue shirts had gone about distributing leaflets and occasionally giving away sample packets of Surf. In the afternoon the vehicle, still crackling with canned music, disappeared in a cloud of dust up the road toward Falaba.

"Yes, I can see what it is."

I knelt down and started picking up the papers that had fallen on the floor. They were already smudged with red dirt from the clerks' shoes.

The jokers appeared embarrassed by this crazy show of sympathy for the old man. They backed out onto the porch, making half-hearted gibes and clutching their bottles of beer. L.K. stared morosely at his glass of Guinness.

"Do you want a lift home?" I asked Mamina Yegbe.

"*Awa.*"

I looked down the unlit street, thinking, the generator's gone again, and wanting to say this to Mamina Yegbe. I also wanted to ask the old man, now sitting in silence in the Land Rover beside me, if he still intended to present his letter to the D.O. and claim his fortune, but it might have seemed like another taunt. What simple faith we all place in the power of printed words, these fetishized markings on a page—the clerks, this benignly deluded old man, myself!

The headlights picked out the mosque and the grove of palms beyond it.

"I'm going back to Barawa on Friday," I said.

Mamina Yegbe made no response.

"I'll come and see you before I go."

In the darkness the town gave forth the sounds of its invisible life: a dog yelping, shouts, a radio badly tuned, an inconsolable child crying, a motor scooter spluttering down a potholed lane, the drubbing of an initiation drum.

I drew up outside the house with the broken verandah where Mamina Yegbe lived.

"*Ma sogoma yo,*" I said, as the old man got down.

Mamina Yegbe stood on the roadside in the glare of the headlights.

"In the old days people were happy," he said. Then he turned and drifted into the darkness.

Almost all his life, Mamina Yegbe lived under a colonial regime. He had imagined it to be like chieftaincy—a source of order and benevolent power. If the great chief Belikoro could conjure thunderstorms at will and slay his enemies with lightning bolts, then surely the British Crown or the Presidents of Sierra Leone and Guinea could pay him his due and make good what he was owed. The clerks in the D.O.'s office, who ridiculed him so mercilessly were no less in thrall to wishful thinking. Indeed, it was the maddeningly elusive nature of fortune in the post-colonial world that compelled them to perform their derision of Mamina Yegbe so publicly. But it was Mamina Yegbe's patience that moved me, his imperturbable faith that justice would be done. He reminded me of the so-called millenarian movements or cargo cults that flourished in Melanesia throughout the twentieth century, in which people often ceased gardening and gave themselves up to waiting for airplanes or ships that would magically deliver the material possessions that had been withheld from them, either because of some ancestral error or European chicanery. Many people were convinced that literacy held the secret to the white man's power. Rather than presume writing to be a substitute for speech, letters were regarded as possessing a sui generis efficacy, "a road to the cargo."[1] The strange thing was that anthropologists would write about these mistaken ideas without ever reflecting on the degree to which they shared similar assumptions. For did we not also believe that the arcane language we deployed and the publications that gave us such satisfaction were our roads to renown and remuneration, yet no more enduring or less illusory than the cargo cultists' fetishistic attitude toward words? Max Weber argued that "the fate of our times is characterized by rationalization and intellectualization and, above all, by the 'disenchantment of the world,'"[2] by which he meant that "ultimate and sublime values" had retreated into the intimate spheres of religious, family, and artistic existence. Writing poetry or telling stories would be for Weber, I suppose, among the last refuges of the enchanted. In which case, my kinship with Mamina Yegbe was more profound than I realized at the time I knew him, and my work of words no less a sustained magical attempt to compensate for personal inadequacies and to seek re-enchantment in a world where political economy had come to be the academic measure of most things.

EIGHT

Flights of Fancy

WHEN I TOOK A JOB TEACHING ANTHROPOLOGY at a provincial New Zealand University, some of my Cambridge friends warned that I would starve for want of intellectual stimulation and slowly go to seed. I didn't need to be reminded; I knew that my future depended on publishing abroad and reaching an audience beyond my native shores.

At the University, I generally avoided the faculty club, preferring to buy a sandwich in the student cafeteria, find a quiet spot on the campus, and eat alone. It was a pattern I'd slipped into during my school days, though now it wasn't shyness that made me keep my own company but the exigencies of writing. I wrote at home every morning before driving to the campus and needed an hour to myself in the middle of the day to take my mind off Africa. But there was always a time lag when I walked about in a daze, jotting down thoughts and images that related to what I had written that morning or planned to write next day. Often I would be startled to realize that I was staring vacantly into space, with only the haziest notion of where I was. I would snap out of my trance to see students walking along the gravel paths, descending the stone steps in the shadow of the great cedars, griping about boring lecturers and onerous assignments, or exchanging gossip about girlfriends, pop songs, and parties. I realized I was living a shadow life, absorbed in Africa, trying to recapture in words the sound and smell and sight of things I might not experience again for many years.

Sometimes it was my colleagues who brought me to my senses. Like the day I was running late for my two o'clock class on the Comparative Study of Myth, and parked my Citroën in a loading zone outside the main building. A week later I received a letter from a "Parking Committee" made up of faculty members, reprimanding me for persistently parking my vehicle in

43

restricted zones. I was asked what gave me the right to act as though I were a law unto myself.

After that I went to the staff club a few times, to put in an appearance and meet people outside my own department. Mostly people talked about television programs or the best wines you could buy locally or the intrigues of various committees they were on. I felt out of place. I was too close to the laterite roads of northern Sierra Leone or too preoccupied by the lecture I had to give on myth. Besides, I didn't watch television, have much interest in local wines, or sit on committees.

One day, a lecturer from the English Department noticed that I had borrowed Michel Foucault's *The Order of Things* from the library. He snidely invited me to explain what it was about. Not realizing that I was expected to dismiss it as bullshit and thereby relieve him of having to read it, I naïvely summarized the argument—that Renaissance thought was characterized by a compulsive search for similitudes and correspondences, but in the early seventeenth century there was a sudden turn from the quest for synthetic resemblances to analytical methods for establishing identity and difference. I then said that I disagreed with Foucault's view that the earlier paradigm was fully eclipsed by the rise of Enlightenment rationality. In my experience, the work of the imagination, including writing, is always driven by this search for signs, syntheses, auguries, blazons, analogies, and figures. "Ask anyone you know to recall the most memorable moment in his life and I'll bet he'll tell you a story about some fateful coincidence, some uncanny and inexplicable event, something that revealed a hidden connection between his life and the life beyond his immediate horizons."

I can't recall whether it was on this occasion or another that the talk got round to Antoine de Saint-Exupéry. Perhaps someone had seen a documentary on television or broached the subject of French wines. In any event, Peter Alcock, who had disapproved of Foucault, now declared that apart from *Le Petit Prince,* Saint-Exupéry had written nothing that excited real interest. I was struck by that phrase, "excited real interest," because Peter looked as if nothing had excited him for a very long time.

I said I didn't think Saint-Exupéry should be dismissed lightly, and that Saint-Exupéry had once been my favorite writer. In my late teens I had read everything by him and about him. I still remembered the revelatory impact of Saint-Exupéry's view that the visible rests in the invisible and that an author's task is to reveal unseen connections beneath the surfaces of our familiar world. Then, for some reason I still cannot fathom, I launched into an account of Saint-Exupéry's last years.[1]

When war was declared in 1939, Saint-Exupéry received orders to report for duty as a flying instructor at Toulouse-Montaudran. When he demanded to be assigned to active duty, he was reluctantly allowed to fly several reconnaissance missions over Germany, and won the Croix de Guerre for his flight to Arras in Belgium in 1940.

After the fall of France, Saint-Exupéry was demobbed. Knowing he could never live in France while it remained occupied, he made his way to America, where he endured two and a half years of isolation and inactivity. In early 1943, he joined a group of Free French sailing with the Americans to North Africa. At Oujda, the French were attached to the American Third Photo Group of the Seventh Army. The squadron was equipped with new P-38 Lightnings—fast, long-range aircraft adapted for strategic photographic reconnaissance. According to regulations, pilots had to be no more than thirty years of age, but an old friend of Saint-Exupéry's in the French Command persuaded the Americans to allow the forty-three year old Saint-Exupéry to fly.

After one successful reconnaissance mission over France he was grounded—the result of a crash-landing. He was to spend almost a year in Algiers before he was permitted to fly again. Some of his friends put pressure on him to accept desk jobs or diplomatic assignments. Others agreed that he should be permitted to rejoin his group.

"The only thing that remained were the war missions," he wrote, "a few hours spent flying over France—something of the dignity of an icy scaffold. It suited me fine. But being unemployed I have nothing to look forward to that means anything to me. Sickening discussions, polemics, slander—I'm bored by the morass I'm entering. . . . Everything is mediocre, I can't stand it. At 35,000 feet I was beyond mediocrity. Now I no longer have that outlet."

Finally, the Americans approved five more reconnaissance missions from a base at Alghero in Sardinia. Saint-Exupéry felt rejuvenated. He flew his five missions, surviving engine failure, fire on board, fainting due to lack of oxygen, and pursuit by German fighters.

In July 1944, the group was moved to Corsica in preparation for the final thrust to liberate France. Saint-Exupéry asked to be assigned further flying missions. His close friends were now desperately concerned for his safety and conspired to have him grounded.

He was permitted one final flight.

It was his tenth reconnaissance mission. Sortie No: XX 335 176. Date: July 31, 1944. Time out: 0845.

At 1 p.m. he had not returned. At 2.30 p.m., after numerous phone calls and radar and radio searches, his comrades and commanding officer knew there was no longer any hope of his still being airborne. At 3.30 an American liaison officer signed the interrogation report: "Pilot did not return and is presumed lost."

For over fifty years, no trace of Saint-Exupéry or his aircraft would be found. What came to light, however, was that the Messerschmitt pilot who shot Saint-Exupéry down over the Mediterranean unwittingly killed his hero and role model. The young German not only owned all the French author's works in translation; he knew everything that was to be known about him, and had enlisted in the Luftwaffe on the strength of his admiration of St-Exupéry's pioneering flights across the Andes and the Sahara.

I have no idea how my colleagues responded to these details, but I do remember vividly running into Peter Alcock a few days later and being taken to task for the unsubstantiated story I had told. "Where did you get all stuff about Saint-Exupéry being shot down by someone who'd read all his books?" Peter asked. "I've been through all the critical biographies in the library and I'm damned if I can find any reference to any German airman who shot Saint-Exupéry down. You sure you got your facts right?"

I told Peter I had read the story in an introduction to one of Saint-Exupéry's books. It had been an English translation. I couldn't remember the title. I said I'd try to remember more details and get back to him.

Peter phoned me at home. He'd been doing some more checking and had come up with nothing. Was I sure of my source?

"Now you've got me mystified," I said. I told him I would go through all the Saint-Exupéry books in the university library and see if I could find the one I had in mind. "It's going back a few years, though," I said. I could tell that Peter was beginning to suspect that I was putting him on.

Over the next few days, I checked through every English translation of Saint-Exupéry's works that I could lay my hands on. I also skim-read several critical biographies. I was certain I had read the story some six years before, when I was living in Wellington. This would, therefore, discount biographies and translations published since that time. To satisfy myself that I had checked everything, I lodged interlibrary loan applications for those of Saint-Exupéry's books that were not held in our own library.

In the faculty club, Peter asked me how I was faring in my scholarly search for the facts about Saint-Exupéry's death. The question brought smiles to the faces of his colleagues.

I was angry, but I also felt fraudulent, as if my reputation as a poet really did debar me from credibility as a scholar. I asked myself, if I had been so convinced of the veracity of my account of Saint-Exupéry's death—an account it now seemed I had largely imagined—then what store could be set by the ethnographic data I had collected in West Africa and was now preparing to publish? Perhaps it was true what people said about me—I should decide whether I was a poet or an anthropologist, and stop trying to be both.

That night I went home, determined to ransack my study, to go through every folder of notes I'd ever accumulated until I found the piece of paper on which I now remembered scribbling, in Wellington some time during 1968, when ill in bed with flu, the details of the story I had recounted at the staff club.

I finally found it.

There were four leaves of bank paper held together with a rusty paperclip. Dated March 20, 1968, the first page was filled with notes about my feelings at the time. . . . Lying in bed, Pauline downstairs translating sagas, her unflagging, cool meticulous routine, each day getting her quota done. Myself cut off and isolated, unable to write, like a businessman who is getting no returns.

The second page recorded my thoughts after reading Anaïs Nin's *Journals:*

I am astounded at the reception accorded them. It doesn't figure. She pretends to have written a faithful chronicle of her life for her own edification, and yet the journals are so self-consciously addressed to the world that one has to conclude that they are in part works of fiction.

The third page consisted of two quotations from Spengler that I'd copied from Camus' *Carnets:*

It was the Germans who invented mechanical clocks, these terrifying symbols of the flow of time . . .

The man who gives definitions has no knowledge of destiny.

The fourth page contained the following passage from Stuart Gilbert's introduction to his translation of Saint-Exupéry's *Citadelle:*

He took off at 8:30 on July 31, 1944; the weather reports were good, the engines running smoothly, and the plane soared lightly into the shimmering morning air, northwards towards France. At one-thirty Saint-Exupéry had not returned and his friends were growing more and more anxious, as by now only an hour's fuel remained in his tanks. And at two-thirty he still had not returned. . . . That evening a young German pilot attached to *Luftflottenkommando* 2, entering up the day's report in his logbook, wrote: "Tribun [i.e., Avignon] has reported one enemy reconnaissance plane brought down in flames over the sea." Everything points to this plane's being Saint-Exupéry's Lightning. By a curious irony of fate this German airman who, after four crashes, had been assigned to an observation post on Lake Garda, was a cultured young man and amongst the most treasured books of his library, now buried under the ruins of his hometown, were those of— Antoine de Saint-Exupéry.

Under this I had transcribed an extract from one of Saint-Exupéry's last letters:

> I do not mind being killed in the war. What will remain of all I loved? I am thinking as much of customs, certain intonations that can never be replaced, a certain spiritual light. Of luncheons at a Provençal farm under the olive-trees; but of Handel, too. As for the material things, I don't care a damn if they survive or not. What I value is a certain arrangement of these things. Civilisation is an invisible boon; it concerns not the things we see but the unseen bonds linking these together in one special way and not otherwise. . . .

It was then clear to me that the story I had told at the staff club was in part a fabrication. I had conflated the young German telephonist, whose name was Hermann Korth with the pilot who shot down Saint-Exupéry over the sea.

Another thing struck me, rereading these lost pages. All the quotations I had recorded were, in a sense, oblique commentaries upon the impossibility of drawing a hard and fast line between fact and fiction.

But I knew that Peter Alcock would not be satisfied with such a conceit.

Was I going to tell him that I'd got my wires crossed? Would I argue that my story of Saint-Exupéry's death was true to the spirit of things if not completely faithful to the facts? Would I dare suggest that we all improvise with what we remember of the past, that no one, not even the most conscientious scholar, lives his or her life faithfully recapitulating what has already been said and done? Would I add that Stuart Gilbert had got *his* facts wrong, confusing Sardinia for Corsica, misquoting the time of Saint-Exupéry's final sortie, mistranslating Korth's log report?

In the end I let the matter drop. I wrote Peter a note, saying that my search had been fruitless. I had failed to find the book, the reference or any details that corroborated my story.

Since the end of the war, various accounts have purported to explain how Saint-Exupéry's met his death. First, there was Hermann Korth's, written in 1949 when he was a theology student in Germany. Then, in 1972, another, ex-Luftwaffe pilot, Robert Heichele, published an account in a German magazine of a mission he flew over the south of France on July 31, 1944. Heichele and his co-pilot took off from Orange in Provence, and were patrolling the Mediterranean littoral between Marseilles and Menton when they encountered a P-38 Lightning flying about a thousand meters above them. Inexplicably, the Lightning descended, and Heichele maneuvered into position behind it. When the Lightning was within range he opened fire. He took another turn and again fired on the Lightning. After a third attack, the Lightning began to lose altitude. It crossed the coast, trailing white smoke. Then the starboard engine burst into flames, the right wing dipped, and the Lightning ploughed and somersaulted into the sea.

Heichele's account was corroborated by Claude-Alain Jaeger, who had been a seventeen-year-old student in Biot in 1944. Jaeger was a spotter, and he kept notes on any military activity he observed in the area. On 31 July he observed a P-38 Lightning with American and French insignia flying at rooftop height and great speed towards the open sea.

On the same day, a German defense company commander, Leopold Bohm, was on duty at a place called Tête de Chien, high above Monaco. He too observed a low-flying airplane, pursued by two others, crash into the sea.

Since all these reports suggest that Saint Exupéry's plane went down well to the west of Marseilles, it is difficult to reconcile them with a fisherman's discovery in 1998, off the coast of Marseilles, of a bracelet engraved with the name of Saint-Exupéry's wife, together with a fragment of a flying suit, or with a diver's discovery two years' later of the remains of Saint-Exupéry's Lightning P38 in the same area. Without any evidence that he was shot down, are we to conclude that Saint-Exupéry committed suicide by crashing his aircraft into the sea?

NINE

Writing Fellowship

DESPITE MODEST SUCCESSES IN PUBLISHING ethnography and poetry,[1] I nursed an ambition to write fiction, and after winning a Writing Fellowship in 1982 I went to the South of France, accompanied by Pauline and our twelve-year old daughter, Heidi, intending to rework the novel I had written eighteen years before in the Congo.

I had never found it easy to reconcile creative and academic work, much as I told myself that scholarship required imagination, and fiction achieved its greatest force when faithful to lived realities. For me, anthropology and poetry involved very different dispositions, and the transition from one to the other was never easy.

We arrived in Menton as the summer visitors were departing, and I found the challenge of writing fiction as daunting as my daughter found the challenge of attending a French lycée. On her first day, as she choked on her words of protest, "I don't want to go, I don't want to go," I felt her anguish as my own. Later that day, as we did the rounds of the local *papeteries,* buying folders, *feuilles,* and narrow-lined Spirax notebooks, she began to cheer up and take an interest. My heart went out to her. If she could adapt, so could I. I bought a notebook for myself, and wrote on the first page, "In the absence of any literary project I decided I would keep my hand in by keeping a journal. Something may come of it. If not, what matter. I need a rest."

As I let myself drift, I found myself awash with memories and dreams, sounding depths where everything was amorphous and only vaguely familiar. By day I would catch whiffs of Africa in the cloying sea air, the decaying foliage, the acrid smell of burning leaves, the stale odor of urine around the bole of a tree. The musty smell of the room in which I wrote reminded me of the old colonial barracks at Fourah Bay College in Freetown where Pauline and I lodged in the days before Heidi was born. Night after night, my dreams returned me to Sierra Leone. Kuranko friends appeared, asking why I had abandoned them. In one dream, a calamity of some kind had forced the people of Barawa to flee their homeland. In another, my friend Noah was venturing into politics. I dogged his heels, but he would not deign to speak to me. What had I done to deserve his censure? Somewhere in this dream I was negotiating a narrow path around the side of a hill, but could find no purchase on the smooth eroded surfaces.

Did these dreams disclose guilt about the self-indulgence of creative writing? Did the allusions to political events suggest that writing must have some pragmatic value?

During the exceptionally cold winter of 1938–1939, William Butler Yeats was living on the French Riviera. In the days before his death, he sat in his room at the Hôtel Idéal Séjour at Cap d'Ail, looking out to sea, perhaps contemplating the moment when he would become the person he conjures in "Sailing to Byzantium," free at last of the physical body and "gathered into the artifice of eternity."[2] At this very moment, Vladimir Nabokov was roaming the hills between Menton and Roquebrune, catching butterflies.

The political pall that hung over Europe concerned Yeats less than the journey into the afterlife upon which he was about to embark and whose lineaments he had spelled out in his esoteric work, "A Vision," inspired by spirit mediums and automatic writing. Yeats was, of course, not the first writer to believe that one's work welled up from subconscious or supernatural sources and that an author was simply a mouthpiece or medium through which such external influences found expression. It would be consoling for a writer who had lost his muse to think that inspiration would return if he or she was only patient enough, but those of us who have direct experience of these long vigils know, as Siddhartha Gautama finally realized, that impatience is incompatible with the openness required for the spirit to move us and that, moreover, our desperation may turn the spirits away. In Yeats, there is an intimate connection between his celebration of the gyre, the paratactic style of his writing, and the notion that the imagination waxes as one's life wanes.

Yeats was temporarily buried at Roquebrune before his remains were removed, under military escorts and with great pomp and ceremony, to Sligo. There he was reburied in sight of Ben Bulben, the subject of his last poem, which in its closing lines imagines the poet lying in Drumcliff churchyard, where one of his ancestors is also buried, and provides the epitaph to be cut on his gravestone:

Cast a cold eye
On life, on death.
Horseman, pass by!

When I was living on the French Riviera in 1982–83, the Hôtel Idéal Séjour was shabby and forbidding, and Pauline and I walked quickly past the padlocked wrought iron gate on our way to the Villa Les Caroubiers, where Edward Hulton and Jillian Robertson had invited us to lunch. Jillian showed us around the villa, which she was in the process of renovating. Walls had been demolished to create a large, sunlit living room and a study where Jillian could write. Downstairs, a similarly expanded space would become their dining room. We ate on the terrace. Expensive pâtés, baguettes, chilled pinot grigio, and a tossed salad in a capacious wooden bowl. The wind-smitten sea was visible between cypresses, pines, and palms. I envied Edward and Jillian their villa and view, but Jillian demurred. "Everything here is a refuge," she said. "Only people without friends or ties would come and retire here. Only those without lives would give up everything for this kind of existence. It is completely artificial. It has no basis, no roots. It is like being in limbo."

Not knowing what to make of this remark, I endeavored to bring Edward out of his shell, though it was only when Jillian urged him to tell me about his Flying Boat that he opened up to me, asking if I had ever seen a Short S.25 Sunderland. Because the Royal New Zealand Air Force had flown Sunderlands and Solents until 1967, I was not only familiar with these aircraft but used to watch them move down their slipways at Mechanics Bay and taxi across Auckland harbor before taking off to Fiji or the Chatham Islands. Astonished to have found someone with whom he could share his passion, Edward regaled me with stories of his five-year struggle to nurse an ailing Sunderland back to life, to hire pilots who could fly it, and to find slipways and hangars in Britain where the aircraft could be housed and maintained. When I ventured to ask how he could afford this expensive hobby, Edward explained that his father had founded the *Picture Post* and owned the *Evening Standard*. Edward not only bore his father's name; he had inherited his father's fortune, and had spent almost two million pounds making his Flying Boat, which he had christened *Excalibur VIII*, airworthy. It was, he said, the love of his life, a comment that proved ironically prescient as, in the months that followed, Pauline and I became more familiar with Jillian's side of the story.

After lunch we strolled down to the foreshore for coffee. Pauline told me later that Jillian had talked about her books, but confessed that her writing was on hold while she supervised the renovation of the house and settled her two-year old son Jamie into a new school. A child of Jillian's first marriage to travel writer Martin Page, Jamie had been in a private boarding school for a couple of years but had become deeply unhappy. Jillian had therefore decided to bring him to live with her and Edward at Cap d'Ail. Pauline sensed that Edward had difficulty relating to Jillian's son and that Jillian was unfulfilled in her marriage. I told Pauline I had formed the same impression while talking to Edward. I had learned that when Edward was a small boy he had been diagnosed with tuberculosis. After preliminary treatment in Britain, his parents sent him to a sanatorium in the Swiss Alps. He languished there for many months, feeling abandoned and forgotten. His parents' visits were few and far between, and though he was showered with gifts he suspected that his parents were more invested in their social engagements in Monaco, Paris, and Rome than in having him return home, even though he was completely cured. It must have been like the dark night of the soul for this child, I told Pauline, waiting for his parents to come and take him home.

In the spring of 1983, Pauline became seriously ill and we left the South of France for England. Five months later Pauline died. I wrote to friends in France and elsewhere, stunned and lost for words as I tried to explain the rapid and tragic course of events that had culminated in Pauline's death. Jillian wrote back with news of her own. She and Edward had gone their separate ways. Jillian had been suffering from an illness she described as similar to the illness from which Pauline died. But rather than support and care for her during this trying time, Edward had persisted in his efforts to get his ailing Flying Boat into the air and had also begun an affair with a wealthy stockbroker's wife in London. Jillian had symbolically ended the marriage by casting her wedding ring into the sea at Cap d'Ail. Now she was in the throes of a legal battle to remain in the Villa Les Caroubiers and claim alimony. I heard from Jillian again in 1988 when she sent me an invitation to her marriage to Angus Alan Douglas Douglas-Hamilton, fifteenth Duke of Hamilton, informing me that she was about to become Jill, Duchess of Hamilton and Vice-President of the Royal Society for the Prevention of Cruelty to Animals.

After Pauline's death, struggling to regain my hold on life, our days in Menton seemed enchanted. Not only had Pauline and I felt at home in

France; we had made new friends, had time to write, and found fulfillment in our life together. I had waited a long time for a sabbatical from anthropology; finally, I had been free to commit myself completely to fiction.

Every morning I left my apartment in Garavan, made my way along Avenue Katherine Mansfield and Chemin Fleuri to the Villa Isola Bella, once described by Katherine Mansfield "as the first real home of my own I've ever loved." Here she wrote some of her most celebrated stories. She was thirty-one when she came to Menton in September 1920, suffering from tuberculosis and other ailments. When she left for Switzerland in May 1921, she had only nineteen months to live. I liked to imagine that the Menton K.M. had known had not changed in the sixty years since her sojourn there. On the steep hillsides, terraces were planted with citrus trees. Villas were shaded by chestnuts, figs, olives, oaks, aloes, and eucalypts. You inhaled the odor of rotten figs, dry grass, pines, juniper, and cypresses. Wisteria tumbled over limestone walls. And African date palms were ubiquitous, though their fruit was inedible. I would inhale the bitter scent of crushed laurel leaves, the hot rust of railway lines, the whiff of a Gauloise, the fresh smell of asphalt in the early morning when the waiters hosed the pavement outside their cafés, my senses alive to everything around me. But there were days when Pauline feared that the cancer she had suffered nine years before had returned, and neither of us could settle to our writing. At such times, the violet blossoms and gigantic leaves of the wigandia became ominous signs that our days in Paradise were numbered, and I would avoid the Avenue Blasco Ibanez, where the shadows of cypresses lay across the road and stirred on the stucco gateway of the Fontana Rosa, the decaying mansion of Vicente Blasco Ibáñez, who wrote *The Four Horsemen of the Apocalypse*.

Fiction brings a temporary semblance of order to what is in its very nature "a fractured and fragmented world." For Lawrence Durrell, "The solace of such work lies in this—that only there, in the silences of the painter or the writer can reality be reordered, reworked, and made to show its significant side."[3] In writing a novel about my childhood, I suppose I was attempting to clear up the mystery and confusion that surrounded my origins, to contrive a resolution that had eluded me in life, and to free myself from the past. But I did not agree with Durrell when he speaks of art as a "joyous compromise," in which the imagination makes good the disappointments and defeats of our quotidian life, for stories must, despite our rage for order, retain a strong sense of the fiery furnace in which they are forged and avoid giving the impression that the patterns we hammer out in art reveal an order that lies within life itself. As Virginia Woolf reminds us, "Every day includes much more non-being than being."[4]

That I turned my hand to fiction during my year in Menton also reflected my belief that it was an art form superior to poetry and ethnography. This made my work especially arduous, postponing the day when I would wise up to the fact that fiction was not my forte. It was a biography of Norman Lewis that finally helped me understand where my talent lay. Lewis wrote fifteen novels, all now out of print, though his travel writing is still read and widely admired. But his failure to write great fiction worried Lewis throughout his career, and he appeared unable to fully admit that "his powers of invention required the pollinating gift of facts."[5] Paradoxically, Lewis was never more of a novelist "than when faced with a road drenched in the mire of actuality or a room beset with real horrors faced by real human beings," and he was at his best when confronted by an actual place or person that pulsed "with the perfect reality of an invented thing."

Had I realized all this in 1982, I could have saved myself a lot of trouble. Lines scribbled in the dead of night that would not survive the dawn. Screwed-up paper littering the floor. Long walks into the landscape to collect my thoughts.

How many mornings did I walk out of my studio, glance up at the limestone bluffs of Ormea, and take the old mule track that led from the coast to Baousset, the rain-rinsed air resinous with pines? When I paused to catch my breath, Menton was far below—the cubist roofs of the old town clustered around St. Michel, the sea ploughed by a stiff wind racing away to Italy, and the promontories of Cap Martin, Monaco, and Cabbé clearer than I had ever seen them. If only my writing could do justice to what was so freely given!

Bypassing Castellar, I take a track through broom, brambles, stunted pines, and untended olives, hoping to reach Granges St. Paul and thence one of the old smugglers' paths along the border with Italy. The air is fragrant with juniper, lantana, and fermenting figs, and not for the first time I find myself contemplating the labor that went into building those dry-stone walls, the terraces crumbling now beneath olives and holm oaks. So many lives vanished from the earth. So many untold stories.

Above me, against a deep blue sky, are the crags of Berceau. After clambering up the scree below the col, I plunge into knee-deep snow and silent pinewoods, marveling at how instantaneously it is possible to pass, in effect, from one season to another, one's mind following suit with fresh sensations and images. Five miles further on I reach Sospel. Another five and I will be in Moulinet, where Nabokov lived in 1938 in "proud emigré destitution"[6] and, on the steep slopes above the village, came close that June to fulfilling a lifelong dream of capturing a new species of butterfly. There are times when I imagine that I am struggling to create a hybrid of my own, a form of writing that balances explanation and description, saying and showing, essay and story—a writing that is without pretention, that does not seek authenticity or authority, but only fidelity to life as lived, the ways it unfolds, the ways in which consciousness oscillates between solipsism and sociability or shuttles between what is past and passing and to come.

It is midafternoon by the time I get back to Menton, too late to do any writing, too early to return home. I buy an espresso at Le Narval and sit at a sidewalk table, facing the boat harbor. A stiff wind is rattling the halyards of moored craft—a loud tinkling of metal against aluminum masts, like the chime and chatter of a Buddhist monastery.

Occasionally, on clear midwinter mornings, Corsica is visible on the horizon. Houses along the coast, dark smudges of forest. "Un trompe l'oeil," my friend Roland Ghersi calls it, pointing out that the island is too far away to be directly visible. "Des différences de densité et de température dans les couches basses de l'atmosphére tendent à courber les rayons de la lumiére provenant de la Corse et provoquent un leger effet de mirage qui améliore notres visibilité de l'île." When I explain this to my twelve year-old daughter, dipping a pencil in a glass of water and showing her how it appears bent, Heidi rejects the analogy of pencils in water and islands in the sea. She wants the substantiality of images.

Perhaps this is why it took me so long to realize that fiction is as unfaithful to life as an academic treatise, and that memory is a misnomer—a shadow cast across the conscious mind, a hypnopompic delusion on waking or falling asleep. We speak of memory as though there is something solid to which our minds return, something in storage that is retrieved. But what if the here and now is *all* that exists and there is nothing behind the screen? What if our compulsive search for closure and completeness were an aberration rather than a justification for science or art? We writers take it upon ourselves to make good the deficiencies of life, says Henry James, "to see people not only as they are but as they might be.[7] "In truth," James says, "everyone, in life, is incomplete, and it is [in] the work of art that in reproducing them one feels the desire to fill them out, to justify them, as it were."[8] I disagree. It isn't that art enables one to complete these mysterious others; rather, we round out *ourselves* in writing about them. Consider Joseph Conrad. In his

"Author's Note" to *Victory,* Conrad recalls the origins of his four main characters. Axel Heyst was a mysterious Swede whose paths crossed Conrad's for only a few days. Though Heyst left no trace of his past or his purposes, he provided Conrad with an unforgettable image of resolute detachment. As for the cadaverous Mr. Jones, Conrad encountered him lounging in three chairs on a hot afternoon in a little hotel in the Island of St. Thomas some forty years before he became the venal character in *Victory.* Ricardo was a fellow passenger on a small and dirty schooner "during a four day's passage between two places in the Gulf of Mexico whose names don't matter."[9] And Conrad met Lena, whose love for Heyst would stir him so fatefully, in a café in the South of France. In a room filled with tobacco smoke, the rattling of dominos and the music of a traveling group of musicians, Lena moved silently and somnolently among the tables, collecting money. When Conrad plots to have Lena meet Heyst, he wants her to be "heroically equal to every demand of the risky and uncertain future." Indeed, he ensures that this is so, and in view of her "triumphant end" asks if he could have done any more for her "rehabilitation and happiness." But Conrad does not broach the question as to whether, or to what extent, his stories of Lord Jim, Kurtz, Marlowe, and Axel Heyst were ways in which he sought "to rehabilitate himself."

TEN

———

There Go I

MY NOVEL ENDED AS ABRUPTLY AS my sojourn in France, and for a long time I wanted to go back to Menton and bring to a close what I felt I'd left unfinished.

On the last page of my novel I describe a local clochard.[1] Our paths crossed every day. We never exchanged a word, but I regarded him as a familiar and got to know his habits and beat by heart.

His hair and beard were grizzled and unkempt, his skin grimy and weather-beaten. Winter and summer he wore the same buttonless, stained overcoat, frayed trousers and plastic sandals. If he was a wild man, then Menton was his cage. All day he shambled along the seafront boulevard between Cap Martin and the Italian border, pushing a supermarket trolley full of rags and scraps of cardboard. He talked relentlessly to himself, berating the pavement, gesturing irritably. Mostly his eyes were averted, but if he happened to meet your gaze he would look straight through you. I thought of him as the Ancient Mariner and wondered what awful events weighed upon his mind. I imagined myself the wedding guest to whom he would one day unburden himself, and sometimes I shadowed him, going far out of my way, in the hope that eavesdropping might give me access to his story. But either he spoke patois or was mad, and in the end I had to piece together his story from hearsay.

According to Madame Picard, my *concierge,* he had been a mathematics teacher. He'd taught at the Lycée André Maurois. She hadn't the faintest idea how he'd become a drifter. You should ask your friend Ghersi, she said, he'll know.

Roland Ghersi had grown up in Menton. His parents owned a small farm on the slopes above Castellar. Roland once took me there, an exhausting climb along old mule tracks to a plateau high above the sea. Each time we stopped to catch our breath, we glanced back at Menton and its littoral huddled far below. Above us soared the eroded limestone bluffs of Berceau.

It was noon when we reached the place—a wilderness of broom and juniper. We sat in the shade of a Mediterranean pine and Roland uncorked a bottle of Gigondas. I carved slices of country bread, spreading them with pâté and sharing out handfuls of black olives. Around us, the shrilling of cicadas.

Roland wanted to know about my book. I said it was called *Rainshadow*—an image of how we live in the shadow of the past, its conspiratorial silences, its fragmentary allusions to events that shaped us but that we can never fully know.

When we had eaten, Roland showed me the ruins of the house his great-grandfather had built. The roof had collapsed long ago, and an enormous fig tree was growing through the broken masonry.

Roland regretted having let his birthright go to rack and ruin, and he kicked at the crumbling terrace in disgust.

"It isn't only places that fall apart," I said. And I mentioned the clochard who pushed his supermarket trolley up and down the seafront boulevard all day, and each night slept shrouded in his filthy overcoat outside the bureau de change at Garavan.

Roland turned his head from side to side, as if trying to pick up the sound of something drowned by the noise of the cicadas. "Yes," he said, he knew the guy, but not by name. "It was true he had been a math teacher. His wife had been killed in a car crash. He had been driving. The accident had happened on the same corniche where Princess Grace met her death."

"What else?" I asked.

"It must have unhinged his mind, his wife dying like that. He went back to teaching for a while, then one morning, in the middle of a lesson, he walked out of the classroom and never went back."

I wanted to know what language he spoke, whether it was French or Mentonnais.

"Don't know," Roland said, "I've never spoken to him."

I pressed Roland to tell me more, but he knew no more. So I had to imagine him, this nameless man, after the death of his wife, convinced that nothing added up to anything in this world, that all our purposes are illusory, and that the sole solution to a problem from which the key integer has been lost is to subtract the other cipher, reducing everything to nothingness. I imagined him pining for a life more perfect for the suddenness of its ending, then craving annihilation, nullifying the arbitrariness of his wife's death by contriving to bring about his own. I imagined him haunted by the hideous stillness of her face, by the conviction he had caused her death. For several weeks he refuses all contact with the outside world. He reads and rereads letters she wrote when he was in Senegal during the war. At night he opens her wardrobe and presses his face into her clothes, inhaling her presence. Friends prevail upon him to rejoin their backgammon circle at Le Narval. He sits listlessly watching the counters move around the board, contemptuous of the significance his friends attach to the outcome of the game. A piece of popular music on the jukebox overwhelms him with an unbearable memory, and he shoves back his chair and stumbles into the street. Perhaps Alpha 60, the computer in Jean-Luc Godard's sci-fi movie, *Alphaville* ("Capitale de la Douleur") offers a glimpse into his mind:

> No one has lived in the past and no one will live in the future. The present is the form of all life, and there is no means by which this can be avoided. Time is a circle that is endlessly revolving. The descending arc is the past and the rising arc is the future. Everything has been said. At least as long as words don't change their meanings and meanings their words. It is quite obvious that someone who usually lives at the limits of suffering requires a different form of religion than a person who normally lives securely. Nothing existed here before us. No one. We are absolutely alone here. We are unique, dreadfully unique. The meaning of words and of expressions is no longer grasped. One isolated word or an isolated detail in a drawing can be understood. But the comprehension of the whole escapes us. Once we know the number 1, we believe we know the number 2, because 1 and 1 makes 2. But we have forgotten that firstly we have to know the meaning of "plus."[2]

A few weeks pass and he is persuaded to return to the lycée. Everyone is full of sympathy and concern. He feels he deserves none of it. Colleagues address him warily and respectfully, as if the slightest harshness will make him fall apart. He shows no gratitude.

It is then that the gossip begins. In the playground and outside the school gates, students relay what they have overheard at home. It is said he was drunk at the wheel of the car the day his wife was killed. In the opinion of some, he should have been charged with manslaughter. It is whispered that he visits the cemetery at night and sleeps on his wife's grave. He begins to take a perverse delight in his growing isolation, though sometimes he experiences himself as a mere shadow and is terrified. At night he wakes in a cold sweat. He hears the Paris-Milan *rapide* thundering through the darkness. He thinks of all the places he might go. There is nowhere. Now he listens to his own heartbeat, waiting for it to falter. But it is like the clock ticking on the table beside his bed, or the *rapide* vanishing into the night, something with a life of its own, with a timetable and ineluctable.

He walks through the deserted streets of the old town and along the seafront, muttering under his breath, whimpering with grief. He contemplates the darkness of the ocean, its hiss and glut upon the shingles. One night he strips naked and swims out to sea, but when he tries to swallow water and sink into the depths he finds he cannot drown.

At the lycée, the absolute and unconditional truths of mathematics oppress him. One and one no longer equal two, since he is alive and she is not. One day, as he is writing equations on the blackboard, two girls start talking behind his back. He turns and stares at them. Again he experiences himself as a mere shadow. He rubs his hand across his chest and stomach to confirm his own substantiality. He opens his mouth to tell the girls to shut up, but his voice is parched and feeble. The girls look at him, taunting him to speak, demanding his anger, but the words stick in his throat. Now everyone is watching him struggling to get the words out. He walks toward the door in a daze, telling himself he is thirsty and needs water. A sinister murmuring follows him from the room.

In the street, the sunlight blinds him. He slumps onto a bench in the shade of a great plane tree. Cars pass up and down the road. Tourists are sitting under parasols in the harborside cafés. Life is going on as usual, yet he is pervaded by a maddening numbness, so that the sound of traffic is dulled and he can hardly bear to look at the light glinting on the sea.

Half an hour passes. The Principal is standing over him, imploring him to speak. When his appeals fall on deaf ears and the math teacher clasps his head in his hands, the Principal asks if he should telephone a doctor. You have been under a lot of strain, he says, and the clamor of the classroom doesn't make things any easier. Maybe you shouldn't have returned to teaching so soon. The Principal asks if he can drive the math teacher to the hospital. Perhaps he could be given something to alleviate his distress.

The math teacher tells the Principal to bugger off. The Principal glances nervously up and down the street. But you can't just sit out here in the street! You might be recognized!

The math teacher assures the Principal that he knows what he is doing; he just needs to be alone for a while, there's nothing to worry about, he'll be all right. He won't be returning to the school though, not today, not next week, not ever. The Principal is no longer solicitous. He tells the math teacher he has a school to run, other people to think about, responsibilities. He wants to hurl the word ingrate at him.

At first the math teacher is hurt to find that the very people who went out of their way to help him when his wife died now spurn him. Colleagues at the lycée, whom he has dined with regularly for years, cross the street when they see him approaching—and this at a time when his clothes are still clean, and he still bothers to wash and shave. But then it occurs to him that this ostracism is exactly what he wants. The only trouble is that he had wanted to repudiate *them;* it had not occurred to him that they would preempt his scheme, comply so readily with his wishes.

It is then that he begins to let his beard and hair grow, to go for days without washing, to allow his clothes and shoes to fall apart, his body to fester. Now, when erstwhile colleagues see him in town, they disappear down side streets with dismay and repugnance on their faces. Now it is he who calls the tune, who drives them from him.

Gradually, his self-imposed exile comes to resemble madness. His debate with his own conscience is interminable. His thinking is never self-protective. Rather than using ideas and dreams to justify or forget the past, which is what so-called normal people do, he mercilessly keeps alive images of what has happened, torturing himself with regret, rehearsing endlessly the things he might have done or should have done to prevent his wife's death. Living vicariously, he lives another life. His absent-mindedness is literal. Oblivious to the present, because he discredits it as an illusion, he plunges back into the past like someone washed ashore from a shipwreck who realizes that his beloved is drowning out at sea and risks his own life returning to save her.

A foul-smelling sack of a man, smoking butts he has picked up from the footpaths, punctuating his inner monologue with hopeless gestures, he crouches at night over his supermarket trolley in the entranceway of the bureau de change. He notices no one. He subsists on what he forages. Sometimes it is a day-old baguette from a boulangerie, smeared with mayonnaise. Sometimes it is a bowl of soup from the Sisters of Mercy. Sometimes it is a bottle of wine. He has no name, and because his identity is constructed so tortuously from events that others know nothing of, he is in effect a nobody, a *quelconque,* an idiot.

Consider now the audacity of the author of these pages. Beginning with some meager autobiographical details, he constructs his fiction. A clochard, with whom he has never exchanged a word, is given a past and a personality—the very things the poor drifter has done his utmost to render opaque. In good bourgeois style, the author has dragged the clochard off the streets, given him a bath, loaned him some of his own clothes, and found him a menial job in the factory where he himself is employed. The clochard has been made to pay for his marginality and mystery! The clochard craved anonymity; the author, refusing him that freedom, dresses him up and turns him into a walking parody of himself.

Countless adages caution us not to judge other people by ourselves, not to rehabilitate others in our own likeness. It is impossible, one is told, to know other minds. Yet we go ahead and grant ourselves all kinds of authorial privileges as if we were exempt from these discretionary rules. We gate-crash the private lives of others, presuming to enter into the consciousness of people whose language we do not speak, whose experiences we do not share, whose concerns are beyond our grasp.

Still, I tell myself, even though we have no good grounds for claiming certain knowledge of others, a writer's task is to try to bridge the gap between himself and those with whom he shares the world. Life would be absurd otherwise. We would become lost to one another, and thought would degenerate into mere solipsism.

Walking home alone the seafront, I think of the risk a writer runs as he fills in the blanks, puts flesh on the bare bones of someone else's story. Perhaps this is why poets and so-called primitive peoples prefer to make stones, trees, and natural phenomena their means of articulating human passions and ideas. Stones, trees, and forked lightning do not, as a rule, talk back if they are misrepresented or maligned.

Perhaps my clochard wouldn't give a damn about knowing what I made of him, what tasks I set him to perform in the workhouse of my imagination. Perhaps if he read these pages he would recognize himself and be astounded that so much could be intuitively known. In any event, there is always a loss and a gain in any dialogue, and every writer has a need for his work to be redeemed by life. It is the vanity of authors to imagine that one day all the books ever written will be balanced by some daemon, and everything created in the minds of writers will match everything that has actually occurred in the world.

It had been raining. A fresh wind was blowing off the sea. A tricouleur snapped against a pole. Offshore, there was a slick of dirty water-froth, old corks, plastic containers, sticks, and cigarette butts. And then the clochard was shambling toward me along the boulevard, trundling his supermarket trolley, upbraiding the sky with his index finger.

For years I have carried in my head these images of him, *mon semblable, mon frere!* At the center of my imaginings is the idea of a man divided between two lives, just as individuals in traditional societies find themselves today divided between two worlds. So deep was the division in his life that one might speak of two incarnations—the life he led before the death of his wife and the life after. Often I find myself returning to those poignant lines of Joyce Johnson's, because they also belong to him: "If time were like a passage of music, you could keep going back to it till you got it right."[3]

ELEVEN

Love Letters

I USED TO FEEL QUITE AMBIVALENT ABOUT composers like Dvorak, Chopin, Kodály, Bartók, Vaughan Williams, Canteloube, and Janáček, who used folk music as the basis for their own compositions, often without specific acknowledgment of their sources. Undoubtedly, these misgivings reflected my experience as an ethnographer, recording oral traditions, interrogating informants, and collecting the stories of strangers. Even when given carte blanche by those who allowed me to live among them and know their secrets, I was not able to rid my mind of the thought that I was profiting from things that did not, strictly speaking, belong to me. To share the meager royalties of my publications with the people whose lives and testimonies had been grist to my academic mill did little to allay this doubt. There remained a lurking suspicion that I was part of an underhand and ongoing Western tradition of pilfering and piracy.

To invoke the higher causes of art or knowledge to justify this predatory activity seems downright dishonest. And it is even more disgraceful when you know that those who exhibit these works of peasant and primitive people in museums, art galleries, and living rooms, generally turn up their noses at the thought of entertaining the original artists in their immaculate and air-conditioned spaces, let alone recompensing the artists properly for their work. I find it all too easy to imagine that these objets d'art, trapped in their rococo frames or glass-fronted cabinets, yearn to end the terrible journey that has taken them so far from home and exiled them in an alien place. Maori people speak of the hau (wind, spirit, breath) that imbues a valued object. The hau enters the gift as it is made. The object embodies the subjectivity of its maker. The hau, therefore, pines to return to whence it came, and when deflected from this course, it brings sickness, desolation, and death to those who have thwarted it.

There is a curious analogy to be drawn between our craving to possess what is beyond our grasp and our notion that inspiration also derives from elsewhere. We must lay ourselves open to it. We must learn to receive it. It must flow into us and through us, like the wind, if we are to create anything exceptional. D.H. Lawrence's famous lines echo Maori thought in this matter:

> Not I, not I, but the wind that blows through me!
> A fine wind is blowing the new direction of Time.
> If only I let it bear me, carry me, if only it carry me!
> If only I am sensitive, subtle, oh, delicate, a winged gift!
> If only, most lovely of all, I yield myself and am borrowed
> By the fine, fine wind that takes its course through the chaos of the
>   world ...[1]

If our real lives await us elsewhere, then what lies at hand may be seen as a drag or a dead weight. In male imaginings, this contrast between ideal and real is often expressed as a contrast between love and marriage. While the muse is a heavenly creature or potential mistress, the wife is earthly and all too familiar. This equation of exotic locations and erotic love is as compellingly present in Paul Gauguin's Tahitian canvases as in Robert Graves' poems about the "white goddess."

> All saints revile her, and all sober men
> Ruled by the God Apollo's golden mean—
> In scorn of which we sailed to find her
> In distant regions likeliest to hold her
> Whom we desired above all things to know,
> Sister of the mirage and echo.[2]

This "unconscious hankering ... after goddesses"[3] recurs in the lives of painters, musicians, writers, and, I dare say, ethnographers. There is always this desire to escape the drudgery of hearth and home, to find space to dream, unfettered, and to be reborn in an intimate relationship with some exotic other. And so the male artist imagines himself transported to some other realm, whether mountain or moon, or held in the arms of a goddess, mermaid, or muse.

For Leoš Janáček, this other realm was associated, in his imagination, with peasant or Gypsy heroines.

Janáček was 31 when he made his first ethnomusicological expeditions in his natal Moravia. Over the next five years (1888–1893), he spent every summer in the field, collecting peasant folksongs and dances, alone or in collaboration with other Czech folklorists. This music soon became integral to his own evolving style, and many of the songs and dances he composed at this time were orchestrations of the Moravian music he heard in village inns and remote villages. "How much love, longing, happiness and joy there is in these songs," he wrote, "how much truth."[4] In his view, the work of many of his contemporaries had lost touch with this truth. When the Ethnographic Exhibition opened in Prague in 1895, Janáček led a colorful procession of Moravian dancers and singers to the exhibition site, dressed in a black *camara* tunic. Slavonic exoticism became de rigueur, though further afield Japonaiserie was all the rage.

Janáček's identification with peasant music was not only a way of breaking free of classical forms; it enabled him to distance himself from his worrying situation at home—an ailing infant son, a distressed wife. But it is already clear that Janáček is as susceptible to the allures of other women as he is entranced by folk music. When his son, Vladimir, died suddenly, Janáček's relationship with his wife also died. "Each of us was alone in our pain," his wife Zdenka would recall. "For some time now, Leoš and I had not lived as man and wife. There were no intimacies between us, not even affectionate words. As long as Vladicek was around, it was bearable. It was my consolation that at least my husband loved the boy, but now it was terrible. Next to one another, mutual unhappiness, mutual pain, and yet each one so alone."[5]

It was not until July 1917, when Janáček was 63, that he finally found his muse. On a visit to the Moravian spa town of Luhacovice, the composer met the woman who would hold him under her spell for the rest of his life and inspire many of his most famous works. Indeed, in a piece written less than a month after meeting Kamila Stösslová, he makes her a key figure in *The Diary of One Who Disappeared,* referring to her as "that black Gypsy girl," the reason "why there's such emotional heat in these works."[6]

Kamila Stösslová was 25, married, with two children, aged four and one. She had an olive complexion, big black eyes under heavy eyebrows, and a sensuous mouth, and Janáček wasted no time in sending her roses "as a token of [his] unbounded esteem," adding "You are so lovely in character and appearance that in your company one's spirits are lifted."

When he left Luhacovice a few days later he wept at the thought of Kamila's laughter, and the happiness he had experienced in the Stössels' home. The war years were harsh. Kamila's husband, David Stössel, had been wounded on the Western Front, food was scarce, and the Organ School where Janáček taught was without fuel. In letters to Kamila, Janáček would complain of these wartime austerities. His maidservant had to travel as far as the Czech border to scrounge for provisions, and everyone had to barter. One of his students paid for his lesson with a sugar loaf.

Over the next decade, before his death in 1927, Janáček would send Kamila at least a thousand letters or postcards, and the Stössels would often visit Janáček and his wife Zdenka in Brno. Now infatuated with Kamila, whom he fantasized as his "dark gypsy girl," and writing music inspired by her, Janáček's passion was, however, unrequited. With her husband often away on business, Kamila may have welcomed the composer's affectionate attention, but she was happily married and wanted nothing more than a platonic relationship with him. That this was not always easy for her to negotiate is clear from a letter written in August 1922, in which she responds to a comment Janáček had made on her "fickleness." "You know only too well why I do not want to come to your house. I have still not forgotten the last time. Why cause someone else pain without a reason? I already thought that I should no longer be writing to you. But as the old saying goes, 'Old love never becomes rusty,' although there is no love between us only mere friendship."[7]

As Janáček became more and more bored and unhappy in his marriage, he enjoyed international success as a composer and longed for the same fulfillment in his personal life. At 70, he did not feel old. He was at the height of his musical powers. And his passion for Kamila was undimmed. After a visit to the Stössels in the summer of 1924, his sense of the "merciless passage of time" was as strong as his longing for Kamila. "With her 'raven black hair undone,' her habit of walking barefoot indoors, her spontaneity and vitality, Kamila continued to infatuate Janáček, and his letters now became open declarations of love: "you are beautiful, exquisite, [judging by] what else I have glimpsed," wrote Janáček in his next letter. "And your eyes have a strange depth, they are so deep that they do not shine.... But enough of my ravings," he added, only to declare his feelings openly a few lines later: "Kamila, if it weren't for you, I wouldn't want to live.'"[8] There is no evidence that David Stössel was aware of Janáček's declarations of undying love, or the composer's struggle between respecting the purity of his friendship with Kamila and his desire "to have all of you and kiss you passionately."[9] As for Kamila, she declined to attend social events with Janáček unless accompanied by her husband, and she would not receive Janáček in her home alone.

Fame only increased Janáček's ardor. In the last sixteen months of his life, he sent Kamila three hundred letters, sometimes writing her several times a day, rapturous and burning with "the desire to have you, to have you!"[10] Inevitably, Zdenka, tidying up her husband's study at the Conservatory, found one of Kamila's letters, signed "Your Kamila." It was not the first of Janáček's infidelities, but it was, for her, the last straw. Faced with a dangerous operation for a thyroid condition, she considered her chances of survival slim and hoped for a "discreet, decent death." After writing her will, she returned a brooch Kamila had once given her, and averred that she never wished to see her again.

By January 1928, both Janáček and Kamila were thinking of divorcing their spouses, and their letters had become intensely intimate. Janáček was also writing a new string quartet that would "describe musically" their correspondence and their relationship. As the work rapidly progressed, Janáček pressed Kamila to reach a decision over leaving her husband and becoming his wife. Finally, Kamila reciprocated Janáček's feelings. "I really don't know what I would have done during this bad weather if it were not for your letters . . . and I find myself thinking of you all the time even if I don't want to. . . . On reading your letter today I thought so much about everything in the past[,] about everything I have lived through and I was happy. You remind me of it when you write how your life was before and how it is now. And what about mine[?] I have not known anything else[,] have not longed for anything else[,] and my life just went by without any love and joy. But I always went along with the thought that it had to be so. Now I think that God was testing you and me and when He saw that we are good[,] that we deserve it[,] He has granted us this joy in life, I steered clear of everything[,] did not look for anything and only you who have known me all these years [know] that this really is the truth. Anyone else would just smile [and say] how is it possible[,] yes, it is possible[,] you are much dearer to me than if you were young. I assure you that my life is pleasant that I don't wish for any better. And this is your doing alone."[11]

Eight months later, Janáček suffered complications from a bout of flu, and he died in his sleep. His relationship with Kamila was never consummated. According to Kamila, he had never so much as kissed her hand.

Though Janáček seems to have done everything in his power to seduce Kamila, one wonders whether, deep down, he knew that this fascination depended on Kamila's unattainability. If she were to be idealized and retain her "nakedly worn magnificence,"[12] he would have to resist the very desire that drew him to her. In this, he would follow Petrarch's example, for when the great fourteenth-century poet fell in love with Laura (like Kamila, a virtuous married woman), he realized that he would have to sublimate his sexual passion if she was to serve as his muse. Undoubtedly, the resulting frustration and obsessiveness fired his creative work, as did Laura's untimely death. Distance not only lends enchantment; it may foster compulsive devotion.

The ethereal figure of the muse stands in contrast with the earthly figure of the wife. While the first promises transcendence, the second anchors the artist in immanence. Psychoanalytically speaking, the male artist splits the feminine into two irreconcilable images. For Karen Horney, this splitting is an expression of men's "womb envy"[13]—their desire to arrogate for themselves the procreative powers of women and, in extreme cases, create a world in which they no longer depend on women to reproduce their kind. For the male artist, mimicking the role of women as bearers and nurturers of children requires physical separation from women and the suppression of images of women as wives and mothers. Only through these sleights of hand can he sustain the illusion that his own creative work is something other than a pale and potentially ridiculous imitation of women's power to bring life into the world. His denial or denigration of the conjugal bond goes hand in hand with an idealization of pure and perfect women and an obsession with the idea of a female muse who will inspire him to produce immortal works, though she herself has no other role than to serve him. Not only does womb envy find expression in the imaginings of male artists; it may explain why many male rituals involve strict separation from women and secret performances of mimetic birthing, rebirthing, and menstruation (through cutting and bloodletting) in order to augment male potency and power. Writes Bruno Bettelheim, "One purpose of male initiation may be to assert that men, too, can bear children." As for the secrecy of such rites, "it may serve to disguise the fact that the desired goal is not reached."[14]

That these psychoanalytic ruminations were prompted by my explorations of Janáček's music ethnography and his passionate attachment to Kamila Stösslová was not unconnected to my preoccupation with the question as to whether an ethnographer can produce something more than a pale imitation of the lifeworlds in which he or she sojourns. Does ethnographic knowledge resemble our knowledge of those nearest and dearest to us, which we think of as "real," despite it being largely implicit and habitual? Or is it like the largely conjectural, intuitive and projective forms of understanding that fill the vacuum between ourselves and strangers, or places we have only imagined? The criticism that is sometimes leveled at ethnographers—that we are academic profiteers, stealing the cultural property of others for our own gain and giving nothing back to the people who gave us so much—is far less pressing for me than the question as to how we may creatively respond to whatever we learn in the field, producing something so genuinely alive that its verisimilitude and vitality become its justification. It is neither a matter of representing the other faithfully nor of betraying the other in our interpretive annotations to what we observe, for the issue is always one of integrating these opposed perspectives. Crafting some kind of interplay between empirical particulars and abstract reflections therefore resembles the integration we hope to achieve in our lives, between realism and idealism. Only when we succeed in this endeavor can we say that the hau that inheres in the gift is finally brought home, or the borrowed airs and dances of another world are redeemed, or the muse and spouse united in the one beloved companion.

TWELVE

Writing for Bare Life

I AM HAUNTED BY A CONTRARY THOUGHT—that while writing may forge connections with others, it can just as readily cut one off from the world. Although writing is an all-consuming fire, it may also reduce one's life to ashes. It is as if nothing can be brought into this world without something else departing from it—a conjecture that underpins the widespread belief that death is not a state of nonbeing but another mode of being, and that we are perpetually passing into and out of this world in a never-ending cycle of death and rebirth.

It was the Congo, recalled through my rereading of Cendrars, the dog-eared, rain-stained notebooks I leafed through, and the remote and imagined sound of a *mbira* in the warm grasslands near Pic Mensi, that set me writing this book—much as Cendrars was moved to write after being visited by his friend Edouard Peisson in August 1943. But no new departure or burst of creativity is without its losses, and on another visit, a little more than two years later, on November 26, 1945, Peisson paid his friend another visit and noticed, on a small table to the left of the entranceway to Cendrars' apartment, a bouquet of flame-red carnations. "Flowers, this morning!" Peisson exclaimed, and asked Cendrars if he was all right. The previous evening Cendrars had received a telegram from Meknès in Morocco informing him that his son Rémy had been killed in a plane crash. He nevertheless seemed calm, and filled with a "kind of quiet pride" as he showed his friend a photo of Rémy. A few days later he confided to Peisson: "They want to bring Rémy's body back to France. I am against it. He is buried in the cemetery of a Moroccan village with his comrades. Don't you think it's better to let these young airmen rest in peace, in the sand, wrapped in their parachute shrouds like the larvae of cicadas in their chrysalids, awaiting the day of the resurrection?"[1]

Would my own work of words presage a death? And why do writers sometimes imagine that the demands of their craft require the sacrifice of family and sometimes friends? In 1965, not long after returning to New Zealand after several years abroad, I found work as a builder's laborer on an insurance building under construction in downtown Wellington. One day, the foreman assigned me to work with an individual who, it turned out, was a fan of Walt Whitman's *Leaves of Grass* and had ambitions to write in the same vein. His confession astonished me; it was simply not the kind of thing one admitted in a working class environment. That I pretended not to know what he was talking about, indicated the care with which I kept my own light under a bushel. It quickly became apparent, however, that Gary was captivated by the idea of being a poet, not publishing poetry, and he would, without a moment's notice, jot down lines on the inside of his cigarette packet before proudly informing me of his accomplishment. His inspiration was almost the death of us. One afternoon, standing on a scaffold, we were about to take the weight of a heavy metal beam onto our shoulders before lowering it to the ground, when Gary was suddenly animated by a beautiful thought. He let the beam slip from his shoulder. Powerless to prevent it falling, I had to jump from the trestle to avoid being crushed as it fell. As I picked myself up, I found him, oblivious to the chaos around him, placidly scribbling on the back of his pay slip.

What struck me more than his bouts of absent-mindedness was Gary's denigration of women who, in his benighted view, were anathema to the full flowering of one's creative genius. I found it difficult to reconcile his misogyny with his passionate pursuit of women in the street or in the pub. "Why chase women if they are a threat to your literary vitality?" I asked him. His response: "The trick is not to let them get their hooks into you. Not to marry Not to settle down."

What is the origin of this widespread male anxiety that sexual intercourse and marriage sap one's creative power? Among the Tallensi of Ghana, men cite the exhausting work, heavy responsibilities and irksome taboos that begin with a woman's pregnancy, as causes of impotence, though their tribulations really begin, they say, with the sex act itself, since ejaculation "is a giving up of something vital that is a source of strength and youth."[2] According to Hindu tradition, semen loss diminishes vigor and shortens life. Semen is "closely associated with the idea of the soul that survives after death"[3] and "the retention of sperm makes a man a hero and a god; its loss makes him low and animal-like."[4] Moreover, in many religious traditions—shamanic,

Buddhist, and Christian—celibacy is a precondition for priesthood, just as in the arena of modern sports, sexual abstinence before a game is thought to preserve an athlete's power.

But what of literature? Does the same superstition hold true? Consider the case of Franz Kafka, and his struggle to reconcile his literary ambitions with married life. Perusing his diary entries for the first half of 1912, one is struck by Kafka's isolation, and by the frequency with which he confesses to having written nothing. Disgusted with himself, he burns old papers (March 10). Wisely, he tells himself "not to overestimate what I have written, for in that way I make what is to be written unattainable" (March 25). A week later he admits to "an almost complete failure in writing" (April 1). "Bad. Wrote nothing today" (June 7). The complaints run on into August. But on the 20th of that month, Kafka writes a thumbnail sketch of a young woman he met seven days earlier at the home of his friend, Max Brod.

In his first description of Felice, Kafka declares, "I was not at all curious about who she was, but rather took her for granted at once. Bony, empty face that wore its emptiness openly. Bare throat. A blouse thrown on. Looked very domestic in her dress although, as it turned out, she by no means was."[5] Seven and a half months would pass before Kafka met Felice again, but in the interim he wrote to her several times a day and in the course of a single exhausting night (September 22-23, 1912), completed a story that was, in his opinion, the first real expression of his literary personality—a story connected in his mind with Felice Bauer, to whom it was dedicated. Entitled "The Judgment," this story later became "The Trial."

Though Kafka's relationship with Felice appears to have given him the confidence to write (tellingly he wrote *The Metamorphosis* during the period he was writing to her[6]), he was increasingly tormented by his inability to reconcile the demands of affection and the demands of his writing. He simply could not imagine a weakling like himself finding the strength to do both. On January 3, 1912, he had written, "When it became clear in my organism that writing was the most productive direction for my being to take, everything rushed in that direction and left empty all those abilities which were directed towards the joys of sex, eating, drinking, philosophical reflection, and above all music. I atrophied in all these directions."[7]

But was his lack of energy the sole source of his tormenting indecisiveness? According to Kafka himself, it was not born of a dread of not being able to write, but of a deeper fear of not being able to live the kind of life that made writing imperative and possible. "I am a writer . . . even when not writing [though] a non-writing writer is a monster inviting madness," Kafka wrote in a letter to Max Brod. "Writing . . . is a reward for serving the devil and descending into darkness. Perhaps there are other forms of writing, but I know only this kind; at night, when fear keeps me from sleeping, I know only this kind."[8] Given his dim view of life, Kafka could never have found fulfillment in the light of day, the monotony of office hours, the obligations of domestic life, the demands of friendship, the bonds of matrimony. "Only with absolute focus, at night and in complete isolation, was Kafka able to work."[9] The closer he was drawn to Felice, the more estranged he felt from his writing. And just as his office job compromised his creative activity, so commitment to Felice would be tantamount, he felt, to being bound by the wrists and led to the scaffold. On May 3, 1913, he wrote in his diary of "the terrible uncertainty of [his] inner existence,"[10] and on July 21, he summarized his arguments for and against marriage, noting that while marriage would make his life less lonely, he needed to be alone a great deal. "What I accomplished was only the result of being alone."[11]

Kafka is partially mistaken here. Although he feared connections and dreaded the thought "of the connection, of passing into the other,"[12] it was, ironically, his sense of being "a total stranger and only an object of curiosity"[13] in the eyes of other people, together with his sense of not being himself when in their company, that drove his writing. He embodied the Sartrean paradox that one can only confirm the truth of one's own singular existence by submitting to the hell of being with others. But Kafka also reminds us of the dangers of writing in the first rather than third person. "For as long as you say 'one' instead of 'I,' there's nothing in it and you can easily tell the story, but as soon as you admit to yourself that it is you yourself, you feel as though transfixed and are horrified."[14]

In what consists this horror of the "I" unless it implies that there is no bridge between one's own experience and the experiences of others? Indeed, it suggests that one is socially dead, dead to the world. And this sense of being doomed to exist in isolation from others may be more horrifying than the prospect of one's physical death. This reduction of one's being to individualized being is *transfixing,* not just in the sense that it paralyses one with fright but because it precludes the possibility of ever being moved by others, falling in love, being carried away by one's passions, or changed. You are little more than a bedridden invalid, a bug pinned to a sheet of paper, a beetle on its back powerless to move.

THIRTEEN

Writing So As Not to Die

IN AN INTERVIEW WITH CHRISTOPHER HITCHENS in July 2010, not long after the British-born writer and iconoclast had been diagnosed with metastasized esophageal cancer, George Easton asked Hitchens, "What would you have done had you not become a writer?" Hitchens replied that he never wanted to do anything else but write. "It's what I am, rather than what I do."[1]

Most serious writers would agree. Although few succeed in making a living as writers, writing is their raison d'être; for them it is as inconceivable not to write as not to breathe. Writing and living are synonymous. This is why Hitchens' first thought after receiving his grim diagnosis was not "I am going to die," but "Will I be able to write?"[2]

This existential anxiety over losing the ability to write leads me to conclude that while writing may sometimes appear to be a solipsistic, self-serving pursuit, it is more profoundly a way of creating and sustaining connectedness to others, a sense of being in the world. This is what Joseph Conrad means when he says that writers speak to "the latent feeling of fellowship with all creation—and to the subtle but invincible conviction of solidarity that knits together the loneliness of innumerable hearts, to the solidarity in dreams, in joy, in sorrow, in aspirations, in illusions, in hope, in fear, that binds men to each other, which binds together all humanity—the dead to the living and the living to the unborn."[3]

Writing mediates relationships with others. Through stories we create avatars who can do what we cannot do, understand what we cannot understand, go where we cannot go. As Aleksandar Hemon, observes, we need narrative spaces to extend ourselves into. We need more lives, another set of parents, someone other than oneself to throw our metaphysical tantrums. Narrative imagination enables us to process experiences that lie beyond our means to grasp or accept.[4]

Even as a teenager, I wrote in order to relate to a world I lacked the confidence to participate in directly. Tongue-tied in the presence of others, I could collect my thoughts in writing. Unable to approach a girl I adored at a distance, I would conjure her in poetry as if this would work like a spell and draw her to me. I had learned from my Kuranko research that people told stories about the intractable issues in their lives, trapped in an unhappy marriage, at the mercy of a tyrant, mistreated by an older sibling, denied love by a stepparent. In stories, one could speak one's mind and share one's adversities, for the storyteller would always begin with a disclaimer, locating events far off and long ago. Once upon a time, in a distant land. Stories for Kuranko were like writing for me—safe places where one could call the shots, reworking one's experience into a shape more just, more coherent, more perfect than reality allowed. After Pauline's death, I spent two years in relative isolation, writing a book about our life together. Keeping her vividly before me, so to speak, until I could let her go, as if the ending of the book would release me to begin a new chapter in my life.

To recount a story about someone else, living in another time or another place, is not always escapist in the sense that the writer is unable to bear his immediate reality; rather, the story enables the storyteller to escape from the prison house of the self. For as long as it takes to tell the story, the storyteller is in touch with others—the characters in his story as well as the people in his audience. He is dwelling in *social* time.

This is the meaning of the story of Scheherazade. She is under sentence of death, physical extinction. She tells a story. Not only does this keep her connected to the world; she annuls time, for instead of night ending with the dawn of the day of her death, it passes through that day into another night and into another story, making any ending inconceivable, including the ending of her life. What has been decided is transformed into the not-yet-destined. She thereby escapes biographical time—the time of being towards death—and enters mythological time—the eternal time of our shared humanity.

The story belongs to the chronicles of the Sassanid kings of Persia.[5] According to this epic, a beloved king has two sons. When the king dies, the elder son, Shahriyar, succeeds his father while the younger son, Shahzaman, is given the Kingdom of Tartary whose capital is Samarkand. After a separation of twenty years, Shahriyar invites his younger brother to visit him. On the eve of his departure, Shahzaman discovers his beloved wife *in flagrante* with a Moorish slave. Shahzaman kills his wife and her lover, then travels to the capital of Persia, where he is welcomed, wined, and dined. But it is clear to Shahriyar that Shahzaman is suffering from some profound sorrow, and after numerous attempts to lift his younger brother's spirits, the Sultan proposes that they go hunting together, hoping that this diversion will succeed where others failed. At the last minute, however, Shahzaman begs to remain in his brother's palace. While sitting alone at a window, dwelling on his own unhappiness, Shahzaman happens to see his brother's wife in the courtyard below, having sex with one of her Moorish slaves. The realization that his brother's wife is as perfidious as his own wife transforms the sorrowing Shahzaman, who now resolves to put the treachery of women from his mind and enjoy the pleasures of his elder brother's palace.

On returning from the hunt, Shahriyar is overjoyed to see his younger brother so cheerful and presses him to explain his change of heart. Though loath to inform the Sultan of the Sultana's infidelity, the truth comes out and Shahriyar has his wife and her black slaves executed. Being now persuaded that no woman can be trusted, he resolves to take a virgin in marriage to his bed each night and have her killed in the morning.

His Grand Vizier, who reluctantly assented to the Sultan's cruel decree, has two daughters, Dunyazad and Scheherazade. Not only does Scheherazade possess courage and wit, but she is also well read in philosophy, medicine, history, and the liberal arts and her poetry excels the compositions of the best writers of her time. She is also surpassingly beautiful. To her father's dismay, Scheherazade prevails on her father to give her in marriage to the Sultan. After a long argument the Grand Vizier says he will accede to his daughter's request, but only on condition that it is just and reasonable. Scheherazade explains that the justice of it lies in her decision to put an end to the barbarous thralldom in which the Sultan holds the families of the city.

Before marrying the Sultan, Scheherazade takes her sister aside and asks her to promise that she will come to the Sultan's palace an hour before dawn the following day for a final adieu. On the night of her marriage to the Sultan, Scheherazade asks of her husband a single favor—that she be allowed to see her sister Dunyazad one last time before she is killed. The following morning, Dunyazad arrives at the palace and, as arranged, she implores Scheherazade to tell one of her stories. Scheherazade addresses her husband: "Sire, may it please you to allow me to afford my dear sister this simple satisfaction?"

"With all my heart," replies the Sultan.

As Scheherazade recounts her story of the Merchant and the Genie, the Sultan is so spellbound that he not only stays her execution, scheduled for that morning, but eagerly awaits the next story, and the next, gradually coming to admire the courage of his wife and renounce the terrible edict he had promulgated.

That Scheherazade had such a fund of stories to draw upon might seem exceptional unless we acknowledged the work of the human imagination. Even without our awareness or determination, our minds are continuously producing an excess of images and inchoate ideas. Storytellers, fabulists, and mystics foster and exploit this surplus production of the natural mind, grateful for its bounty and aware that it may one day save their lives. But we are taught to place such an inordinate value on our role as actors, responsible for plotting the course of our lives, that we often overlook the strategic value of subjecting ourselves to the actions of others, and of yielding to fate. This is the example that Martin Heidegger finds in the poetry of Hölderlin. Misguidedly, we act as though we were the masters and shapers of language, Heidegger writes, when in "in fact language remains the master" of us.[6] We must learn to allow language to speak through us and "to let something be seen"[7] through the images that come to mind, whether these assume the form of ideas, stories, characters, or divinities. Accordingly, writing is not a sui generis phenomenon. It is a technique that bears a family resemblance to falling in love, spirit possession and madness, in which the realm of otherness is invited to take us over, to give us guidance, to work its will upon us. Only by trusting in our capacity to be filled with the spirit, for an answer to find us, for the germ of a lifesaving story to enter our minds, can we hope to have the raw material we then consciously hammer into shape and share with others.

FOURTEEN

Chinese Boxes

STORIES ARE NOT ONLY EMBEDDED IN LIFE—in the biography of a
storyteller and the epoch in which he or she lives; stories are often embedded
in stories. *One Thousand and One Nights* exemplifies this tradition of frame
stories, examples of which can be found in ancient Persian, Arab, and Indian
folklore. *The Manuscript Found in Saragossa*—written by a Polish aristocrat,
Count Jan Potocki in the first decade of the nineteenth century—is a modern masterpiece of this genre.

Potocki (1761–1815) was an adventurer, political activist, polymath, and
pioneering ethnologist. Brought up in the Ukraine and in Switzerland, he
spoke eight languages fluently, though chose to write in French. A real-life
Münchausen, he served twice in the Polish army, fought pirates with the
Knights of Malta, ascended in one of Europe's first hot-air balloons, and
traveled the length and breadth of Europe and Asia, venturing as far afield
as Mongolia and Morocco. His published accounts of his expeditions—
including *Research on Sarmatia* (published in Warsaw 1789–1792), *Historical
and Geographical Fragments on Scythia, Sarmatia, and the Slavs* (published
in Germany in 1796), and *Prehistory of the Peoples of Russia* (published in
Petersburg in 1802)—contain considerable ethnographic, historical, and linguistic detail. Czesław Miłosz calls Potocki "a precursor of Slavic archaeol-
ogy,"[1] and Ian Maclean notes that Potocki's "published writings helped found
the discipline of ethnology."[2]

At 51, politically disillusioned and in poor health, Potocki retired to his
castle at Uladowska in Podolia (now in the Ukraine). Here he completed
the *Manuscript* that he had begun many years earlier, inspired by his travels
in Muslim Chechnya. In December 1815, he committed suicide. Legend has
it that he fashioned a silver bullet from the knob of a teapot or the handle

of a sugar bowl given him by his mother, then had the bullet blessed by the chaplain of the castle before blowing his brains out in his library.

The *Manuscript* is set in 1739. A young Walloon officer, Alphonse van Worden, travelling to Madrid to join the Spanish army, takes a shortcut through the perilous marches of the Sierra Morena—a region where the influence of Europe succumbs to the Orient and Africa. Detained here for 66 days, he falls under the erotic and hallucinatory spell of gypsies, Muslims, and Jews and listens to their stories. Over successive days, one story frames and entails another, until they come to resemble a set of Chinese boxes or *matryoshka* dolls.

In 1964, a movie of *The Manuscript Found at Saragossa* was released in Europe. I saw the film in London the following year, though three decades would pass before I laid my hands on a translation of the book. In the film, the part of Alphonse van Worden is played by Zbigniew Cybulski, best known at that time for his role as the disillusioned nationalist militant in Andrzej Wajda's *Ashes and Diamonds* (1958). In the 1960s, Cybulski's tough yet sensitive features earned him the nickname "the James Dean of Poland." The first Polish superstar in the Hollywood tradition, a 1964 *Time* profile described him as having an unpronounceable name, "but women in a couple of dozen countries have developed a sudden passion for linguistics in order to fondle his exotic consonants."

Cybulski died on January 8, 1967 (coincidentally my birthday is also January 8) at the age of 40, under mysterious circumstances. On the day he died, he had been due in Warsaw for a theatrical engagement. He reached the station at Wroclaw at 4 a.m., just as the Warsaw train was pulling out. He ran for the train and leapt from the platform onto a running board, but missed his footing and fell under the train and was killed. The accident may have been the result of fatigue or alcohol, but rumors spread that his death was premeditated. Unlike James Dean, who died at the height of his powers and glamour, Cybulski had become a paunchy, weary imitation of himself, giving lackluster performances under second-rate directors. Better to burn out than to fade away.

Quite apart from the fact that *The Saragossa Manuscript* has remained, for more than forty-five years, one of the influential movies in my life, I have never ceased to be intrigued by the role that disenchantment and isolation seem to have played in the deaths of Potocki and Cybulski, and how these elements conspired with the wars and partitions that devastated Europe at the turn of the eighteenth century, and again in the midtwentieth century, to lead both the author of the *Manuscript* and the man who starred in the movie to take their own lives. There are stories within stories here. Author within actor. The Orient within Europe. Europe within Africa. Nightmares within dreams. And, of course, ethnographer within fabulist. How can one endure such multiplicity, and cope with such disparate origins and beliefs? And what creative possibilities might this fragmentation yield?

Here is another story, another ironic sequel to Cybulski's possible suicide. At the time of Cybulski's death, Andrzej Wajda had been contemplating making a film about the actor. Devastated by the news of the death of his close friend, Wajda decided to go ahead with his plans but to focus the film on the question of absence. *Everything for Sale* is a film about film making, in the same way, one might say, that the *Manuscript* is a story about storytelling. The film splices fiction and fact, just as the *Manuscript* fuses truth and illusion. Documentary footage of Cybulski's funeral and reminiscences by fans are included, and Cybulski's wife and many of Cybulski's friends figure in the film. Indeed, one of them—Cybulski's closest friend, Bogumił Kobiela (who would be killed in a car crash the following year)—walked off the set in protest at Wadja's opportunistic mixing of documentation and make-believe. Wajda defended himself: "I used all the facts, events and anecdotes that I was aware of or which I witnessed during my many years of friendship with Zbigniew Cybulski. But I could never pretend to make a film of his life or about him in person. *Everything for Sale* will mostly be a film showing the impossibility of defining a man without his presence."[3]

The movie opens with an apparent recreation of Cybulski's death: a man is seen running to catch a departing train, then slips and falls and is dragged to his death beneath the wheels. Here we come full circle. If Potocki's *Manuscript* is made up of stories within stories, Wadja's film about the life and death of the actor who starred in the film of the book is made up of films within films. For no sooner has the man on the railway platform fallen under the train than the train grinds to a halt and an actor emerges from beneath the wheels to ask "How was that?" It's a take in a film. But it's not the film's star who asks the question, but the film's director, who has had to stand in for the star who has not turned up on the set. Some time later, searching for the missing actor, the director will hear a radio broadcast with news of the actor's death the previous night in a train accident remarkably similar to the one in the movie. The director rewrites his scene. He now decides to make the star's absence a key element in the film, to create a movie around a person who never actually appears. Thus, Cybulski's actual death is reenacted again and again: by the director standing in for the missing actor on the film set, then by the actor, in reality, each replay dissolving being further into nothingness.

Henry James observed that for any writer "there is the story of one's hero, and then, thanks to the intimate connection of things, the story of one's story itself." It is possible to understand James' observation in two ways. First, no matter how remote from biographical truth a story seems to be, it is inevitably tied, obliquely and mysteriously, to the circumstances of its author's life. Second, just as every story implicates other stories, so the subject of every story implicates other subjects.

Stories are *about* the lives of individual subjects—persons living among other persons, subject to inner passions and compulsions, and under the sway of circumstances they can never completely comprehend or control. Stories are also authored and told *by* individual subjects—again, persons acting in relation to others, subject both to the influence of stories already told, and the impinging pressures of their society and their situations. But the term *subject* has a third and abstract meaning, as when we speak of the subject matter or theme of a story. The term *subject* is thus "patently equivocal," for it refers simultaneously to particular *persons* as well as to universal attributes of human *thought,* including abstract, categorical, and logical generalities such as race, culture, and nationality. As Theodor Adorno points out, it is fatuous to attempt to disentangle these two senses of the subject, for both the particular and the abstract connotations of the term have "reciprocal need of each other."[4] It therefore makes no sense to speak of individual lives without reference to the social and historical conditions that bear upon them, nor to invoke universals without reference to the individuals who embody, experience, objectify, perpetuate, and struggle against them. In the case of Jan Potocki, his book is more than a picaresque about fantastic characters in a fantastic land; it encapsulates and allegorizes the disillusion felt by many Poles when the promise of the Revolutionary Era proved tragically empty. The bizarre interplay of dream and reality, reason and superstition, that permeates the fiction reflects not only the exotic range of Potocki's personal experience, but it also suggests the terrible conflict in late eighteenth-century Poland between nationalist dreams and the reality of foreign domination. Though 100,000 Poles would serve in Napoleon's Grande Armée in the belief that Napoleon would guarantee the nation's liberation from Russian, Prussian, and Austrian rule, only 20,000 would survive the retreat from Moscow in 1812. The Poles' last heroic stand was at Leipzig, on the banks of the Elster. Surrounded by Prussian and Russian forces, and wounded by three bullets, General Jósef Poniatowski scorned surrender, and spurred his horse into the river under furious sniper fire. It is tempting to see in Potocki's retreat from public life that same year, and in the book he completed in isolation before taking his own life three years later, a symbolic recapitulation of Poniatowski's heroic suicide—the melancholy culmination of dashed nationalist aspirations.

The *Manuscript Found in Saragossa* thus points in two directions—to the author's own itinerant life that blurred the borders between so many religious and cultural domains, and to the political life of the nation that surrounded him with its fire.

FIFTEEN

The Writing on the Wall

IN HIS NOBEL LECTURE OF 2006, Orhan Pamuk says that experiences that initially seem unique to oneself come to be shared with others, and it is on a writer's ability to reveal this common ground that his or her writing stands or falls. "My confidence comes from the belief that all human beings resemble one another, that others carry wounds like mine—and that they will therefore understand. All true literature rises from this childish, hopeful certainty that we resemble one another."[1]

I recalled these words as I read Pamuk's *The Museum of Innocence,* for it seemed to me that the objects Kemal collects in an apartment that he and his beloved will never inhabit is a poignant image of a writer's struggle to strike a balance between his narcissistic relationship with his own experience and his desire for constant renewal in the world that lies about him. In the novel, Kemal collects objects whose origins or associations promise to bring the object of his love within reach. But the apartment in which these souvenirs collect dust becomes a museum to her memory, a place of desolation and regret. "My mother used to say no one would read my novels," Pamuk once said. "My novel honors the museums that no one goes to, the ones in which you can hear your own footsteps."[2] He might have added, it honors those with whom we have lost touch, whom we cannot reach. . . .

Even today, I cannot enter a museum without feeling that I am entering a mortuary. Despite the creative innovations of contemporary curators in contextualizing the objects on display, and in giving a semblance of life to the masks, carvings, bas reliefs, tomb offerings, and articles of clothing in their care, the objects are as confined in their solitude and as lost to the world as long-term inmates in a maximum security jail. My longing to liberate these memento mori from their atmospherically controlled, hermetically sealed environments is the same longing I feel when I hear of people unjustly oppressed, silenced, and incarcerated.

Unlike museum objects, which lack language and imagination, prisoners may summon these very resources to break down the walls that hem them in. Writing is often the file that cuts through the bars, a means of escape, a way of reconnecting with the outside world. In 1981, Republican prisoners in the notorious H-Block of Belfast's Maze Prison began a hunger strike. Ten men would die, including Bobby Sands, before the strike was called off. But as these men lay dying, a veritable industry of writing communicated their political message to the world. "These texts constituted a literature of conversion, letters to international organizations, political groups, unions, governments, and prominent individuals which publicized the Hunger Strike and asked support for the protest. Certain prisoners writing with pen refills on cigarette papers were able to produce 200 letters a day. It was a remarkable literary production which seemed to flow directly from the dying body of the hunger striker. The tortuous process of composing four thousand-word letters on cigarette rolling papers was an uncanny evocation of the equally tortuous production of monastic calligraphy in medieval Ireland."[3]

Sometimes, a prisoner writes letters that cannot be sent, like Oscar Wilde in a "dark cell in convict clothes, a disgraced and ruined man,"[4] penning his unrequited love letter to Alfred Lord Douglas (nicknamed Bosie). The worst experience of Wilde's two years in prison was not his remorse at the ruin and public infamy he had suffered but Bosie's indifference to his fate. Aware that his letter might never repair the relationship, Wilde writes as much for Bosie's sake as for his own. And so he instructs Bosie to send a letter, addressed to The Governor, H.M. Prison, Reading. "Inside, in another, and an open envelope, place your own letter to me: if your paper is very thin do not write on both sides, as it makes it hard for others to read. I have written to you with perfect freedom. You can write to me with the same."[5]

Just as there is a continuum from sociality to solitary confinement, so there is a parallel continuum from being able to exchange letters with others to being condemned to write letters that will never reach their destinations, or keep a journal that no one else will read.

"We are being hunted to death all through Europe," wrote Etty Hillesum on August 24, 1943.[6] Etty was twenty-nine, one of more than 100,000 Dutch Jews incarcerated in Westerbork, a transit camp near Assen in the northeastern Netherlands, "the last stop before Auschwitz." For two years, in mud and misery, sickness and fear, Etty wrote letters to friends in Amsterdam, as if in writing she could keep hope alive and sustain some sense of contact with the world she had known before the war. "I have told you often," she wrote to her lover Han Wegerif, "that no words and images are adequate to describe nights like these. But still I must try to convey something of it to you. One always has the feeling here of being the ears and eyes of a piece of Jewish history, but there is also the need sometimes to be a still, small voice. We must keep one another in touch with everything that happens in the various outposts of this world, each one contributing his own little piece of stone to the great mosaic that will take shape once the war is over."[7]

Three weeks after this letter was written, a postcard was thrown from a transport leaving Westbork. It was addressed to Christine van Noorten. "We shall be traveling for three days," Etty wrote. "Thank you for all your kindness and care. Friends left behind will still be writing to Amsterdam; perhaps you will hear something from them. Or from my last letter from camp."[8]

The card was found by farmers who posted it to Christine.

Two and a half months later, Etty was dead.

We write so as not to die. "We tell ourselves stories in order to live."[9] But to live is to be connected with others. And for such connections to be made and maintained, we need the literary devices of script and plot, of moral coherence, coincidence, and closure. These can be conjured in writing or speech, in stories or treatises, and to some extent in the privacy of one's own mind. Without these bridges to the wider world, our lives are crippled and incomplete. "We live entirely, especially if are writers, by the imposition of a narrative line upon disparate images, by the 'ideas' with which we have learned to freeze the shifting phantasmagoria which is our actual experience." So writes Joan Didion, at a time in her life when she had come "to doubt the premises of all the stories" she had told herself.[10] "I was supposed to have a script, and had mislaid it. I was supposed to hear cues, and no longer did. I was meant to know the plot, but all I knew was what I saw: flash pictures in variable sequence, images with no 'meaning' beyond their temporary arrangement, not a movie but a cutting-room experience."[11]

Few writers better capture this "shifting phantasmagoria which is our actual experience" than Samuel Beckett, in whose work logical conundrums and existential impasses combine to create devastating images of human absurdity and indecisiveness, as in his *Three Dialogues with Georges Duthuit*, in which he speaks of "the expression that there is nothing to express, nothing with which to express, no power to express, no desire to express, together with the obligation to express."[12] Clearly, it is not God or Godot or inspiration that eludes Beckett's characters, but Being itself. Godot is but one of the names we might give to the unnameable sense that our very existence is in flux, waxing and waning like the weather, one day threatening rain, the next unpredictably sunlit, though all the while outside our ability to know or control.

Like Beckett, and Kafka before him, I am skeptical of claims that "we *are* the stories we tell,"[13] that "life, as lived, is a story being told",[14] and that "stories are lived before they are told."[15] These glib phrases naturalize and fetishize the imagined parallels we like to draw between stories and lives, such as the tripartite structure of beginning, middle, and end that glosses over the messiness of lived experience, the turbulence of our streams of consciousness, and the absence of absolute beginnings and determinable endings.[16] As Frank Kermode observes in *The Sense of an Ending*, many writers—at least in the modern world—find difficulty in sustaining the illusion that life is as orderly and rounded as our fictions make it appear to be.

> How good it would be, [Robert Musil] suggests, if one could find in life the simplicity inherent in *narrative order*. This is the simple order that consists in being able to say: "When that had happened, then this happened." What puts our mind at rest is the simple sequence, the overwhelming variegation of life now represented in, as a mathematician would say, a unidimensional order. We like the illusions of this sequence, its acceptable appearance of causality: "It has the look of necessity." But the look is illusory; Musil's hero Ulrich has "lost this elementary narrative element" and so has Musil. *The Man Without Qualities* is multidimensional, fragmentary, without the possibility of a narrative end. Why could he not have this narrative order? Because "everything has now become non-narrative." The illusion would be too gross and absurd.[17]

It is not only the postmodern shattering and scattering of subjectivities—personal or cultural—that robs narrative of its credibility as a model of existential order. Nor can we entirely attribute the delegitimation of narrative to the abstract, denotative, nonnarrative forms of understanding that permeate the postmodern world. For the new technologies of communication that have virtualized reality in such manifold ways since the Second World War have, ironically, been countered by a resurgence of literary, journalistic, and cinematic realism during the same period, and it may well be that it is a desire to bear witness to the brute facts of human experiences "after Auschwitz," a desire to speak "without flippancy, about things that matter,"[18] to do justice to lived experience by eschewing literary artifice, wishful thinking, and romantic stereotypes, that has, as much as anything, undermined the authority of traditional narrative. Though fiction provides us with ingenious ways of escaping reality into fantastic or virtual worlds where everything is predictable, simple, and solvable, it is equally true that in times of *extreme* hardship people sometimes repudiate such legerdemain, spitting on language as a travesty of life and seeing in silence the only decent way of respecting it. Though such silence is a far cry from the speechlessness that accompanies terror and trauma, deliberate silence is a familiar strategy among refugees, survivors of death camps, abused children, shell-shocked soldiers, victims of torture and rape, and the bereaved and is often enjoined in ceremonies of remembrance for the victims of catastrophes.

In a poignant and powerful short story, Lorrie Moore goes straight to the heart of such experience. The story concerns a mother struggling to come to grips with the fact that her only child has a cancerous tumor on his liver. The mother is a writer. Throughout the crisis, her husband urges her to "take notes." She takes notes. She has recourse to narrative to cope with her confusion and stress. But she feels contemptuous of narrative. "I write fiction," she cries. "This isn't fiction." She says, "I mean, the whole conception of 'the story,' of cause and effect, the whole idea that people have a clue as to how the world works is just a laughable metaphysical colonialism perpetrated upon the wild country of time."[19] After her child has undergone surgery and is recovering, the mother renders her final angry judgment on the work of narrative:

> How can it be described? How can any of it be described? The trip and the story of the trip are always two different things. The narrator is the one who has stayed home, but then, afterward, presses her mouth upon the traveler's mouth, in order to make the mouth work, to make the mouth say, say, say. One cannot go to a place and speak of it; one cannot both see and say, not really. One can go, and upon returning make a lot of hand motions and indications with the arms. The mouth itself, working at the speed of light, at the eye's instructions, is necessarily stuck still; so fast, so much to report, it hangs open and dumb as a gutted bell. All that unsayable life! That's where the narrator comes in. The narrator comes with her kisses and mimicry and tidying up. The narrator comes and makes a slow, fake song of the mouth's eager devastation.[20]

Though many people act *as if* the patterning of events in their fictions corresponded to the patterning of events in reality,[21] the truth is that our lives are for the most part, as Lorrie Moore says, "unsayable," and emplotted only in our imaginations. "The trouble with life," observes Martin Amis in a more ironic vein, "is its amorphousness, its ridiculous fluidity. Look at it: thinly plotted, largely themeless, sentimental and ineluctably trite. The dialogue is poor, or at least violently uneven. The twists are either predictable or sensationalist. And it's always the same beginning; and the same ending. . . ."[22] In the face of the idea that human lives are orchestrated and symphonic, we need to remind ourselves of Schönberg's atonality, with its rejection of classical harmonies and eternal formal laws. The idea that any human life moves serially and progressively from a determinate beginning, via a middle passage, towards an ethically or aesthetically satisfying conclusion, is as artificial as the idea of a river running straightforwardly to the sea. Lives and rivers periodically flood and run dry; rapids alternate with calm stretches, shallows with depths; and there are places where eddies, countercurrents, undertows, cross-currents, backwaters, and dark reaches make navigation unpredictable.

Literature is often celebrated as a manifestation of genius, evidence of a civilizing process that began with the imprint of a hand on the wall of a Paleolithic cave or rock shelter. But writing is but one means of making a life livable. Of connecting with others, of transforming one's experience. Regardless of what value may be placed on any finished work, it helped someone recover something that she had lost. Before it circulated as a product to be marveled at or imitated, it enabled someone to regain some purchase over events that confounded him, humbled him, and left him helpless, salvaging a sense that he had some say in the way his fate unfolded. In telling stories we renew our faith that the world is within our grasp.

Following a devastating stroke, Jean-Dominique Bauby awoke from a deep coma and learned how to dictate his memoir, using only his left eyelid.[23] In *The Man with a Shattered World,* the great Russian neuropsychologist, A. R. Luria, describes a long-term patient of his who suffered massive damage to the left occipital–parietal region of his brain when hit by shell fragments in 1942. Alexandr Romanovich Luria was not only a pioneer in neuropsychological studies of memory, language, and cognition, but he also refused to allow the abstract models of science to eclipse the lived reality of human beings—the ways in which they saw their world and struggled to live even under the most debilitating circumstances. If science often gives the impression of writing off individuals in order to grasp the external forces that shape their lives, Luria's detailed case histories do justice to the individuals with whom he is concerned, illuminating the worlds of their experience. He therefore describes how, for twenty-five years, Zazetsky painstakingly filled volume after volume of notebooks with accounts of his fragmented world, even though he was unable to write connectedly about his life. Writing, observes Luria, "was his one link with life, his only hope of not succumbing to illness but recovering at least a part of what had been lost."[24]

Zazetsky was under no illusions that his scribblings would constitute a coherent narrative, help recover his memory, or be of much use to anyone else. Perhaps that is why he referred to his writing as "morbid," though it was something he had to do. "If I shut these notebooks, give it up, I'll be right back in the desert, in that 'know-nothing' world of emptiness and amnesia."[25] What sustained him was a primitive existential imperative—to act rather than be acted upon. "The point of my writing, he said, is to show how I have been, and still am, struggling to recover my memory. . . . I had no choice but to try."[26]

In March 1995, the anthropologist João Biehl visited a place in the south of Brazil that a human rights activist described to him as "a dump site of human beings."[27] Ironically named Vita (life), the place had been founded in 1987 by Zé das Drogas, a former street kid and drug dealer. After his conversion to Pentecostalism, Zé had a vision in which the Spirit told him to open a place where people like him could find God and regenerate their lives. Zé and his religious friends squatted on private property near downtown Porto Alegre, a comparatively well-off city of some two million people, and inaugurated a precarious rehabilitation center for drug addicts and alcoholics. Soon Vita's mission enlarged. An increasing number of homeless, mentally ill, and dying persons began to be dumped there by the police, by psychiatric and general hospitals, by families and neighbors. Vita's team then opened an infirmary where these human beings—most of them without documents or names—awaited death. Two years after first visiting Vita, João met a woman "of kind manners, with a piercing gaze, whose speech was slightly slurred."[28] João was struck by Catarina's mobility. While others lay on the ground or crouched in corners, abject, withdrawn, immobilized, Catarina "wanted to communicate."[29] Her ties to her family had been severed, her voice was ignored, and her actions appeared to matter to no one, yet she wanted to engage, and João responded. "I lived kind of hidden, an animal," Catarina would later tell him, "but then I began to draw the steps and to disentangle the facts with you."[30]

Clearly, this woman refused her exclusion. Not only did she struggle to rise above silence, to transmit her sense of the world; she sought to reconnect with the world from which she had been ostracized, as ill, as mad, as "a maimed statue."[31] Even before João began working with her, Catarina had been working nonstop on what she called her dictionary—an extraordinary compendium of key words and cryptic phrases that resembled Zazetsky's journal, piecing together the evidence of her ties with the world from which she had been banished.

Recovery of my lost movements
A cure that finds the soul
The needy moon guards me
With L I write Love
With R I write Remembrance

João remarks, "Catarina writes to remain alive."[32] But it is also true that João writes in order to keep Catarina alive. Although she died in September 2003, João's book, published two years later, is a testimony to her life and struggle.

In the closing pages of his book, João describes how a Vita volunteer called Oscar, reflecting on the work they had done together for many years, turned to Catarina and said, "I came to see myself in you."[33] Undoubtedly, this was as true for João as it was for Oscar, for he had grown up in the same town as Catarina, just outside Porto Alegre (Novo Hamburgo), though without any awareness that places like Vita existed. As a boy, João once told me, "I would find myself riding on a bus through these poor neighborhoods and become vaguely aware that a couple of generations back my own family would have been struggling to make a living under similarly dire conditions, and that a strange kinship connected me to these places, these people, and their destinies." Perhaps, I suggested to João, this is why, even before your first encounter with Catarina, you were open to such a relationship, disposed to such an identification, for is it not true that just as we have shadows so we carry within us images of who we might have been under other circumstances and that it is this other who is the unacknowledged subject of everything we write?

SIXTEEN

Writing out of the Blue

WRITING NEVER CEASES to astound me. Not for what can be conjured or conveyed with words, but for how language allows us to go beyond ourselves, to become other than what we are or have ever been. To imagine that a voice out of the blue, without a face, is addressing us and holds clues as to our true destiny. To contemplate another life, and think "there but for grace of God go I." To see a stranger in a waiting train and imagine for a fleeting moment that you two belong together.[1] To feel the presence of God after a church service has ended and the church has been reclaimed by silence.[2] To speak of a beehive as if it were one's innermost self, aswarm with "unintelligible syllables" like a Roman mob.[3] To suppose that one can feel "the tug of the halter at the nape" of the neck of a girl unearthed from a Danish bog.[4] To see heaven in a wildflower and a world in a grain of sand.[5] To feel that the tragedy of five Franciscan nuns, drowned off a wild Welsh coast, commissions one to speak, who has for many years kept silent because of a "higher" religious calling.[6] To respond to a distraught woman waiting outside a Petersburg prison for news of her son by saying you can describe what it is like.[7] To believe that a vision of an Abyssinian damsel with a dulcimer, singing of Mount Abora, is the same vision that moved a thirteenth-century Mongolian emperor to build a palace and pleasure dome.[8] To become a windhover "in his riding of the rolling level underneath him steady air."[9] To imagine a prayer as "the minims sung by a tree, a sudden gift,"[10] or describe the blur of distant rain as "an arrow-shower sent out of sight."[11] Does such magic not take one's breath away?

The metamorphosis of self into other, and vice versa, lies at the heart of all literature. When Rimbaud turned Descartes on his head and declared, "Je est un autre" (I is somebody else), he was acknowledging that the ego was not the center of the universe. I am where the world itself finds expression. I am not a sovereign subject; I am subject to the influence of others. It is not I who thinks; I am thought. In the same way, I do not write; I am written. "To me this is evident: I witness the birth of my thought: I look at it, I listen to it: I give a strike of the bow: the symphony begins to stir in the depths or comes bursting onto the stage."[12]

This is why poetry and religion are often spoken of in the same breath. One lays oneself open to nature, to the world, or to God, allowing "it" to drown out the "I." Rather than seeking to be an author of the world, one allows oneself to be "written-by-the-world."[13] When, after years of grueling apprenticeship, Eugen Herrigel acquired the art of Zen archery, he remained somewhat confused about what exactly he had acquired. "I'm afraid I don't understand anything more at all," he said to his master, after loosing a commendable shot, "even the simplest things have got in a muddle. Is it 'I' who draws the bow, or is it the bow that draws me into the state of highest tension? Do 'I' hit the goal, or does the goal hit me? Is 'It' spiritual when seen by the eyes of the body, and corporeal when seen by the eyes of the spirit—or both or neither? Bow, arrow, goal and ego, all melt into one another, so that I can no longer separate them. And even the need to separate has gone. For as soon as I take the bow and shoot, everything becomes so clear and straightforward and so ridiculously simple. . . . "

"Now at last," the Master broke in, "the bow-string has cut right through you."[14]

Literary analogues are legion. Confessed Vladimir Nabokov, "The pages are still blank, but there is a miraculous feeling of the words all being there, written in invisible ink and clamoring to become visible."[15] When questioned about the design of his strange book, *Tristram Shandy,* Laurence Sterne replied, "Ask my pen; it governs me; I govern not it." Malcolm Lowry confesses a similar experience in a letter to Conrad Aiken on the writing of *Under the Volcano:* "I do not so much feel as if I am writing this book *as that I myself am being written.*" And in *If on a Winter's Night a Traveler,* Italo Calvino asks us to imagine using the verb "to think" in the impersonal third person, saying not "I think" but "it thinks" in the same way that we say "it rains." "Will I ever be able to say, "Today it writes," just like "Today it rains," "Today it is windy"? Only when it will come naturally to me to use the verb "write" in the impersonal form will I be able to hope that through me is expressed something less limited than the personality of an individual."[16]

Sitting under an ancient chestnut tree in the park of the Military Academy of Wiener Neustadt in the autumn of 1902, a young German military student named Franz Xaver Kappus read Rilke's poetry for the first time and was inspired. When he learnt that Rilke had also been a military student some fifteen years before—albeit at another school that Rilke would later describe as a place of "one long terrifying damnation"—the nineteen-year old Kappus decided to send Rilke some of his own poems for critical evaluation. Several weeks later, Kappus received a blue-sealed letter, postmarked Paris, February 17, 1903, in which Rainer Maria Rilke told Kappus that his "verses have no style of their own"[17] and suggests he desist from trying to publish his work or even secure the advice and opinion of others. "There is only one thing you should do. Go into yourself. Find out the reason that commands you to write; see whether it has spread its roots into the very depths of your heart; confess to yourself whether you would have to die if you were forbidden to write. This most of all: ask yourself in the most silent hour of your night: *must* I write."[18]

For me, there was never any doubt. From my teenage years I wanted to write as much as I wanted to love and be loved. But writing came painfully and slowly to me. My friend Harry St. Rain wrote with enviable fluency, but he wanted to avoid the pain of writing. Not surprisingly, he later turned to screenwriting because, as he put it, "you cannot afford self-mortification in that business." Another close friend, Fletcher Knight, had as much talent as Harry, but after a few initial forays into print, he never published a line, arguing that he was too fond of the company of others and could not endure the solitude of writing. I did not mind either the pain or the solitude, and taking my cue from "East Coker," I renewed my raids on the inarticulate, knowing that for the likes of me "there is only the trying,"[19] and that, as Rilke observed, "most experiences are unsayable"[20] and we are in the "deepest and most important matters, unspeakably alone."[21] What prolonged my apprenticeship, however, was my inability to realize that I would never write anything worth reading while I dwelled upon my own emotions and took refuge in my own thoughts. What I lacked was something to write about—a subject far removed from my own subjectivity, something that would wrench me out of myself.

During the winter of 1911–1912, Rilke was a guest in the castle of the Princess Marie von Thurn und Taxis Hohenlohe in Duino. Rilke's hostess was as fascinated by telepathic and spiritualist phenomena as she was renowned for her hospitality. Writers, antiquarians, and philosophers were made to feel at home in the castle and invited to participate in séances and experiment with automatic writing. Rilke's room was in a quiet corner of the castle, with windows on three sides overlooking the Adriatic Sea and a hidden stairway that led down to the oratorium. On the landward side of the castle was a zoo, with pathways winding between oaks, laurel, and pines. It seems, however, that Rilke felt less inclined to explore the landscape than brood in his eyrie, "looking out into the empty sea-space, directly into the universe."[22]

Since completing his novel, *Malte Laurids Brigge* more than two years earlier, he had felt exhausted and uninspired, and every few weeks he would move to another city or country, fretting about his dwindling finances, the insufferable weather, and his physical ailments, which included toothache, migraines, hemorrhoids, sore muscles, and "an influenza-like debility" that made him "incapable of doing anything."[23] Though Rilke was often forlorn and self-pitying, Marie Taxis succeeded in drawing him out with flattery and teasing banter. But his life at Duino became more and more of an ordeal. "A great sadness befell him," Marie Taxis would write, "and he began to suspect that this winter would fail to produce anything. Then one morning he received a tedious business letter. Wishing to deal with it right away, he had to sit down and devote himself to figures and other dry matters. Outside, a strong bora was blowing, though the sun was shining and the sea was a radiant blue seemingly overspun with silver. Rilke climbed down to the bastions, which were connected at the foot of the castle by a narrow pathway. From there the cliffs fall steeply, perhaps as much as two hundred feet down to the sea. Rilke walked back and forth deep in thought, preoccupied by his answer to the letter. Then all at once, in the midst of his brooding, he stopped dead, for it seemed to him as though in the roar of the wind a voice had called out to him: *'Wer, wenn ich schriee, hörte mich denn aus der Engel Ordnungen?'* ('Who, if I screamed out, would hear me up there among the angelic orders?') He stood still, listening. 'What is that?' he half-whispered. 'What is it, what is coming?' He took out the notebook he always carried with him and wrote down the words, and right afterward a few more that formed without any effort on his part. Who came? He knew it now: the god. Quite calmly, he climbed back up to his room, laid his notebook aside, and took care of the business letter. But by evening the whole elegy had been written down."[24] A few days later, the first elegy was followed by a second, though a year and a half would pass before the third came to him, and he would have to wait another year before the angel of the unsayable visited him again.

A surviving description of Rilke in 1910 would appear to fit the melancholic and restive individual who haunted the Schloss Duino with his blue childlike eyes, his prominent nose reminiscent of a well-bred hunting dog, his mouth surrounded by a Chinese-style spiral moustache, and the color and expression of his face changing rapidly as he spoke.[25] Punctilious in the matter of arrivals and departures, he did not give the impression of striving for mystical experience but on the contrary seemed anxious to be in touch with the divine only in order to return to the world and his work.

SEVENTEEN

A Storyteller's Story

A WRITER MAY GIVE THE IMPRESSION OF leading an insular life, lost in the hinterlands of subjective thought or fantasy. But despite appearances, the writer may not be absorbed in himself or herself but in other times, other places, other lives. The same paradox holds true of a tribal raconteur. Often in the company of others, with little time to call his own, he is no less absent-minded than the writer in his "long-tongued room," toiling "towards the ambush of his wounds."[1] Like his literate counterpart, the oral storyteller inhabits an invisible life of reverie and dream, his mind wandering, casting about, making connections. So when he begins a story with the phrase, "Once upon a time," he is letting slip that his mind was never entirely on the hoeing, plowing, or threshing, but rather it was elsewhere, preparing another kind of harvest, food for thought.

Researching Rilke's life, I found myself drawn ineluctably back to my sojourns in Sierra Leone and the weeks I spent in the Kuranko village of Kondembaia recording stories. One would be hard put to imagine more dissimilar settings: Keti Ferenke Koroma's humble mud-brick house, with its gloomy rooms, cement floors, and shabby furniture, the porch where we sat as villagers passed to and fro along the street, women with pails of water balanced on their heads, and small boys trundling hoops or skeletal trucks made of wire and tin cans and the Schloss Duino, with its square tower and fortified medieval walls, its associations with Dante, who sheltered there after being banished from his native Florence, its grand salons, beautiful frescos, priceless porcelain, and rare books.

Yet in these two artists' experiences of the creative process, and their recourse to times and places far removed from their own, there are such striking parallels that one is led to doubt the view that culture and history make us complete strangers to one another. Moreover, for both men, war obliterated their lifeworlds. In early 1916, Rilke was called up. Though discharged from the army six months later, traumatic memories of his years in military school from age eleven to sixteen shocked him into silence, and it was not until 1922 that he was able to complete the Duino Elegies, by which time the greater part of the Duino castle lay in ruins, destroyed in the various battles along the Isonzo River when Austro-Hungarian and Italian armies clashed and half a million soldiers lost their lives.

When I went back to Sierra Leone in 2002, a decade-long civil war was coming to an end. I revisited Keti Ferenke's village only to find that it had been pillaged and burned to the ground in rebel attacks. The great cotton tree that had overshadowed Keti Ferenke's house was dying, and for a hundred yards in every direction there was nothing but bare laterite. I was stunned that not a vestige of the street or the houses along it had survived the destruction, and wondered whether the sorrowful state of the great cotton tree was symptomatic of the grief it had witnessed as drug-addled rebels used its buttressing roots as butcher's blocks to sever the limbs of innocent villagers. I knelt by the concrete-edged grave of the forty men, women, and children who were murdered during the 1999 incursion, imagining that I was hearing the voices of the damned on that terrible day as sporadic gunfire signaled the arrival of the rebels and people cried, *Yuge bi nala* ("Badness has come"), and later, as word spread of what was happening, *Ma faga yo* ("We are being murdered"), *A bi na faga* ("They are killing us"), and *Ma bin na faga* ("We are all dead"). And then, *Allah ma ma dembe* ("God help us") and *Kele na l bama* ("The world is coming to an end").

When stories are told, they are told in the past tense, as if in distancing ourselves from what cannot be borne or comprehended we recover a sense that we can remake the world that has momentarily unmade us. I would discover that Keti Ferenke had not lived to see the horrors of the war. But his stories were much on my mind that day as I realized that I had been deceived by the bucolic atmosphere of more peaceful times and had never really reckoned with the violent episodes in many of his stories. Only now did I remember that the great cotton trees that shaded Keti Ferenke's house had been planted as part of a defensive palisade against Samori Ture's mounted horsemen who descended from the north one hundred years ago, sacking and burning Kuranko villages, including Kondembaia, which was rebuilt at the end of this epoch as a place of refuge and rebirth, though for many years piles of skulls could be found beneath creepers and regenerating bush on the edge of the old settlement.

Rilke observes that "a work of art is good if it has arisen out of necessity."[2] But there is a world of difference between the need to express oneself and the need for one's self-expression to have significance for others. Keti Ferenke Koroma disguised his personal preoccupations in the stories he composed and told and attributed his inspiration to Allah, much as Rilke referred his to the angelic orders. And while Keti Ferenke enjoyed his fame as a storyteller, his hope was that his stories would enable others to find a way of respecting the bonds of friendship, of being dutiful sons and daughters, and of honoring the ancestors.

"It is Allah who endows a person with the ability to think and tell stories," Keti Ferenke once told me. "It was my destiny to tell stories. When my father went to a diviner before I was born, the diviner told him that his next-born child would be very clever."

These remarks are consonant with the Kuranko idea that a storyteller simply "sets down" or "lays out" something that has been given to him or put into his mind; he is, therefore, a *til'sale*—"one who sets down *tileinu* [stories]." In this sense a storyteller is like a diviner. The diviner is "one who lays out pebbles," though it is God or a bush spirit who implants the idea of how to interpret the patterns in the diviner's mind.

"When you are told something," Keti Ferenke said, "it is good if it stays in your mind. Ideas come into my head just like that. I am not asleep. I am not in a dream. But when I think of them, I put them together as a story. I could never stop thinking of stories, though I could stop myself telling them." And he went on to describe how, as he worked on his farm or lounged in his hammock at home, he would try to develop a narrative that did justice to the idea that had been seeded in his mind, bringing it to life in an entertaining and edifying way.

Not only did ideas come to him when he was relaxed and susceptible to "divine" (we might say "unconscious") inspiration; it soon became clear to me that his stories themselves were plotted, like folktales throughout the world, as a series of critical episodes or encounters, usually three in number, that interrupt the narrative flow, creating moments of impasse and heightened suspense that are preludes to a breakthrough, a surprising intervention, a novel perspective. In Kuranko stories, these moments of hiatus and tension usually occur at a socio-spatial threshold—a river's edge, a ford, a crossroads, a bridge, the outskirts of a village or chiefdom—or at the temporal borderland between the rainy and dry seasons or night and day. Spatial and seasonal boundaries thus provide Kuranko with concrete images of existential limits in the same way that images of the no-man's land between *ius humanum* and *ius divinum* or of a censoring ego that regulates traffic across the threshold between the unconscious and conscious provide the European social imaginary with its metaphors of border situations. But in both lifeworlds, it is quasi-human figures—djinn and fetishes, scapegoats, angels and gods—that demarcate and embody the ambiguous zone where we cease to be recognizable to our everyday ourselves and confront sides of ourselves that belong to the shadows.

I see him now—self-assured, risible, indefatigable—spellbinding us in a crowded and shuttered room. In the penumbra of a hurricane lamp I take notes and adjust my tape recorder. Children clamber over one another, trying to get closer to him. Babies sleep, oblivious, on their mothers' backs. Old men, chewing kola, unmoved by the commotion, sit in the shadows. Before the night is out, Keti Ferenke will boast that he knows more stories than I have tapes to record them. He will challenge me to stay on after the others have drifted off. But weariness will defeat me and I too will wend my way home through the darkness of the village and fall asleep, dreaming already of the fantastic figures and images he has seeded in my mind.

At the time this particular story begins, the yimbe drum—the source of such sweet music during initiations—is in the hands of the hyenas in the bush. But hearing it night after night, the villagers become entranced by its sound and present an ultimatum to their chief: If you do not bring the drum to us in the village, we will go into the bush. Concerned to keep the community together and maintain his authority, the chief promises a "hundred of everything" to anyone brave enough to bring the yimbe from the bush to the town.

A young man decides to try his luck. After saying goodbye to his mother—who fears she will not see her son again—he sets off on his quest. Deep in the bush, he encounters a man-eating djinn. But the djinn, impressed by the young man's audacity and courage, decides not only to spare his life but to help him by giving him a fetish, with instructions on how to address it in an emergency, as well as an egg, a live coal, and a piece of bamboo.

That night the young man reaches the village of the hyenas. Though suspicious and wary, the hyenas offer him food and lodgings, and accede to his request to be allowed to sleep in the courthouse—where the yimbe drums are kept. In the middle of the night he steals the sweetest-sounding yimbe and flees. Hyena Sira, the canniest of the hyenas, who has not slept for fear of what the young man might do, rouses the other hyenas and leads them in pursuit of the thief. However, each time the hyenas threaten to overtake him, the young man summons the fetish. The first time it tells him to throw down the bamboo, which becomes an impenetrable forest that hyena Sira has to gnaw her way through. The second time it tells him to use the live coal to set fire to the grass, though hyena Sira quickly douses the flames by pissing on them. The third time it tells him to throw down the egg; it turns into a great lake that enables the young man to reach the safety of the town with the yimbe drum in his possession.

Now, the djinn had given the young man the fetish on condition that he kill a red bull and offer it as a sacrifice to the fetish when his quest was ended. But the young man forgets his promise, and when hyena Sira, disguised as a seductive young woman, comes to the village and entices him to accompany her home, he sets off with no thought for his safety.

Once they've crossed the lake, hyena Sira leads the young man into an ambush. As the hyenas close in for the kill, he shinnies up a tree and summons the fetish for help. The fetish says nothing. Desperately he summons it again. Again no response. It is then that he remembers his broken promise, and declares that he will sacrifice two bulls to the fetish if it saves him. As the hyenas are about to tear him limb from limb the fetish breaks its silence. It tells him to take a branch from the tree. It turns into a gun. The fetish then tells him to take some leaves. These turn into bullets. He fires on the hyenas and they flee for their lives.

The young man returns home, and makes the promised sacrifice to the djinn.

I have always liked to compare this story with Defoe's *Robinson Crusoe.* Both are allegories of the wilderness in which the protagonists, separated from their ordinary lives, struggle not only to survive but to triumph. But while the hero of the Kuranko story succeeds in keeping his community together, the world Crusoe creates is entirely his own. Beholden to no one, he is the self-made man, the possessive individualist, a law unto himself, captain and savior of his own soul.

With whom might the anthropologist identify—with Crusoe, or with the young man who belatedly makes good his promise to the djinn? And how can we write in ways that satisfy ourselves yet make our writing accessible and useful to others? Summing up his philosophy of film making, the great Russian director Andrey Tarkovsky observed that while art is by nature aristocratic, any artist is responsible to the world in which he or she lives. In this sense, the artist is *vox populi,* since the work not only satisfies a need for self-expression but also an obligation to others. "When I finish a work, and, after a longer or shorter interval and more or less blood and sweat as the case may be, it is finally released—then I confess that I stop thinking about it. The picture has sloughed me off, it has gone out on its own, to start an independent adult life away from its parent, and I no longer have any say in what will happen to it."[3] There are echoes here of Eugenio Montale's essay on the second life of art, in which the Nobel Prize–winning poet observes that the divorce between art and the ordinary citizen is a relatively recent development. The convoluted syntax, willful obscurantism, fragmentation and formlessness of much contemporary poetry or, for that matter, the indwelling and ethereal works of a sensitive soul like Rainer Maria Rilke, possess in Montale's view "a misguided respect for the ineffability of life and a fear of walking down already-traveled streets."[4] Undoubtedly, the Italian poet would have approved of Keti Ferenke Koroma, for whom stories seem to originate in an unnameable space beyond oneself, yet, after being given form, pass into circulation in the public sphere, available to everyone. Thus, an art born of life always has to flow "back into the very life from which it took its first nourishment," serving and speaking for all humanity. Initially, the inspiration exists solely in us, holding us in thrall for as long as it takes to send it packing into the world. Then it is not longer ours. It is for others to judge or use as they see fit. Accordingly, the story of the yimbe drum has become, for me, an allegory of anthropology—my debt to those, like Keti Ferenke Koroma, who gave me the wherewithal to write and without whom my own work of words would have been stillborn.

EIGHTEEN

Writing in the Dark

PREFACING HIS *ESSAYS*, Michel de Montaigne says that he writes not for the world at large, in prose decked out to secure public favor, but for a select audience of close friends and kinsmen, so that when he dies they will find in his writings some traits of his character and of his humors. "They will thus keep their knowledge of me more full, more alive."[1] As it turned out, Montaigne's writing outlived his friends and family and found favor in quarters to which he claimed to be indifferent. There are many like myself who are beneficiaries of his unintended bequest. But grateful though I am for these remarkable writings, published posthumously by his widow in 1595, I often ponder the anonymous graveyards of history in which so many individuals, as brilliant as Montaigne, disappeared without a trace. Though one's own work is indebted to a long line of named precursors, one is bound also to pay homage to those whose names have not survived and whose absence is also a precondition for our own presence.

In a typically aphoristic vein, Walter Benjamin observes that "Death is the sanction of everything that the storyteller can tell," and that the storyteller "has borrowed his authority from death." That is to say, Benjamin continues, "it is natural history to which [all] stories refer back."[2] To illustrate his assertions, Benjamin summarizes a story by Johann Peter Hebel, called "The Unexpected Reunion," that builds on the events surrounding the mysterious death of a young Swedish miner named Mads Isaksson in 1687. Benjamin is particularly fascinated by the way in which Hebel embeds his story in natural history, so that the devastating loss suffered by a young woman whose fiancé vanished without a trace on the eve of the midsummer day she was to be married reminds us of the historical calamities and countless deaths that occurred in Europe in the forty-two years before the fateful day Mads Isaksson returned from the dead.

A few years ago, I was in Western Sweden, attending a conference, and seized the opportunity to visit the great copper mine at Falun, now a World Heritage Site.

The first thing you see as you approach the mine are various eighteenth-century buildings clustered around the open-cast pit—the old mine entrance, the dressing plant, the machine director's house, the miner's lodge, the shaft heads, and hoists and water wheels. Then you come to the edge of the great pit itself, 325 feet deep and between 1,000 and 3,000 feet across, its present shape the result of a massive cave-in on June 25, 1687, when underground galleries and chambers collapsed down to a depth of 1,000 feet, together with the rock walls dividing what were at that time three separate open pits. Time did not allow me to tour the old buildings, some of which were now museums, but after putting on a waterproof cape and gumboots I joined a tour party that was making the first descent of the day.

I was immediately aware of how different this was from George Orwell's experiences of going down a mine. Where Orwell had been obliged to walk hunched over or to crawl on hands and knees along dark tunnels for hours on end to reach the coalface, a modern elevator carried our party comfortably and quickly 180 feet underground from where we walked along a newly driven drift to the oldest sections of the mine. And while Orwell visited a working mine, and saw at first hand the hellish conditions under which miners toiled far beneath the landscapes of Yorkshire, we found ourselves in a place of ghosts. A working mine, as Orwell so vividly describes, is a place of infernal noise and suffocating dust, of backbreaking work in a dark, confined space. But at Falun, the galleries were as vacant and silent as a graveyard, and the artificial lighting imparted a grey and ghostly pallor to the stone. Dwarfed by the gigantic chamber in which I found myself, its jagged vaults reminding me of a decayed tooth, I had to imagine the labor that had created the underground passages, the explosions that had brought down the ore, the men who had hewn and hacked at the solid rock, carrying the spoil away in wooden barrows and shoring up the shafts with stacked pine logs.

When people die, houses are abandoned, wars end or mines are shut down, these moribund lifeworlds live on for a time in the memories of those who knew them at first hand. Recounted as stories, these memories may be passed on to the next generation, but thereafter all direct experience of the past is lost. Yet we remain haunted by the historic past, as if those who lived long ago had permeated the earth, continuing to speak to us in ghostly whispers, their presence felt in the dank air that recalls their dying breath. But how exactly can we explain our attraction to the past, our interest in sorting through surviving documents, rummaging in archives, visiting industrial museums? Is it the same impulse that compels us to explore lifeworlds remote from our own, as if in comparing ourselves with others we stand to gain a better sense of who *we* are? Or do we seek in these excursions into the past to compensate the dead for something we feel was tragically withheld from them? Perhaps, in salvaging a sense of the reality of labor from the monumental products that both outlast the laborer and extinguish his identity, we may also recover a sense of the lives that history has consumed in its wake, but still linger at the periphery of our consciousness as names on untended graves or cenotaphs or as photographs that give us a brief glimpse into the actual existence—so uncannily like our own—of our predecessors.

These were my thoughts as I followed our guide down old wooden staircases where the only sound was dripping water or the amazed murmurings of some of our party as they spied wooden wheelbarrows and implements lying in the rubble, having been perfectly preserved for hundreds of years.

We now entered the vast chamber adjacent to the Creuz shaft that plunges 680 feet into the bowels of the earth on the fringe of the central ore body. The shaft, bisected by an enormous wooden wall built between 1833 and 1836, was perhaps the world's tallest wooden structure. Behind the wall were manways and pumps; in front hung an immense wooden bucket with iron hoops, in which, our guide explained, workers and equipment were lowered into the mine and the ore was hauled to the surface. At every shift change, the bucket was packed with men, some standing on the rim and clinging to the leather cable. Those coming on shift would move their collective weight to and fro in order to swing the bucket close to the edge of the chamber, whereupon they would jump out.

The copper mountain at Falun was worked from late Viking times, possibly as early as the eighth century, until well into the nineteenth century and was only officially closed on December 8, 1992. In the seventeenth century—the heyday of Sweden's power—the mine was the source of the nation's wealth, and Falun was the country's second largest city. At this time, Swedish copper accounted for 70 percent of world production, and many of Europe's great buildings, including the Palace of Versailles and the Christiansborg Castle in Copenhagen, were roofed with Falun copper. One thousand Swedish miners worked below, though most of the engineers and explosive experts were German. Our guide also reminded us that the red paint with which houses were treated throughout Sweden derived from the rock from which the copper ore was extracted. Rich in iron ochers and silicic acid, this waste rock was allowed to oxidize in the open air before being slurried, dried, and calcined. The ruddle was then ground into Falu Rödfärg, or red pigment.

After a short walk through damp passages, we assembled in yet another chamber, where the guide drew our attention to the signatures of visiting dignitaries and member of the Swedish family who, for centuries, owned the wealth from the mine. In 1687, our guide continued, a major cave-in occurred. Miraculously it happened on the one day of the year—midsummer—when the mine was deserted, and so it was thought that there were no casualties. But forty-two years later, a young man who had mysteriously gone missing on Midsummer Eve was found in a disused section of the mine. The copper sulfate in the water had perfectly preserved his body, and when he was brought to the surface the locals recognized him as Mads Isaksson. He had been due to marry on that long ago midsummer day, and his bride-to-be, now a woman in her sixties, found herself face to face with the still youthful man who had unaccountably disappeared on the eve of their wedding. It was conjectured that he had gone down the mine on a drunken dare, fallen asleep, and been entombed by the cataclysm. Our guide invited us to imagine this aging woman, who had never married, finally meeting her ageless paramour and discovering his fate. However, Fed Mads was not to rest in peace, even now. His body was placed in a glass casket. And even though it was quickly reclaimed by the elements from which it had been protected for so many years, the legend of the "petrified miner" spread throughout Europe and inspired Richard Wagner to sketch the outline of an opera about him and Johann Peter Hebel (1760–1826) to write his famous story.

That night in my hotel room at Dalarna, I could not sleep. I was haunted by the Piranesi-like images of those underground chambers with their gigantic stacks of pine logs caulked with gangue, supporting the rough-hewn vaults and rock walls. I went to the window and looked out at the dark pinewoods and the snow, trying to figure out what it was that had so troubled me about my visit to the Falun mine. Was it the gap between the way the Falun mine was now advertised to the visitor and the way it had been experienced as a workplace in the past—a gap between representation and reality? Or was it the thought of the tens of thousands of men who had toiled in that mountain over the centuries and were now unknown to us? Walter Benjamin cites Pascal's observation that "no one dies so poor that he does not leave something behind."[3] This is wishful thinking, a sign of how hard it is to accept, when confronted by a past that survives only as a few poignant remains, that it is forever beyond reach. And it occurred to me that many of us want to refuse the estranging effects of time, to countermand the narratives and statistics that render the meaning of human toil in terms of the conversion of raw material into monumental buildings, human dwellings, and fleets of battleships. They spoke of Fed Mads as "the petrified man." Perhaps, however, the people of Elsborg saw in his miraculous reappearance the possibility of redeeming their lives from the thankless labor that made the nation great but left their own lives unchanged. For though the names of kings and bishops are still inscribed on the rock faces of the mine, Fed Mads is the only worker whose name survives and who, as it were, has not been buried in the adytum of history and the darkness of the mountain.

Among the fascinating books and essays I read in the weeks after my visit to Dalarna and Falun, was a book of "interesting sketches" by Thomas W. Knox, published in San Francisco in 1878, that included an account of his descent into the Wieliczka salt mines near Cracow, Poland. Then the most productive and largest salt mine in the world, the Galicia mines employed 1400–1500 men who worked twelve hour shifts for a wage of 30–40 cents a day, though the mine generated a revenue of $6 million per annum. In Knox's eyes, these Polish and Austrian miners were sub-men who, being "densely ignorant, were not tortured by brighter memories, nor haunted by pictures of the possible."[4] The Poles in particular, he noted in passing, possessed "a certain kind of stupid contentment" and had "no ambition, and no future." All bore "the marks of undevelopment, all the traces of an animal and undisciplined nature. Mind, in the strict sense, is omitted in their composition. They are merely machines of flesh and blood, obeying physical instincts, and impelled by the law of self-preservation."[5] Knox makes no bones about the extent to which such views were shared by his guides, and undoubtedly these benighted attitudes were shared by those who profited most from these men's subterranean toil, for it is always comforting to tell oneself that "undeveloped" persons are paying the price of one's own and one's nation's development, though these days we probably rely as much on external as internal censorship to blind us to the true costs of generating wealth and fuelling an urban–industrial state.

The theme of the degradation of labor has a long history. The back-breaking and soul-destroying character of manual labor often leaves one feeling that one's hands have become like the stone on which one toils, one's body as hard and one's mind as unfeeling as the materials on which one works. Nowhere is this image of petrification and mineralization more vividly conveyed than in the photographs by Sebastião Salgado that document the Brazilian gold prospectors or *garimpeiros* of the Amazon. Enrique Rodríguez Larreta describes the appearance of the human beings in these photographs as:

> grey and uniform under the sacks of earth, which they transport up and down the rudimentary staircases of the mine. The dark skin is covered with mud. The photographs transfer a motionless expression. It is as if the strong bodies have become an appendix of that violated and disturbed Nature. The dirt partially hides the trademarks on the T-shirts and shorts—Coca-Cola, Harvard, Princeton University—so common in the shantytowns of Brazil. Dirt provides the uniform grey color of the gold diggers just as it did that of the slaves in Fritz Lang's film *Metropolis*. All the associations of contemporary critical social theory from Theodor Adorno to Michel Foucault seem to be confirmed by these images: the anonymity of the bodies transformed into productive tools, the febrile agitation produced by the bewitched fetishism of gold.[6]

Larreta goes on to say, however, that "every image simultaneously obscures and reveals," and in his own remarkable study of the *garimpeiros* he brings to light the experience of the workers and their lifeworlds—the gold diggers who dream of striking it rich, their dread of losing everything, their sense of being adventurers, explorers and frontiersmen, staking their lives on a lucky break or a change in their fortunes; the system of debt-servitude that binds them to local entrepreneurs; the camaraderie that binds them to one another; the violence and illness that threatens their lives at every turn; the accursed world of local nightclubs where the *garimpeiros* converts his meager gains into moments of masculine triumph and communitas. One wonders whether Knox, whose book is as forgotten as it was misbegotten, would have appreciated the irony of recent events in Chile, when thirty-three mine workers, entombed for sixty-nine days 2000 feet beneath the Atacama Desert became household names and national heroes, or whether he would have been moved by the humanity of these men who, despite the media circus that celebrated their stoic endurance and "miracle" of rebirth, spoke bitterly of the criminal neglect of safety in the mine and of the dark night of the soul as they waited for death under the granite weight of the collapsed shafts above and around them.

If writing is sometimes a lonely and profitless occupation, it is seldom life threatening, which may explain why writers often agonize over how they can do justice to the extreme experiences to which they bear witness. It is as if we are under an obligation to honor those whose lives were sacrificed to the pitiless demands of capital, imagining these lost souls in purgatory, awaiting the day of judgment when all that has been stripped from them in this world, their labor exploited, their names erased, their rights denied, will be redeemed. But can writing ever set the world to right, or is it doomed to fall short of its redemptive goal, resembling, as Adorno warns, "the musical accompaniment with which the SS liked to drown out the screams of its victims"[7] in the death camps of the Third Reich?

When she was thirteen, Judith Sherman was transported in a cattle wagon, along with countless others, from Kurima, Czechoslovakia, to "resettlement" in the east. Her father and mother, and her brother Karpu, would perish in the lagers, though she would survive Ravensbrück to marry, bring children of her own into the world, become a grandmother, and remember her parents when they were younger than her own offspring and her brother who would "forever be nine." When Davíd Carrasco introduced me to Judith Sherman at Harvard in 2007, I did not know what to say to her. My inability to conceive of the experiences she had undergone more than sixty years ago became translated into a sense that I was unworthy of her and that anything I might say would be foolish or inappropriate. Just as we think of the SS as monsters, so we think of their victims as angels. Judith quickly put me in my place. She related to me as a fellow poet. We exchanged poems and e-mails. In commenting on mine she called into question the value of metaphor and imagination. "I want an exact, literal hearing of my words. The reality is there, concrete and indisputable. It must not be subject to fancy or escapism." When I asked her why we are compelled to write, she replied, "It prevents nothing, but helps us feel our way through the darkness." On another occasion she said, "We are owned by a past we cannot abandon." Judith then asked me a question. "Should we ever forgive?" I quoted Hannah Arendt, who argued that forgiveness has less to do with absolving our tormentors than with wresting back our lives from their grasp. "This, you have achieved," I said. "You sum it up in that phrase about living two existences at the same time, the presence of bread today never erasing the memory of the absence of bread in the past."

> I am here and I am there, when I have a shower, when I eat potatoes, when I am hungry, when I am not. When I sneeze I think in hiding that would be a give away. If an infant cries, will there be milk? Water? . . . In supermarkets I do not select fruits or vegetables. I just take those from the top. I cannot engage in "selections" because of Auschwitz—because of Mengele.[8]

But it is not for us to write the holocaust, Judith said. This is God's work, for in our darkest hour, beaten and abused by the SS, we were so visible to them and so invisible to Him. Judith was therefore prepared to wait for all eternity, if necessary, for God to account for his absence, and her memoir can be read not only as a testimony to man's inhumanity to man but as an epistle to God. And I think here of Hélène Cixous's compelling lines about writing as a way in which we "confront perpetually the mystery of the there-not-there. The visible and the invisible. Writing: a way of leaving no space for death, of pushing back forgetfulness, of never letting oneself be surprised by the abyss. Of never becoming resigned, consoled; never turning over in bed to face the wall and drift asleep again as if nothing had happened; as if nothing could happen."[9]

In Ravensbrück, Judith would wake at three-thirty every morning and go the washroom. "There would be dead bodies on the floor. Either nothing flowed from the tap into the rusty basin, or it would cough out brown and slimy water. But in turning on this tap, I felt empowered. In going through the motions of washing my hands as my mother had taught to me, I kept her alive." Now, aged eighty, Judith Sherman walks barefoot from her house to the street every morning, sun, rain or snow, to collect the newspaper, answering the *appell,* keeping in mind that place of terror and death where so many were lost. "The morning, shoeless, I stand with them. The rest of the day I wear shoes."

Even if it is true that "to write poetry after Auschwitz is barbaric,"[10] poetry will be written, for the very reason that, despite the mass destruction of human lives, life itself goes on. This is not a choice.

The aftermath of the civil war in Sierra Leone brought this home to me. Counting or grieving one's losses, or seeking revenge, are sometimes luxuries one cannot afford. What matters is feeding one's family, surviving the day, having a chance at tomorrow.

Amputees' Camp, Freetown

Heaney with his Grauballe and
Tollund men might have focused on
the missing arm, its walnut burr and whorl
of skin from which I shrink, gone as far
as making their phantom pain
a metaphor for memory—the day
that they recall, slow-motion as in space,
a blunt machete sawing through a limb,
a screaming child, and all that followed
not in thought but flight.

We are voyeurs
whom bog-dark centuries keep safe.
Distant, these are not our kin.
He knows this best who has no words for it:
"They came at noon. By evening they were gone.
Twenty of us were dead, or bleeding
from our wounds. We were farmers.
What had we done to them?
We cannot forget,
cannot forgive,
though life goes on."
    The halter at the neck
is nothing they can use. No fingerprints
identify the enemy, divine a cause.
Images of ridge and river, grain or tar
make damn all difference.
    Here is no "tribal, intimate revenge".
Only the matter of fact phrases:
"Seed rice is all we ask. With seeds we can begin again."

NINETEEN

Writing in the Zone

IN ANDREY TARKOVSKY'S UNFORGETTABLE FILM, *Stalker,* a scientist, a writer, and a tormented individual known simply at Stalker, move through a mysterious landscape that resembles a devastated industrial zone. Somewhere in this forbidden and nightmarish place there is a room where one's wishes may be granted and happiness found. Though Stalker himself appears indifferent to this room, accepting who he is and desiring nothing more, the scientist hopes that in explaining the mystery of the zone he may be awarded a Nobel Prize. When the scientist berates the writer, calling him a blabbermouth, good for little more than painting walls in public toilets, the writer sneers at the scientist's "purchased imagination." "Let's imagine I do enter this room," he says, "and return to our God-forsaken town a genius. A man writes because he's tormented, because he has doubts. He needs to constantly prove to himself and to others that he's worth something. And if I know for sure I'm a genius? Why write then? What the hell for?"

Considering the anguished lives of writers, one might be forgiven for concluding that writing is an obsessive–compulsive disorder that can only cause great misery and ruin. Think of W.G. Sebald, for instance, working on his account of Max Ferber:

> It was an arduous task. Often I could not get on for hours or days at a time, and not unfrequently I unraveled what I had done, continuously tormented by scruples that were taking tighter hold and steadily paralysing me. These scruples concerned not only the subject of my narrative, which I felt I could not do justice to, no matter what approach I tried, but also the entire questionable business of writing.[1]

Even writers who found the going less rough have had recourse to odd stratagems to keep their noses to the grindstone or find inspiration. Rudyard Kipling demanded the blackest of inks before he could begin writing.[2] Truman Capote required yellow paper. Schiller was obsessed by the smell of apples and kept several in the drawer of his writing desk. Flaubert kept Louise Colet's slippers and mittens in *his* desk drawer. And the names are legion of writers who needed nicotine, caffeine, alcohol, or opiates to stimulate their imaginations. There are also, however, the Anthony Trollopes of this world, among whom I count myself, who go about their business with minimal fuss, find considerable happiness in their work, and manage to strike a balance between writing and other pursuits. Trollope reports in his autobiography that he would awake well before first light and write from 5:30 a.m. to 8:30 a.m. with his fob watch in front of him. He required of himself two hundred and fifty words every quarter of an hour. If he finished one novel before eight-thirty, he took out a fresh piece of paper and started the next. For much of his life, his writing sessions were followed by a day job with the postal service. Even so, he went hunting at least twice a week. Under this regimen, he produced forty-nine novels in thirty-five years, and would urge his method on all would-be writers. "Let their work be to them as is his common work to the common laborer. No gigantic efforts will then be necessary. He need tie no wet towels round his brow, nor sit for thirty hours at his desk without moving."

In Copenhagen, I worked for six years at the Institute of Anthropology on Frederiksholms Kanal, within hailing distance of the Christiansborg Castle and not far from the Black Diamond on the upper reach of the harbor. Because I had no Friday classes, I would write for more than my customary two hours, and by the end of the day would often have completed a chapter or achieved some minor breakthrough in the work on which I was engaged. With a sense of quiet satisfaction, I would put on my coat and head out onto the damp and windswept street beside the canal, then along Gammel Strand toward Amager Square, where I would buy a *Herald Tribune* before walking north along Købmagergade toward home. A kind of post-coital calm would overcome me as I reflected on the work I had done or the prospect of our homely apartment in Nørrebro with candles lit on the window sill, glasses of wine on the dining table, our children returning from school as the darkness descended, and the voice of Cesária Évora filling the room: "If I write that I not write, if I forget that I not forget, until the day I return. . . ."

Walking up Sankt Hans Street, just before coming in sight of our apartment building, I would pass the house where Knut Hamsun, on his return from the United States in 1888, rented a cheap room under the roof at number 18 and began writing *Hunger*. Hamsun lived on rye bread without butter or cold cuts and was often without food at all for several days at a time, during which he chewed match sticks to stave off hunger pangs.

The year my contract came to an end was also the bicentenary of the birth of Hans Christian Andersen, and not long before my family and I left Denmark, a series of painted size 12 footprints appeared on the streets of downtown Copenhagen, leading to sixty-two places associated with the Danish writer. Curious to know where these trails might lead, I followed them over several days to the Tivoli Gardens; to Nyhavn, where Andersen wrote his first fairy tales; to the Royal Theatre, where, newly arrived in the city, he had hoped to be hired as a ballet dancer; and to the Rundetårn, where the University Library was located and the aspiring writer spent many hours trying to make up for his woefully inadequate education. Andersen had always fascinated me, for while folk music had inspired many European composers—including Janáček, Dvorak, Brahms, and Bartok—very few writers had succeeded in using the folktale as a narrative form, let alone preferred it to the novel. It also intrigued me that one anonymous reviewer of Andersen's first collection of fairy tales expressed the hope that "the talented author, with a higher mission to follow, will not waste any more of his time in writing fairy tales for children,"[3] since many years ago I had explained to my supervisor at Cambridge that I had collected scores of Kuranko folktales in the course of my fieldwork and that these tales shed considerable light on people's existential dilemmas and moral preoccupations, only to be advised not to bother with such trivial material. As for the African novel, some critics disparage it as overly influenced by folktales, with their episodic structure, one-dimensional characters, unbelievable happenings, and didactic motives.[4]

If Andersen sometimes appears naïve it may be because he often felt more comfortable with children than with adults, an affinity that reflects his own humble beginnings. In his final autobiography, Andersen describes his life as "a beautiful fairytale, rich and happy." He paints a picture of his grandparents as well-to-do farmers who had fallen on hard times and persuades us to believe that his parents, despite their poverty, were very much in love.

In fact, Andersen's early circumstances were very different from those he described. His father, a cobbler, died when Hans was eleven, his grandmother was a pathological liar, his grandfather was insane, his aunt ran a brothel in Copenhagen, and his mother was a washerwoman who drank heavily. This is not to say that Hans was not loved or that his parents did not do all they could to give him a start in life, only that lowly origins may have a similar effect on a person as childhood abuse, leaving him or her with a sense of unworthiness and shame that no amount of success will ever erase.

For many people whose childhoods were impoverished or degraded, good fortune can never compensate for this inner inadequacy. They carry it with them as long as they live, and they will return, time and time again, in their imaginations, to the bleak places from which they started out and from which they never really escape. Whether in the guise of an Aladdin-like soldier, an ugly duckling shunned by those around it, a mermaid heartbroken by unrequited love, a tin soldier unable to reach the object of his desire, or a hypersensitive princess who must pass a strict test to prove herself worthy of marrying a prince, Andersen chose oblique ways of recounting the story of his own tribulations, leaving Odense at fourteen to seek his fortune in Copenhagen only to suffer humiliation and rejection not only as a singer, actor, playwright, and dancer, but also as a man. He thought of himself as a swamp plant. Down at heel, wearing ill-fitting clothes, and cutting an ungainly figure, he inspired derision or pity.

Even when welcomed into the Collin family, Andersen felt ill at ease, and though his friendship with Edvard Collin came to mean the world to him, the upper-class, classically educated and reserved Collin could never bring himself to treat Andersen as an equal or use the familiar *Du* when addressing him in public. For Andersen, the unstinting help Collin gave him—correcting his spelling mistakes, discussing his work, or negotiating with publishers—seemed insignificant beside the recognition that was withheld and the aloof and supercilious attitude Collin appeared to adopt toward him. Indeed, reading Andersen's Copenhagen journals and letters, one gets the impression of someone constantly slighted and ridiculed, even though other evidence suggests that he was "much more esteemed by literary critics and the general public than he would himself allow."[5]

Perhaps the effects of poverty on a small child are ineradicable, no matter how cleverly a writer might disguise these effects in his fiction. One thinks of Andersen's admiration for Charles Dickens, whose unhappy childhood resembled his own. When the celebrated writers first met, in London in July 1847, there was, it seems, instant rapport. Over the next few months, the two writers went out of their way to renew their friendship, and a warm correspondence followed Andersen's return to Copenhagen at the end of December. But Andersen's infatuation was only partially reciprocated, and despite Dickens's obvious sympathy for "The Dane," his letters were sometimes condescending, as if he found it impossible, like Edvard Collin before him, to respond to Andersen's childlike effusiveness and devotion.

Six years after his first visit to England, Andersen returned. He stayed with the Dickens family at Gad's Hill for five weeks, his room overlooking a landscape that, he wrote, resembled a garden. "From the Hill one can follow for many miles the windings of the Thames, catch a glimpse of the open sea, and see far around over woods and fields. There is a scent of wild roses and of hay here; the air too is so fresh; and in the house itself live happy people."[6] Andersen, however, was not regarded very highly by his hosts. It wasn't only the visitor's limited English and social gaucheness; Dickens was convinced that Andersen did not even speak his own language very well, and grew exasperated by The Dane's suspicion of cabbies who he thought were bent on robbing him. When his guest finally departed, Dickens could not resist writing a card and pinning it over the dressing-table mirror: "Hans Andersen slept in this room for five weeks—which seemed to the family AGES."[7]

At around the time I was researching Andersen's Copenhagen years, I was spending occasional weeks in London, where my friend Sewa Koroma was experiencing difficulties reminiscent of Hans Christian Andersen's. I was particularly struck by Sewa's conviction that he had no right to be in England, even though he had a valid visa. "Living here," he said, "you are living in fear, fear of no life. These are the things that make this place really hard for people, I mean people living underground." Whenever Sewa saw a policeman, he would cross the road to avoid contact. The sirens of police cars freaked him out. He experienced himself as someone whose validity was constantly in question. He seemed to live in imminent danger of being found out, of making some inadvertent yet irreversible mistake, of being picked up by the police and deported. In Sierra Leone one's destiny was determined by a network of face to face relationships with people to whom you were obliged or who were under obligation to you, people whom in local parlance you could "beg" or from whom you could borrow money, expect a meal, or a roof over your head. But in London, Sewa discovered that he had passed from a patrimonial to a bureaucratic regime in which power seemed to reside less in people to whom one could appeal than in an impersonal force field that found expression in a stranger's stare, a policeman's orders, a supervisor's demands, or the letter of the law. In this inscrutable and Kafkaesque world of bureaucratic protocols, indecipherable documents, abstract rules, and official forms of validation, Sewa came up against a politics of indifference.

The "living spirit" of community had given ground to the "dead letter" of a system that recognized no one because it was nobody.[8] Among strangers, whom Sewa simply called "those people" ("dem people"), one could expect nothing but indifference, disparagement, or outright menace. "They shame me," (*An ya na moliya*), Sewa would say. "They make me feel small" (*An ya na dogoye*).

This constant exposure to a negative social environment will easily lead one to feel under attack, fearful of ostracism or deportation, and prey to a nagging guilt that the price of one's own improved chances in life is the loss of one's homeland, one's kith and kin, and one's heritage. At the same time, the impossibility of being accepted into the society in which one has sought asylum translates into a sense that one is worthless, that one is good for nothing, that one is doomed.

Hans Christian Andersen endured his demoralizing years in Copenhagen by daydreaming and reading:

> When on my first arrival in Copenhagen I walked the streets, poor and desolate and often without money for a meal, I gave the few pence I had to get a novel by Walter Scott from the lending library, and that made me forget coldness and hunger, I was rich and happy. How dear do I not hold Bulwer, how fervently do I not wish to press Boz's hand; when I read his books I often think: that have I myself experienced, that could I portray![9]

In fact, Boz's early life was possibly more harrowing than Andersen imagined, for Dickens had experienced several idyllic years before his father was thrown into debtor's prison and he was obliged, at age 12, to begin work in Warren's Blacking Warehouse, the site of which was hard by the Nissan Hut under Hungerford Bridge where I worked among the destitute during the winter of 1963–64, often giving away the little I earned in attempt to ease my conscience at the hardship I witnessed.

> The blacking-warehouse was the last house on the left-hand side of the way, at old Hungerford Stairs. It was a crazy, tumble-down old house, abutting of course on the river, and literally overrun with rats. Its wainscoted rooms, and its rotten floors and staircase, and the old grey rats swarming down in the cellars, and the sound of their squeaking and scuffling coming up the stairs at all times, and the dirt and decay of the place, rise up visibly before me, as if I were there again. The counting-house was on the first floor, looking over the coal-barges and the river. There was a recess in it, in which I was to sit and work. My work was to cover the pots of paste-blacking; first with a piece of

oil-paper, and then with a piece of blue paper; to tie them round with a string; and then to clip the paper close and neat, all round, until it looked as smart as a pot of ointment from an apothecary's shop. When a certain number of grosses of pots had attained this pitch of perfection, I was to paste on each a printed label, and then go on again with more pots. Two or three other boys were kept at similar duty down-stairs on similar wages. One of them came up, in a ragged apron and a paper cap, on the first Monday morning, to show me the trick of using the string and tying the knot. His name was Bob Fagin; and I took the liberty of using his name, long afterwards, in Oliver Twist.[10]

What sustained Sewa in London were thoughts of home, as if evoking memories of his late father, his natal village, and his happy childhood could compensate for the state of eclipse that made it sometimes impossible for him to see any way ahead in London. He once cited a Kuranko adage: If you move a chicken in the evening from one place to another, it will be agitated all night and only become settled when the new day dawns. After three years in London, Sewa confided, "I am still not settled. So it must still be night."

"What unsettles you?" I asked.

"When I worked in a restaurant," Sewa said, "I hated to see so much food left uneaten and thrown away. I hated to see people stuffing food into their mouths and talking with their mouths full. At home we eat in silence, out of respect for the food, which is always scarce and to be savored."

He mentioned a friend of his from Mali. Some English women asked if he had ever experienced a famine in Mali. Sewa's friend could not answer. He was in tears. Only when he had dried his eyes could he tell them that he had not known what it was to have a full belly until he was twenty. And he described a famine so devastating that he sometimes had to drink cow urine and eat leaves or wet clay to stave off hunger. In London, he found it difficult to watch the garbage trucks picking up furniture and clothing that would be dumped and never used. "In England," Sewa said, "life is a choice between cellphones, what we will wear to work today, which shoes, which shirt. At home we sometimes did not even have a choice between rice and cassava, meat or fish, only between eating enough today or going without tomorrow."

Is there a room, or a zone, where wishes can be granted and fulfillment found? Where one can get the measure of the world? Or should we think of fairy tales and utopian fantasies not as promising the impossible but in breaking the spell that makes us believe that virtue is necessarily rewarded, justice will be done, and the damsel in distress rescued from her tower? Sometimes the writing that satisfies us most is the writing that does not seek a happy ending, but attests to our inconclusive struggle for existence, that attends to life's surpassing detail and surprising shifts without attempting any synthesis in the name of explanation or moral insight. In his holocaust memoir, Elie Wiesel is unable to say how he survived or why he felt compelled to give meaning to his survival:

> Did I write so as not to go mad or, on the contrary, to go mad in order to understand the nature of madness? Was it to leave behind a legacy of words, of memories, to help prevent history from repeating itself? Or was it simply to preserve a record of the ordeal I endured as an adolescent, at an age when one's knowledge of death and evil should be limited to what one discovers in literature? [11]

TWENTY

Writing, Naturally

WITHOUT A READERSHIP, a writer's work remains unconsummated. This is nowhere more evident than in a haiku, whose brevity, ambiguity, and syntactical compression require someone other than the author to fully realize its potential. The same principal holds true of a folktale. Its minimalism fools many into thinking that it is a childlike form of storytelling, lacking depth of character, and bereft of the descriptive detail that supposedly makes the novel more psychologically sophisticated and satisfying. Yet it is by stripping a story of the author's presence and preoccupations that it becomes available to others. There is, accordingly, a close relationship between the submergence of the ego in Buddhist practice and forms of writing that erase an author's identity in order to let the reader enter fully into it, fleshing it out in his or her own way.

This is the only meaning I can find in the notion of objectivity—exact description takes precedence over interpretation or explanation. When Gaston Bachelard observed that there are "forces manifested in poems that do not pass through the circuits of knowledge,"[1] he did not mean that the pursuit of knowledge is intrinsically pointless, but merely that knowledge must be "accompanied by an equal capacity to forget knowing."

"In poetry," Bachelard said, "non-knowing is a primal condition."[2]

Similar phenomenological precepts may be found in Thoreau's conviction that "the roots of letters are things," and that "natural objects and phenomena are the original symbols or types which express our thoughts and feelings."[3] William Carlos Williams's dictum, "No ideas but in things," also echoes this view:

> so much depends
> upon

a red wheel
barrow

glazed with rain
water

beside the white
chickens

Nevertheless, I share Wallace Stevens's doubt that "pure" and "discursive"
modalities of consciousness can be separated out, since "things as they are/
Are changed upon the blue guitar."

Poetry is the subject of the poem,
From this the poem issues and

To this returns. Between the two,
Between issue and return, there is

An absence in reality,
Things as they are. Or so we say.

Still, we cling to the idea that the world may speak *through* us, that our own
thoughts may be silenced for this to occur, and that in stilling the discursive
mind we can transcend knowledge and allow "that which shows itself [to] be
seen from itself."[4]

To say that this goal is unattainable may be to miss the point. For what
phenomenology asks of us is that we cultivate, as best we can, a disinterested
attitude toward the world, such that it may be seen from a standpoint other
than our own, and thereby continually seen anew. Writing creates connections, not knowledge. Writers should not be in the business of confirming
what is assumed to be true, but in apprehending the world as a source of
perennial surprise, "gleaning the unsaid off the palpable."[5] Such selflessness
opens up the possibility that the world may write us to the same extent that
we write it. Said Bashō:

Go to the pine if you want to learn about the pine, or to the bamboo if you
want to learn about bamboo. In doing so, you must leave your subjective preoccupations with yourself. Otherwise you impose yourself on the object and
do not learn. Your poetry issues of its own accord when you and the object
have become one, when you have plunged deep enough into the object to see
something like a hidden glimmer there. However well phrased your poetry

may be, if your feeling is not natural—if the object and yourself are separate—then your poetry is not true poetry but merely your subjective counterfeit.[6]

Every writer who writes in this vein relives Chuang-Tzu's dilemma of not knowing whether he was happily dreaming of a butterfly or was a butterfly dreaming of a man called Chuang-Tzu.

In a letter dated October 11, 1917, to the painter Dorothy Brett, Katherine Mansfield describes this elision of the boundary between self and other:

> What can one do, faced with this wonderful tumble of round bright fruits, but gather them and play with them—and *become them,* as it were. When I pass an apple stall I cannot help stopping and staring until I feel that I, myself, am changing into an apple, too, and that at any moment I can produce an apple, miraculously, out of my own being, like the conjuror produces the egg. . . . When I write about ducks I swear that I am a white duck with a round eye, floating in a pond fringed with yellow-blobs and taking an occasional dart at the other duck with the round eye, which floats upside down beneath me. In fact this whole process of becoming the duck (what Lawrence would, perhaps, call this "consummation with the duck or the apple!") is so thrilling that I can hardly breathe, only to think about it. For although that is as far as most people can get, it is really only the "prelude." There follows the moment when you are *more* duck, *more* apple, or *more* Natasha than any of these objects could ever possibly be, and so you *create* them anew.[7]

I had Katherine Mansfield in mind when I gave a talk at Indiana University Bloomington in 1987 on Kuranko shape shifting. A year later, I was appointed to a professorship at IU. But in returning to academic life after several years of unemployment, it was I who was now the shape shifter, and I had no idea whether my new identity would stick.

In the early fall of 1951, Gary Snyder traveled a similar road. Hitching across the Nevada desert on his way to begin graduate studies in anthropology at Indiana University, he found himself waiting for a lift on the old Nevada Route 40. A few days before, he had bought a copy of D.T. Suzuki's *Essays in Zen, First Series* in a "metaphysical" bookshop in San Francisco. During his long wait for a ride, he began reading Suzuki's book. It signaled a complete change of direction in Gary Snyder's life. "I didn't know it at the moment," he wrote almost thirty years later, but "that was the end of my career as an anthropologist." In fact, Snyder lasted one semester at Indiana University, and when he dropped out he confided to his friend Nathaniel Tarn, "I realized that I didn't want to be the anthropologist but the informant."[8]

After six years in Bloomington, Indiana, I resigned my position. It wasn't that I wanted to be the informant rather than the anthropologist; I wanted to be both, free to shift between the two perspectives without settling for either one.

On the day I left the Midwest, I watched from a porch as a fallow deer grazed nervously in the gully below me, biting off clumps of moss, lifting its head, sniffing the air, listening for menace. It was perfectly camouflaged in the russet colors of the late fall, calm despite the possibility of being disturbed in the open, and I felt a deep affinity with it.

When the limo appeared like an apparition in the driveway, I shouldered my bags and descended the steps. The limo driver got out of the car and hurried to get to the trunk before me.

"No need," I said. "I'll keep the bags with me."

Why did I think of the limo as a hearse, the driver an undertaker, this journey across the Styx?

The limo glided down the road toward the pike. Some rotting jack-o-lanterns grinned toothlessly on a porch. Dead leaves skittered against the curb. And out on Highway 37 the billboards advertised Fast Food outlets, Day Mortuaries, and Insurance Companies (*Wrongful Death Claims, Animal Attacks, Auto & Truck Accidents, Slip, Trip & Fall, Defective Products*). It was all a familiar part of my life in America, yet suddenly it felt as strange as it had been when I first arrived, unable to work out the cardinal points, missing the mountains and the sea.

The truth is that no one leaves home and casts himself adrift in the world without good reason; no one, not even Bashō, abandons his life unless it has first deserted him. Bashō lived in Edo (Tokyo) for several years, writing poetry, recognized and comfortable. But his soul was in turmoil as he struggled to empty his life of worldly attachments, and recover the face he had had before he was born. When his students built him a small house in Fukagawa, at an isolated spot on the eastern bank of the Sumida River, Bashō gladly moved there and borrowed his new name, Bashō, from the species of plantain that had been planted beside his house. "The leaves of the Bashō tree are large enough to cover a harp," he explained. "When they are wind-broken, they remind me of the injured tail of a phoenix, and when they are torn, they remind me of a green fan ripped by the wind. The tree does bear flowers, but unlike other flowers, there is nothing beautiful about them. The large trunk of the tree is untouched by the axe, for it is completely useless as timber. I love the tree, however, for its uselessness. I sit under it, and enjoy the wind and rain that beat against it."[9]

> storm-torn banana tree
> all night I listen to rain
> in a basin

He practiced Zen during this period, still struggling to see the world for what it is, but in the end it was two entirely fortuitous events that opened his eyes. In 1682, after two years beside the river, a great fire engulfed Edo, and Bashō's house was destroyed. The following summer his mother died. One year later, aged thirty-eight, "in the August of the first year of Jykōyō among the wails of the autumn wind," he left his "broken house on the River Sumida" and set out on the first of his great journeys.[10]

> weather beaten
> wind pierces my body
> to my heart

> ten autumns
> Edo has become
> my native place

So where was my native place? Where, for me, was home?

My fieldwork in Central Australia had persuaded me that such questions are best answered, not by reference to substantives or essences, such as house, country, nation or family, but by paying attention to whatever gives one, in any particular cultural or social situation, a sense that one's actions matter, that one possesses some say over the course of one's life, and that one's humanity is recognized. Home is not so much a roof over one's head as it is a state of mind.

> A place we travel from
> and pine for
> when the going's hard,
> a sense of living
> as we choose.

But even states of mind can be divided, and my own sense of being at home in the world had, for me, always involved an oscillation between, and a struggle to reconcile, opposite poles of experience: north and south, solitude and soci-ality, poetry and ethnography.

"Why burn your bridges?" one friend asked me. "If things don't work out in Sydney, at least keep open the option of coming back."

"You're committing professional suicide," another said, as though she already knew intuitively that the job I had found in Sydney would fall through, and I would find myself, for the second time in my professional life, out of work.

At the airport, people were being conveyed along the moving walkways or streaming and eddying around the check-in counters like so much flotsam. The washed-up were soliciting for alms.

In the corner of the bar where I waited for my flight, the TV sets were advertising the next NFL Sunday Night game and corporate men in shirt-sleeves were drinking bourbon on the rocks and strategizing. "The thing is," I heard one of the young executives say, "we're in a transitional phase right now; we've got to see ourselves as in transition."

What of me, I thought; should I also see myself, not as washed up, but in transition?

Bashō

In Edo
city of red shrines,
a banana tree
ripped by the wind.

Its flowers grace
no state rooms
its wood has no earthly use.

From it
you took your name,
preferring
anonymity.

That winter
fire destroyed your house
and your mother died

Turning your back
on poetry
you set out on the journey
"of a weather beaten skeleton"

Then the hardest
journey of all,
north with farewell gifts
a burden on your thin
shoulders

Tempted to discard
ink bottles and rainwear
and travel free.

Sabi: the serenity
of being at one
with rivers,

So that we return to the world
a bystander, smiling
Build another

shelter,
plant
another tree.

TWENTY-ONE

Writing Workshop

WHEN INVITED TO GIVE A BRIEF TALK ON ETHNOGRAPHY at a writing workshop in the Scottish Highlands, I decided to share some anecdotes about the importance of what Jane Bennett calls "the wonder of minor experiences."[1] I wanted to demonstrate that detail determines good writing, not bright ideas. Ideas will come to light, but only if one first yields to the ethnographic particulars. And so I began by citing Arundhati Roy, author of *The God of Small Things.* "Little events, ordinary things, smashed and reconstituted. Imbued with new meaning. Suddenly they become the bleached bones of a story."

In *Flaubert's Parrot,* the English writer, Julian Barnes, takes Flaubert's most distinguished British biographer to task for accusing the great French writer of failing to "build up his characters, as did Balzac, by objective, external description. In fact, so careless is he of their outward appearance that on one occasion he gives Emma [Bovary] brown eyes (14); on another deep black eyes (15); and on another blue eyes (16)."[2] In fact, Barnes says, what appears to be carelessness is evidence of his phenomenological care, for when one examines the passages in which Emma's eyes are mentioned it is clear that her eyes were brown though appeared black when Emma was in shadow, and blue when she was in full sunlight, seeming to "contain layer upon layer of colours, which were thicker in hue deep down, and became lighter towards the enamel-like surface."[3] Indeed, if one is to achieve excellence in ethnography one would do well to make Flaubert an exemplar, as did Guy de Maupassant. The story goes that when the master, Flaubert, decided that his young friend was worthy of tuition, he sent Maupassant out onto the street to observe what was happening there. When Maupassant reported that nothing much had happened, that the day was much like any other, Flaubert sent him back to the street until he returned with a story to tell. Reminding his pupil that "talent is a long patience," he told him again and again: "There is a part of everything which is unexplored, because we are accustomed to using our eyes only in association with the memory of what people before us have thought of the thing we are looking at. Even the smallest thing has something in it which is unknown. We must find it."[4] To find it we must be patient and attentive, to be sure. But we must also be prepared to go along with what another person is saying or trying to say, even though we find it tedious, irrelevant, or outrageous.

I went on to refer to Franz Kafka, who also set great store by training the memory and keeping a record of one's quotidian observations. Elias Canetti was particularly struck by the richness of Kafka's memory, citing the minute details Kafka was able to recall seventy-five days after his first meeting with Felice Bauer on the evening of August 13, 1912.[5] Kafka remembered, for instance, passing to Felice across the table some photographs he had taken during a visit with Max Brod to the Goethe House in Weimar. What Kafka did not confide, however, is that he had succumbed to the charms of the custodian's daughter, spent time in her company, and photographed her in the garden and at the entrance to the house. These photographs were among those he passed to Felice Bauer six weeks later.

From Weimar, Kafka journeyed alone to a sanatorium at Jungborn in the Harz Mountains, from where he sent postcards to the beautiful girl he had met at the Goethe House. He copied one of her replies in a letter to Max Brod, asking Brod why she would bother to write to someone as humdrum as he was. "Could it be that one can take a girl captive by writing?"[6]

The word is arresting, not only because we speak of photographs as capturing likenesses but because ethnographers have sometimes reported on people who fear that in being photographed something of themselves will be taken away or lost.[7] Indeed, just as Kafka dreaded losing his literary soul to the women who captured his attention, so the people with whom anthropologists live and work sometimes dread the possibility of losing control over their cultural property.

This means that ethnographers must work hard to strike a balance between what they take and what they give in return.

Among the students who found my random comments of some use was a young Russian woman, Maria (Masha) Nakhshina, who confessed that she had reached an impasse in her writing, and sought my help in organizing her field notes and bringing more intellectual clarity to her project. That afternoon, eager to clear my head and reconnoiter the landscape beyond the hotel where we were lodged, I was about to head off for a long walk along Rannoch Loch when Masha asked if she might join me and talk a little more about her work. We passed black-faced sheep in lowland pastures, plantations of pine, and a roadside cairn inscribed with the names of two hundred local men who had died in two world wars. As for the loch itself, its untroubled waters reflected the rocky heights of the glacial valley and great mounds of cumulus cloud that seemed to collect on the ridges like sheep's wool on barbed wire. I apologized to Masha for not being able to give my attention entirely to her project, for the war memorial and the drab green fighter plane that roared over the loch on a strafing run had turned my mind to old clan clashes over grazing rights or a grudge, and the land clearances that sent so many crofters to the ends of the earth in search of a secure livelihood and a new life. The bleating of a lost lamb, the lichen-covered stones of a crumbling boundary wall, made me shudder at what history had wrought in even this pastoral setting, though it was not until much later that Masha spoke of the impact of war on her own homeland and family. Over the next few days, I was accompanied on further walks along the loch or up into the heather-and-windswept hills by Masha and some of the other students, and I gradually became familiar with Masha's story and began to admire her adventurous and uninhibited attitude toward life. Indeed, I rather envied her openness to new ventures—climbing and skiing in the Khibiny Mountains on the Kola Peninsula, experimenting with a raw food diet, taking flamenco classes, relishing her long train journeys across Russia and the strangers she met along the way. In Masha, I began to remember myself at her age and identify with her struggle with questions of home and belonging.

After my return to Boston, Masha wrote me from time to time, broaching the question of how long it takes to adjust to life in a new country and commenting on the irony that we often make that difficult adjustment only to find that we have become estranged from our homeland in the process.

Sometimes, I told Masha, we will be accused of having betrayed our homeland by leaving it, just as we will be censured when we walk away from a loveless marriage. But the true betrayal lies not in anything one has done or not done. It arises from the imperceptible and implacable erasure of one's original experience of home, the atrophy of close relationships, the freezing of the past, the impossibility of creating new friendships to replace the old. It is as if life slowly drains out of the living relationship between oneself and one's homeland, leaving only a hulk behind. Masha wrote that in the years since leaving Russia for Scotland she had become increasingly unsure about the locus of home. Despite frequent trips to Petersburg, her life in Aberdeen had been so replete with new experiences—experiences she could not have had in Russia—that her homeland had began to fade like an old photograph in the darkness of an album or drawer. "Now," Masha said, "I do not know where I want to live. I think I could make my home anywhere. It isn't that I am more comfortable in the UK than Russia. In fact, my Russianness is often an obstacle, as when Dr. Witherspoon responded to the first essay I wrote for him by telling me it was too Russian! And when I am back in Russia, I sometimes feel strange because I was raised during the Soviet era, which makes me very different from people even two years younger than I am, whose first memories don't predate the end of communism. And then there's the gap between me and my father."

Masha's father was born in the aftermath of the Great Patriotic War. His father had perished in the war, and his mother was imprisoned for economic fraud when he was four. After seventeen years in a State orphanage, Masha's father began two years of mandatory military service. But in his second year in the army, his mother reappeared, demanding that he now take care of her. Discharged from the army, Masha's father struggled to make ends meet. His mother's heavy drinking used up his earnings, and he wound up doing her cleaning job for her. When his mother was arrested for the second time, and jailed, he headed north to the Kola Peninsula, where he married. Again, his mother tracked him down, demanding money and care. When he refused to give her anything, she took her case to court. The court ordered him to make monthly payments to the old woman. Masha remembers the gifts her parents sent to the Psychiatric Hospital in which her grandmother was confined. But her father never shared details of this story. In fact, Masha told me, we seldom talked about anything that mattered. "My father was like a stranger to me. I know this was because no one cared for him when he was a child, and I know he cannot change who he is. Sometimes I feel like working in an orphanage."

"Perhaps we are all orphans," I wrote back. "Existential orphans, I mean. Cut off from our roots, estranged from our origins or kept from realizing our full potential, even when events do not conspire to destroy our connection to the past. And so we build our homes out of homelessness, out of not belonging."

When Masha next traveled to St. Petersburg, she sent me a round tin of mint pastilles from the Moscow Station. I placed the tin on my desk, but left it unopened. On the tin lid was a picture of the Palace Bridge over the Neva. The central spans of the bridge were raised like two hands whose fingertips were about to touch in prayer. In the middle distance, between the two uplifted ramps of the bridge, there was a baroque building with a gray cupola. Built by Peter the Great to house his bizarre collection of malformed fetuses and curious anatomical specimens, it was now the Museum of Anthropology and Ethnography. I found this metamorphosis both ironic and disturbing.

I would pick up the tin from time to time, examine the picture and put it down again, unsure why I did not want to open it. Perhaps the open bridge and the view of the Kunstkamera was an oblique summons, I thought, to leave behind the deformed memories of my early life, the stillborn, crumpled homunculi in their glass jars, and follow some river to sea, just as I had dreamed of doing as a child. Perhaps I hesitated to break the plastic seal on the tin because the untasted is to be preferred to the tasted (something Masha coincidentally touched on in an e-mail, expressing disappointment in the pastilles she had bought: "They tasted nothing like the old Soviet ones"). I also wondered if the time had not come for me to finally visit the city of Lenin, Pushkin, Nabokov, Brodsky, Dostoevsky, Blok, and Akhmatova.

A week after the arrival of the tin of pastilles, I received another gift from Masha: a CD and some pamphlets from the Anna Akhmatova Museum in St. Petersburg. The Museum was known as the Fountain House. It was located in the northern wing of the Sheremetev Palace. Masha had first visited it several years ago—the high-ceilinged austere rooms, the bare wooden floors, the furniture, personal belongings, and manuscripts as cold and claustrophobic as a tomb. On that occasion, only the linden trees in the courtyard outside had spoken to her, resinous in the autumn wind. "I heard a voice—oh it was soothing!—that cried: 'Come here, leave your wild and sinful country, leave Russia forever.'"[8]

This was Akhmatova's home from the autumn of 1918, the year of her divorce from Nikolai Gumilev. Her eight years of marriage were not happy. Although Gumilev was one of the most colorful poets in pre-Revolutionary Russia, celebrated for his exotic allusions to Abyssinia, he saw his wife's poetic genius as a threat to his own, and Akhmatova lived, unloved, in his shadow. A year after their marriage, she wrote:

> Three things enchanted him:
> white peacocks, evensong,
> and faded maps of America.

He couldn't stand bawling brats,
or raspberry jam with his tea,
or womanish hysteria.
... And he was tied to me.

The Bolshevik revolution that began in Petersburg in March 1917 threw
the city into chaos. And though she was now living in the Fountain House
with Vladimir Kazimirovich Shileiko, a gifted linguist, Assyrianist, and
Orientalist, Akhmatova's energies were drained taking care of the ailing
scholar and supporting his scientific pursuits. "I left Gumilev, taking nothing
with me," she would write. "Vladimir Kazimirovich was ill. There was nothing
that he couldn't do without, except his tea and tobacco. We rarely cooked—
there wasn't any food, and there was nothing to make it in. We had to borrow
every pot from the neighbors: I had neither fork, nor spoon, nor pan."

When I thought of Akhmatova inhabiting the now abandoned palace of
the Sheremetevs, haunted by its erstwhile magnificence, its former servants
still in residence, and the crackle of gunfire in the winter streets, I thought
of the civil war in Sierra Leone, when villagers fled into the bush and lived
without soap or salt, uncertain when it would be safe to return to their sacked
and plundered villages. And in Akhmatova's description of Petersburg in
1920, I recalled the opening pages of Nabokov's *Speak Memory,* in which he
suggests the heart-rending possibility that in writing about lost time we are
magically transported back to the world from which violence has forever
sundered us, and momentarily released from the spherical prison of time.[9]

The Petersburg shop-signs were still there, but behind them was nothing
but dust, darkness, and gaping emptiness. It was a time of typhus, famine,
shootings, pitch-dark apartments, damp firewood, and people so swollen
up as to be unrecognizable. In Gostiny Dvor [the great department store on
Nevsky Prospekt] you could pick a large bunch of wild flowers. The famous
wooden blocks with which the streets of Petersburg had been paved were
finally rotting away. You could still smell chocolate from the basement windows of Kraffts. All the cemeteries had been pillaged. The city had not merely
changed, it had turned into the antithesis of itself.[10]

In 1949, Akhmatova's son, Lev Gumilev, was arrested for the third time by
Stalin's secret police. Fearing that her own arrest was imminent, she burned
her papers in the stove of her apartment, destroying the "poetry of an over-
wrought upper-class lady who frantically races back and forth between
boudoir and chapel [and] is mainly concerned with amorous-erotic themes

which are intertwined with elements of sadness, nostalgia, death, mysticism and doom . . . [the work of] a nun and a whore who combines harlotry with prayer."[11]

But preserved in her memory was *Requiem*—conjuring the Yezhov Terror of 1937, when Lev Gumilev was incarcerated in Leningrad and Akhmatova spent seventeen months waiting in line outside the prison. "One day somebody in the crowd identified me. Standing behind me was a woman, with lips blue from the cold, who had, of course, never heard me called by name before. Now she started out of the torpor common to us all and asked me in a whisper (everyone whispered there): 'Can you describe this?' And I said: 'I can.' Then something like a smile passed fleetingly over what had been her face."

Sometimes it is necessary to remind oneself that what makes it impossible to speak is not always our inertia or lack of inspiration; it is because the state decrees that writing is dangerous. What Orwell called "the prevention of literature" is tyranny's attempt, in the name of morality, security or social order, to determine what can and cannot be said. And whenever the obliterating keystrokes of the censor come into play, the agents of the state are also abroad, hammering on doors at dawn, seizing those who have spoken out, banning or burning books, destroying websites, throwing writers into prison.

But sometimes, it is not an external censor that stays one's hand, but the struggle to do justice to what one is given to write about.

The night I left for Freetown in January 2002, I bought a copy of W.G. Sebald's *Austerlitz* from W.H. Smith's bookshop at Gatwick airport, knowing nothing of this author whose tragic death would occur eleven months later. Sebald helped me find the elegiac voice I sought in writing about the devastated lives, livelihoods, and landscapes I encountered in Sierra Leone. I read only a few pages each night, not wanting the book to end, but by the time I left Sierra Leone I had read it several times from cover to cover. Among the most haunting passages were those in which Sebald described Austerlitz's ambition to write a monumental book on the history of architecture, touching on subjects as diverse as hygiene and sanitation, prisons and forts, and secular temples such as railway stations and war memorials. When Austerlitz finally settled to the task of organizing his compendious notes he discovered to his great dismay that he could hardly compose a single sentence without being stopped in his tracks, overwhelmed by the inadequacy of words. The more hesitant he became, the more daunting and terrifying seemed the task before him. He had only to pick up his pencil to feel panic-stricken and oppressed by the hollowness of language whose entire structure, "the syntactical arrangement of parts of speech, punctuation, conjunctions, and finally even the nouns denoting ordinary objects were all enveloped in impenetrable fog."[12] Austerlitz concluded that our sentences only appear to mean something; in truth they are "at best a makeshift expedient, a kind of unhealthy growth issuing from our ignorance, something which we use, in the same way as many sea plants and animals use their tentacles, to grope blindly through the darkness enveloping us. The very thing which may usually convey a sense of purposeful intelligence—the exposition of an idea by means of a certain stylistic facility—now seemed . . . nothing but an arbitrary or deluded enterprise."

If Sebald shared the pessimism of his alter ego, he must have found a way of overcoming it, presumably by making this spectral other a means of distancing himself from his own despair. And I was reminded of Doestoevsky's *Memoirs from the House of the Dead* and of the strange identifications that made it possible for this writer to come to terms with experiences that might otherwise have destroyed him.

> On 22 December 1849, in the bitter cold of a St. Petersburg winter, twenty young men in white shirts stood in the enormous Semënovksy Square awaiting the execution of the sentence of death that had just been read to them. A priest had passed among them, offering them an opportunity to make their confessions (of which only one availed himself) and presenting a cross to their lips. Now three of them, with their eyes covered, were bound to posts driven into the ground and faced a platoon of soldiers with leveled rifles. One of the three who were next to occupy those places was Fëdor Mikhaylovich Dostoevsky, at that time twenty-eight years old. The order to fire was never given; instead, an officer waved a white handkerchief and once more the prisoners heard their sentences read out, the real ones this time. One of them was pardoned; the Tsar's clemency assigned to the others varying terms of service in penal battalions or of penal servitude and exile. Dostoevsky's sentence was to four years of hard labor in Siberia followed by four years as a private soldier in a Siberian regiment of the line.[13]

According to Jessie Coulson, the lapse of time between 1854, when Dostoevsky was released from the Omsk stockade, and 1861–62 when his book was published, combined with his fear of censorship, "softened much of the bitterness of the story and gave it a certain quality of detachment, almost of impersonality."[14] I prefer to see the continuities. In Siberia, Dostoevsky died to the world only to be resurrected through the grace of God. Memories of his fellow prisoners would provide the raw material for some of his greatest work, in particular the dissolute, debt-burdened nobleman who had, after a fierce quarrel with his sixty-year-old father, allegedly murdered the old man in cold blood in order to inherit his wealth—the model for Dmitry Karamazov. But this leaves unanswered the question as to what draws me to these people in prison, falsely accused or made the scapegoats of a tyrant's paranoia, or their loved ones waiting at the prison gates for news that never comes, unless it is the social death they suffered, their names obliterated even though they remained alive.

TWENTY-TWO

The Books in My Life

WHEN HE WAS FIFTY-NINE AND LIVING AT BIG SUR, Henry Miller wrote *The Books in my Life*.[1] It was an oblique memoir. The books that had inspired the American writer also marked turning points in his life. "They were alive and spoke to me,"[2] Miller says, and concludes his homage to these "kindred spirits" with a list of the hundred books that influenced him most, including works by Blaise Cendrars, Élie Faure, Knut Hamsun, Sherwood Anderson, and Hermann Keyserling—all of which I would read on Miller's recommendation, so that they became books in *my* life.

Sometimes the books that have the greatest impact on us are neither classics nor best sellers, but obscure titles by authors who won few plaudits or awards. Ernest Hemingway alludes to these subordinate figures in his Nobel Prize acceptance speech when he remarks that the loneliness and anonymity of a writer's life may be his or her best guarantee of integrity—a view Camus also shared, though more bitterly, when he declared that many of his contemporaries wrote:

> in order to obtain that final consecration which consists of not being read. In fact, from the moment he can provide the material for a feature article in the popular press, there is every possibility that he will be known to a fairly large number of people who will never read his works because they will be content to know his name and to read what other people write about him.... To make a name in literature, therefore, it is no longer indispensable to write books.[3]

Walter Benjamin takes this thought even further. He suggests that "to read what was never written, to read from the entrails, the stars, or dances," predates the reading of runes and hieroglyphs.[4]

Benjamin's remarks put me in mind of the times in Central Australia when my second wife Francine and I would stop our Land Cruiser on a desert track and our Warlpiri traveling companions would get out and walk around, examining the ground for the spoor of snakes or goanna, the footprints of other travelers, or the imprints of tires. Not only could a sharp eye, sound memory, and practiced skill enable one to reconstruct exactly what had transpired at a given place, and who had passed that way; it could bring more significant traces to light—the petrified foam from a long ago flood, the imprint of a mythical kangaroo in a granite slab, the seedcakes hurled by emus in an ancient fight, the semen of an ancestor discernible as a smear of white clay. In this way, the ordinarily invisible world of the Dreaming reveals itself, closing the gap between the here and now and the ambient, eternal space-time from which every life emerges and into which every life form inevitably passes.

Scrutinizing another's face or trying to divine another's thoughts belong to the same set of techniques for making the world more legible, and may explain why the imprint of a human hand precedes all other depictions in the cave art of our Paleolithic forebears, and why the original meaning of the verb to read was to interpret, render explicable, and advise. Just as reading exists before the emergence of written language, so our lives may be said to rewrite the lives of those who came before us.

When I was twenty-one and working for the Alexander Turnbull Library in Wellington, I would seize every opportunity to make a trip to the downtown book depository where entire libraries of donated books were stored on metal shelves. It was there that I discovered the autobiography of Jacob Epstein and read of the eighteen sculptures he created in 1908 for the façade of the British Medical Association building on The Strand in London. Two years later, I made a pilgrimage to what was then Rhodesia House and saw the sculptures, each in its unique niche, mutilated by prudes, and eroded by acid rain. During the winter of 1963–64, when I worked in a welfare office for the homeless under Hungerford Bridge and passed these vandalized masterpieces every day, I imagined that my ritual visits would somehow keep these sculptures alive and connect me to the man who made them. I adopted a similarly proprietal attitude to Edward Arlington Robinson whose "stark and unhappy" childhood in Gardiner, Maine, I identified with my own, and whose portraits of ill-starred locals like Reuben Bright, Cliff Klingenhagen, and Richard Cory paved the way for the poetry I wished to write. Ironically, one of Robinson's most compelling sonnets is to an author whom the centuries had also consigned to oblivion.

George Crabbe

Give him the darkest inch your shelf allows,
Hide him in lonely garrets, if you will, -
But his hard, human pulse is throbbing still . . .

Whether or not we read him, we can feel
From time to time the vigor of his name
Against us like a finger for the shame
And emptiness of what our souls reveal
In books that are as altars where we kneel
To consecrate the flicker, not the flame.

That I am attracted to the idea of "lost" books may be because I am preoccupied by "lost" souls, and by the anonymity that sooner or later claims the best of us, clearing a space for new names and new work, much of it to be proclaimed as ground-breaking and original. I prefer to see history as an infinite succession of repetitions, or at least a series of variations on primordial themes, there being nothing new under the sun. And so, when I read Bruce Chatwin's "Lament for Afghanistan", published in 1980, I was struck not only by the fact that Chatwin did not live to see America repeat the tragic blunders of the Soviets but by the uncanny way that, following in the footsteps of the British travel writer Robert Byron, Chatwin brings his precursor back to life. Chatwin refers to *The Road to Oxiana* as a masterpiece that he raised to the status of sacred text. "My own copy," he writes, "now spineless and floodstained after four journeys to Central Asia—has been with me since the age of fifteen. Consequently, I am apt to resent suggestions that it is a 'lost book' or in need of being 'rescued from the library shelves.' By a stroke of luck, it was never lost on me."[5]

The kinship one may feel for a literary ancestor or near contemporary may lead one to feel, at times, that one can speak for the other or even embody the other's voice. Thus, Anthony Kerrigan, one of the finest English translators of Jorge Luis Borges, expresses the view to a fellow translator of Borges that they were "intrinsically and extrinsically . . . collaborators in his existence, collaborators in existing him."[6] In these words, Kerrigan echoes Borges' observation that the Victorian translator Edward Fitzgerald and the eleventh-century Persian poet, Umar ben Ibrahim al-Khayyami, may be regarded as mysterious collaborators who might have become close friends had seven hundred years not separated them. In a metaphysical vein, Borges conjectures that "the spirit of Umar lodged, around 1857, in Fitzgerald's. In the Rubáiyát, we read that the history of the universe is a spectacle which God conceives, stages, and then contemplates; this speculation (the technical name for it is pantheism) would permit us to believe that the Englishman could have re-created the Persian, since both were, in essence, God, or momentary faces of God."[7] W.G. Sebald has written in a similar vein, of Fitzgerald's genius in drawing us "word by word, to an invisible point where the mediaeval orient and the fading occident can come together in a way never allowed by the calamitous course of history."[8] And Sebald finds in this peculiar conjunction echoes of the unconsummated relationships that formed the core of Fitzgerald's deliberately reclusive life in the county of Suffolk—his scholarly devotion to the correspondence of Madame de Sévigné, "who became far more real to him than even his friends who were still alive,"[9] and his love of William Browne, "who probably meant more to Fitzgerald than anyone on earth" but who died of injuries sustained in a hunting accident when Fitzgerald was fifty.

The lifeworld that an author creates and inhabits is a virtual universe, a terra incognita of the mind. That it often remains in the shadows or unrevealed makes it no less real than the firmer and more visible realms to which we apply the terms social or cultural.

Henry Miller compares his encounters with books with his "encounters with other phenomena of life or thought," and observes that all such encounters "are configurate, not isolate."[10] From a shelf of books one can divine a life, and sometimes recount a hidden history. Even the books one seldom opens may be kept because they recall a moment long ago when they edified and guided. A book that came into one's possession as a gift from a friend may have proved disappointing; but the friendship is commemorated by its enduring place on one's shelf. A literary classic may impress one less profoundly than a fleeting encounter with its author, as I discovered when I almost collided with E.M. Forster, rounding the corner of Kings Chapel on a wintry afternoon in 1968. As for one's own books, they are like dolmens marking one's passage through life and one's haphazard progress toward a perfection that one knows to be unattainable. These extrinsic narratives are often more fascinating than the narratives the books contain, for they take one out into the world from which their subject matter was derived, suggesting affinities that defy the so-called constancies of personhood, place, and time and revealing living contexts for texts that often pretend to have set a seal on what it is possible to do, to say, or to know. When Wittgenstein argued against our attempts to say what cannot be said, preferring to show what can be shown, he inadvertently approved Anton Chekhov's view that the writer's task is not to provide definitive solutions to the mysteries of existence but to describe these as they are encountered and endured in our everyday lives. I am surprised how long it has taken me to fully embrace this view.

TWENTY-THREE

Writing Utopia

WHENEVER I VISIT LONDON I am returned to the winter of 1963–64, when I worked among the homeless and like a latter-day Jack London wrote about "the people of the abyss."[1] Perhaps this is why, even now, I tend to notice only the dark side of the city and fear I might become trapped in some somnambulant routine, like the derelicts and drifters I used to know, unable to return to the place from whence they had been cast out and equally unable to find a place in which they could take refuge. And so, like Elias Canetti who left Austria after the Anschluss of 1938 and spent thirty years of exile in London, I have always had to "dim part of my recollection, to show the other, which is there, in plenty."[2]

It was two days before Christmas, and I had planned to spend only a night in London before flying on to Zürich. But heavy snowstorms blanketed the southeast, and my flight from Boston to Heathrow was the first in three days. I was therefore concerned lest I become another hapless traveler stranded in the airport, unable to reach his destination. Memories of another night in Gatwick airport came back to me when I was obliged to wait from midnight to 6.00 a.m. with a couple of hundred Sierra Leoneans before boarding our flight to Freetown. Surrounded by padlocked Duty Free shops, I sketched what would become the opening chapter of my book on well-being,[3] a book that drew heavily on Ernst Bloch's *The Principle of Hope*, which he researched and wrote in the reading room of Harvard's Widener Library during the years of the Second World War, stranded between a homeland he had been driven from and a new life that eluded him. "From early on we are searching. All we do is crave, cry out. Do not have what we want . . . what is ours slips away, is not yet here."[4]

Airports are windows onto other worlds. Worlds of the imagination, of the collective unconscious, of "a more colorful or lighter Elsewhere" to which we travel, not as pilgrims but as consumers.[5]

At Heathrow, I bought a snack at a bar serving "global food." Nearby were two gleaming supercars that could be won in a £20 raffle. The winner had a choice of a Lamborghini, an Aston Martin Rapide, a Bentley Continental, or a Mercedes-Benz SLS. Above the concourse hung a backlit sign, *Ecomagination,* and a large moving screen flashing *Nokia Connecting People.* I also noted the Sony shop, where one could *Capture Everything,* the ads for Tag Heuer watches *Making Chronographic History Since 1860,* and images of Marrakech, where *There Are Feelings That Nurture Your Soul.* Our quotidian existence, it appeared, was something to get away from. Fulfillment lay elsewhere, though you needed a luxury car, a timepiece, and money to get there. What, then, was I in flight from, and what was my magical means of transport?

Writing was my antidote to academic life, and ethnographic fieldwork and travel were the sources of my writing. For as long as I can remember the burning question for me was how art—or whatever else one might turn one's hands and mind to—could be made to enhance life rather than impoverish it, a supplement to, rather than an escape from, our everyday existence. I had therefore sought a style of writing that took its departure from lived experience, but kept faith with it, refusing to take refuge in literature or philosophy, or any other fool's paradise of our own fashioning.

Awaiting their own departure times, the people around me seemed spaced out from jetlag, wearied from lugging suitcases along crowded corridors, from small children crying in pain or protest, from the hubbub of voices, trundling carry-on bags, whirring air-conditioning fans, chimes, and flight announcements. Many sat staring into space. Some texted, played video games, or sent e-mails. Others chatted, amused their children, read newspapers, or, like me, took notes. There was a strange lack of fit between the *World Duty Free* that surrounded us and the exhausted travelers awaiting the sign that would permit them to proceed.

I took the Central Line tube to the West End, passing through Hammersmith, where I spent my winter of discontent, often living on vegetables scavenged from under the stalls of the local market and without even the means to heat my small room, having foolishly given the best part of my pittance to the dossers that I felt obliged to help whatever the cost. As the train clattered through the familiar stations, I opened my notebook. But the lurching train made it difficult to steady my pen on the page, and I was distracted by the clatter of bogies, the intermittent hum of an electric motor, and the broken rhythm as we banged across switches. Flowing past were grimy brick walls, thick cables slung over brackets, iron footbridges, destitute trees, and a leaden sky. A floodlit hoarding advertised a movie called *The Way Back*. Travel posters showed white sand beaches, translucent water and palm trees.

Sitting opposite me was a middle-aged man in a bomber jacket, Arsenal T-shirt and blue jeans. He had a worker's hands, with one index finger missing, and he was reading a paperback novel called *The Mask of Troy*, by David Gibbins. A yellow sticker on the cover said *2 for £8*. Between his feet was a grubby gray rucksack, seemingly empty. I wondered where he was going, rapt in his book, his thoughts elsewhere, perhaps in Homer's Troy.

I flew to Zürich the following day. By the time I reached my hotel on Hottingerstrasse, snow was falling. The streamlined tramcars glided noiselessly through the near whiteout. That it was Christmas Eve only increased my sense of being in solitary confinement, isolated from friends and family, with only a tenuous connection with anything real. This unnerving sensation of being adrift in time undoubtedly explained my reactions to the Picasso show that I saw that afternoon. The curator's goal was to reproduce the artist's first museum exhibition in 1932, also sponsored and curated by the Kunsthaus Zürich. Despite Picasso's fascination with the poor and the marginalized, I felt little sympathy for his aesthetic attitude to suffering. A hungry waif was on a par with a bather throwing a beachball, or a woman wearing a yellow belt, or fruit and musical instruments on a table—objects to be creatively manipulated and reworked as novelties.

I spent the rest of the day warming myself in cafes or trudging about in the snow-besieged city, visiting old haunts and pondering the human quest for utopia through travel, through art, or through academic work. I thought of the misfits and exiles who had made Zürich their temporary home—James Joyce, Elias Canetti, Vladimir Ilyich Lenin, Tristan Tzara, Carl Jung—and wondered whether Ernst Bloch's distinction between abstract and concrete utopias could be clearly drawn, since our temporary escapes into irreality, motivated by a need to take stock of a vexing situation the better to reengage with it, sometimes lead to permanent or pathological forms of retreat. What led Jean-Jacques Rousseau "to wander for twelve years among alien cities and conflicting faiths, rejected by society and civilization, repudiating Voltaire,

Diderot, the Encyclopédie, and the Age of Reason, driven from place to place as a dangerous rebel, suspected of crime and insanity"[6] unless his utopian conception of a state of uncorrupted nature, represented by the innocence of childhood and archaic societies, was not only a product of his own sense of always being out of his element, moving in social milieus to which he did not really belong, afflicted by a yearning for a life that seemed to have passed him by, but also the reflection of an older grief, his mother having died in giving birth to him and his father never overcoming the loss of his beloved wife or able to forgive his son for causing her death? "Of all the gifts with which Heaven endowed them, they left me but one, a sensitive heart. It had been the making of their happiness, but for me it has been the source of all the misfortunes of my life."[7]

To distract myself on Christmas Day, I read Geoff Dyer's amusing if ego-centric account of his search for D.H. Lawrence. Dyer is particularly astute in his remarks on Lawrence's perpetual dissatisfaction with where he is, and his unflagging desire to be elsewhere. Like Rousseau, whose avowed sense of being different, of being singled out and special, pervades his *Confessions*, Lawrence's sense of having a unique sensibility may have been born of an equally lonely childhood. Certainly, both shared a conviction that they had been exiled from a paradise that might, however, be recovered at some future time or in some other place. It was the same for Elias Canetti, who spent an idyllic childhood in Zürich and returned there to live out the last twenty years of his life: "It is true that I, like the earliest man, came into being only by an expulsion from Paradise."[8] Still, no sooner does Lawrence escape from a parochial world that censures sensuality and stifles thought, than he finds the alternative equally constricting. Like Rousseau, Lawrence is always on the move, railing against the forces that he imagines to be mustered against him, while rationalizing his nomadism, hypersensitivity, and utopian vision. As Geoff Dyer puts it:

> People need to feel that they have been thwarted by circumstances from pur-
> suing the life which, had they led it, they would not have wanted; whereas the
> life they really want is precisely a compound of all those thwarting circum-
> stances. It is a very elaborate, extremely simple procedure, arranging this web
> of self-deceit: contriving to convince yourself that you were prevented from
> doing what you wanted.[9]

Dyer is right, I think, in concluding, "most people don't know what they want: people want to be prevented, restricted." Utopia (*u-topos*) is no-where.

A few years ago, I also went in search of D.H. Lawrence. I was in New South Wales, Australia, and wanted to see the house where Lawrence had lived when writing *Kangaroo*. After driving south from Sydney through a fire-blackened National Park, I asked a clerk in the Thirroul Post Office if he could give me directions to the bungalow that D.H. Lawrence and Frieda rented in 1922. He said he was unsure, but told me to drive back along the main street and take the first left. "You drive down Bath Street until you get to the beach, then you gotta go a fair way down the coast. The road twists and turns a bit. I dunno zactly where the house is but you kin ask."

I did. A woman climbing out of her car with two plastic bags of groceries nodded toward the high fence across the road. And there it was, number three Craig Street, a pine tree, a cactus growing against the wall, a disheveled oak, and a glimpse of the sea beyond. "There's that little park, too, if you're rinterested," she sang out, nodding this time toward the big araucarias at the end of the street.

The park, named for DHL, had been created in 1998. After reading the brass plaque, I scrambled down to the rocky foreshore, and made my way to the foot of the sandstone cliff from where I could see, perched above me, a deck and the back of the house, but little more. I returned to the park and sat on a bench, taking notes. The ocean churned on the rocks. Far out it was dark blue and scarified by the wind. I thought of Lawrence's quest for renewal and naturalness, faithful to that dark interior sun that makes us burn with a passion for life, a life far from the abstractions and traditions of Europe, that can be touched and tasted and smelled, like the wind-lacerated water on which a lone wind-surfer in a wet suit is blown seaward, the oak bent and beaten by the wind, the weathered araucarias and the pine. And I wondered whether our dreams of a utopia on earth are born of the same desire that throws up images of heaven, and that the distinctions we make between the secular and the sacred are artifacts of language, not facts of pure experience.

Back in Sydney, at a New Year's Eve party, I was introduced to Anne Whitehead, whose book *Paradise Mislaid* interleaves a chronicle of the 1893 utopian socialist settlement in Paraguay called "New Australia" with the author's own journeys between Australia and South America, tracing and interviewing descendants of the original colonists, and seeking to understand why the socialist dream proved impossible to realize.[10] "I was fascinated by this drive in all of us to start afresh," Annie told me, "to break with tradition and create a new world. It's like the search for the Holy Grail, for the elixir of life. But you can't create a new world without recreating yourself, and this was the stumbling block. For all their ideals of gender equality and a classless society, the settlers could not kick their engrained habits. Old habits die hard."

"It reminds me of D.H. Lawrence," I said. "He wanted this new life-form, wanted to slough off his old self and create himself anew. Didn't he come to Australia, thinking this might be his Rananim? Is that the word?"

"Exactly," Annie said. "He wanted to open himself up to Australia, to make a go of it here, just as he did later in Mexico, but much as he railed against the staleness and heaviness of Europe the poor sod couldn't break free of his own past. All that talk of his in *Kangaroo* about the white unwritten atmosphere of Australia, the tabula rasa, the new leaf, the new unspoiled country, untainted by authority, he simply couldn't get rid of the old world in himself, and his own need to dominate the world with his own vision."

"You know *Kangaroo* better than I do!"

"I should. I wrote a screenplay from it."

I hesitated to tell Annie about my pilgrimage to Thirroul, or the mini-essay that I was sketching about utopian dreams, in case she concluded that I was stealing her ideas, and I thought of the last line of Ecclesiastes: "Is there anything of which one can say: this is new?"

Overnight the snow ceased. Though bitterly cold, the sky was clear, the lake like ice, and the wooded hills beyond transformed into a gigantic crystalline formation. In the bracing, pellucid air the clock towers were azure and gold in the wintry sunlight. I walked down to the Central Station, bought a *Herald Tribune* and ordered a *cornetto classico* and *doppio* at an Italian espresso bar. As I sipped my coffee I read of Kenyan villagers installing $80 Chinese solar panels so they could charge cell phone batteries and provide lighting for children doing their homework. A second article also caught my attention. Facebook users tend to access no more than 150 friends, but we "devote 40 percent of our limited social time each week to the five most important people we know, who represent just 3 percent of our social world and a trivially small proportion of all the people alive today. Since the time invested in a relationship determines its quality, having more than five best friends is impossible when we interact face to face, one person at a time."[11]

As I walked along Bahnhofstrasse in search of Pelikanstrasse 8—the location of a bar that James Joyce frequented during his years in Zürich—I wondered whether there was any limit to the number of writers one might name as kindred spirits or seminal figures—writers essential to one's own evolution, and to one's own struggle for a voice, a style, an identity. And what motivates one to visit the houses these writers once inhabited or the graves where they are buried unless it is a desire to seek some kind of confirmation that this circle is as real as any other—a kind of family, community or network of close friends?

When I entered the bar, my thoughts took a very different turn. Joyce's world and mine were not the same. Little could be shared. On a previous visit to Zürich I had tried to establish what Joyce, Jung, Lenin, Canetti, and Tristan Tzara—five people who were, incidentally, *not* best friends—were doing in February 1917. Joyce's *Portrait of an Artist as a Young Man* had just come out in England, Jung was writing *Psychological Types,* Lenin was preparing to leave for Russia, Tzara was publishing the first issue of the periodical *Dada,* and the 12 year-old Canetti was beginning Secondary School. In his *Memoirs,* Canetti fondly and gratefully recalls his teachers in words that suggest that he too was searching for the hidden connections between disparate individuals and seemingly unrelated events. "They were the first representatives of what I later took in as the intrinsic factor of the world, its population. They are non-interchangeable, one of the supreme qualities in the hierarchy; their having become figures as well takes nothing away from their personalities. The fluid boundary between individuals and types is the true concern of the real writer."[12]

The clientele in the James Joyce Bar consisted of young or middle-aged men in business suits. I tried to imagine what fluid boundary existed between them, or between them and the writer who had inadvertently given his name to the bar. Did they select Irish Stew from the menu for its association with Joyce's Dublin, a means of communing with the great man? Did they patronize this bar in homage to a man who used for his defense the only arms he allowed himself to use—silence, exile, and cunning? And could I, for that matter, for all my love of *Ulysses,* bridge the gulf between my world and his by buying a meal beyond my means in a bar whose dark wooden paneling, art deco tiles, somber landscape paintings of misty mountains and waterfalls, windows of stippled glass decorated with wild flowers, tendrils, and foliage evoked, as far as I could tell, nothing Joycean whatsoever? I stood in a corner by the door. Worked into the windowpanes were female figures, dressed like Greek goddesses, standing on pedestals and signifying the four seasons. I was beginning to wonder what in the world I was doing—separated from my family at Christmas, wandering about Europe with only the haziest idea of how my divagations might relate to the book I was writing on writing.

What could possibly be revealed by visiting places connected with writers I admired? What affinities could be affirmed in unearthing old photographs, reading biographies, visiting places they had long ago deserted?

I walked out into the winter afternoon, crossed Bahnhofstrasse and took the number 6 tram to the Fluntern cemetery, a stone's throw from the Zürich zoo.

TWENTY-FOUR

Writing in Search of Lost Time

THE CEMETERY WAS UNDER SNOW. Only the main path, leading slightly uphill from the main gate, had been cleared. After examining a notice board that showed the layout of the cemetery and identified the numbers of some of the more famous graves, I followed a well-trampled path between serried gravestones, amazed to see how many footprints there were, though not a soul was in sight. Joyce's grave was the first I found. His statue was encrusted with snow—the gangly, self-absorbed figure with cigarette and cane almost a mockery of the heroic individual I had conjured when I read his work as a young man. A few feet away I found the snow-obscured, less-visited grave of Elias Canetti. Someone had placed a Chinese candle on the grave—protected from the weather by a crimson tube with gold filigree. Judging from the snow around its base, it had been set there before the recent snowstorm. I swept the snow from the grave with my gloved hand, then used my ballpoint pen to dig snow out of the spidery holes in the brass slab, deciphering Canetti's signature. Nearby was a stand of cedars overburdened by snow. I heard the caw of a rook, a snatch of distant voices and the hum of traffic before the snowbound muffling silence reclaimed the place and I was alone with my thoughts.

In 1968, my wife and I were living in Wellington, completing our masters degrees before taking up scholarships at Cambridge. Our landlady, Kay Miller, was an eco-activist who had gotten media attention for building a hut on the Porirua rubbish dump from where she supervised a recycling project and campaigned against the pollution and desecration of the environment. Kay would make us salads from edible weeds, to be washed down with her home-brewed dandelion wine, and she would regale us with stories of her student days in London, when she had become close friends with Elias Canetti.

When Pauline and I left for England, Kay entrusted us with a package that we were to deliver into the hands of her old friend in Hampstead. The package contained copies of correspondence between Kay and Canetti, possibly for use in the memoirs Canetti had begun to write. In any event, Kay impressed upon us the importance of the documents and the absolute necessity of delivering them to Canetti himself. In 1968, I had read nothing by Canetti and was unaware that Veza (Venetiana Taubner-Calderon), his wife and literary collaborator, had died in 1963. So when Pauline and I went to the address that Kay Miller had given us and rang the doorbell, we did not know if the woman who opened the door was a wife, research assistant, housekeeper, confidante, or passing acquaintance. What was made very clear to us, however, was that Canetti was not to be disturbed. She, whoever she was, would ensure that Kay's precious package was safely delivered to him. There seemed no alternative but to give her the package and leave. But our failure to fulfill our promise to Kay weighed on our minds and led me to ask who this man was, sequestered in this grand Victorian house in Thurlow Road, not far from where Freud had lived, a neighborhood where almost every home was associated with "the guttural sorrow" of some famous émigré intellectual, or the names of legendary English poets.[1] When Canetti and Veza observed the Battle of Britain from Hampstead Heath "they probably stood in almost the same spot as D.H. Lawrence and Frieda, who in 1915 had here watched a German Zeppelin attacking London."[2]

In *Crowds and Power,* Canetti writes that "it is not always veneration for some famous man" that draws us to cemeteries. "Even where this is the original motive, the visit always turns into something more."[3] This remark proved prescient.

I quickly found the grave of the man I had narrowly missed meeting over forty years ago. The dark green cedars were deathly still and a milky sun showed through laundered layers of cloud. But I was unable to write down my thoughts because the pen with which I had traced the cut out letters of Canetti's name had seized up. But Canetti had anticipated my own reflections in a posthumously published collection of autobiographical writings that includes a brief essay on the Hampstead Parish Church cemetery where John Constable is buried. Some of the graves in the churchyard date to the seventeenth century, when Hampstead was a minor spa on a hill north of London. Canetti says it was not until late in his life that he "learned what cemeteries are." He speaks of the gravestones, half sunk in the ground or standing askew with their weather-eroded dates and names, as offering themselves to be gazed upon, and of the "peaceable feeling" that comes upon you from this elementary act of looking at the stones. Standing there, mindful of the passage of time that stands between you and your predecessor is a kind of homage. "You read his name, you perhaps spoke it half-aloud to yourself, you had no reason to bear him any ill-will, and if you didn't feel gratitude to him as such, you did, in a simple, natural way let him participate in the time in which you were contemplating him. It may sound strange, but it helps to explain the warm feeling you had, when you came up to some of these stones, and gazed at them, as if you had known the people."[4] Canetti goes on to say that after his frequent visits to the Church Row cemetery he felt that he had discharged a debt. But he leaves open the question as to how one might explain this sense of owing something to the dead, whether it be recognition or care or an acknowledgment of our common mortality.

As I returned to the main path, I felt an inexplicable reluctance to leave. It was as if I was deserting someone who had placed his trust in me. And I later wondered, whether the calm and righteousness of which Canetti speaks eluded me because I had failed to discharge a moral debt. But at that moment, my attention was diverted by a young African man standing in front of a large gravestone, and wearing a knitted skullcap and black woolen overcoat. I was struck by his stillness and concentration. His only movement was to gently stab his Blackberry with a stylus as if texting or taking notes. As I walked past him, our eyes met, and there was a flicker of mutual recognition. Stealing a glance backward, I tried to decipher the names on the gravestone, intrigued by what connection this visitor had with the four family members buried there. The further I went toward the main gate, the more my curiosity increased. I could not leave the cemetery without knowing more, or coming up with a satisfying fictional answer to the question that now bothered me. So I wandered slowly around the perimeter of the cemetery, assuming he would soon end his vigil and I would be free to examine the names on the gravestone. Five minutes later he was still there, a short black contemplative figure in the snow, as improbable and provocative as an apparition. I could curb my curiosity no longer. Sidling up to him, I asked if he spoke English.

"Yes."

"Do you mind me asking what is the connection between you and the names on that grave?"

"I am Opus Dei," he said. "We are working for the canonization of Toni Zweifel."

He was a student in Geneva, finishing doctoral studies in biotechnology.

He had come to Zürich for an Opus Dei retreat. They were praying for Zweifel's beatification, and praying for peace.

I asked where he was from.

"Côte d'Ivoire," he said.

Only that morning I had read the latest news from Ivory Coast—the growing violence between the followers of the former President, Laurent Gbagbo, and the President-Elect, Alassane Ouattara, and the thousands of West Africans immigrants already fleeing the country, fearful of the threats being made against them.

"What of your family?" I asked. "Are they safe."

"They are safe. I am praying for them. And for my country."

"What is the root of the conflict?" I asked.

"International interference. The colonial powers don't want to give up their interests in Côte d'Ivoire."

We strolled to the tram stop together. He asked where I lived and what I did for a living. I told him I taught anthropology at Harvard Divinity School. I could see he took a dim view of anthropology, but he brightened at the mention of Harvard and asked for my card. When I explained that I did not carry a card, he entered my address into his Blackberry. "God brings people together," he said. "There is always a reason."

He then asked if I was a Catholic.

"No, I adhere to no faith."

I presumed he would board the tram with me, but as it pulled in he extended his hand to say good-bye.

"I hope your prayers are answered," I said.

He looked at me as if an atheist could know nothing of the power of prayer. Then he smiled.

I smiled too, in the tram, writing notes of our brief conversation, descending the long hill back to Zürich. I had made a pilgrimage to the graves of two writers, believing nothing much would come of it, only to be surprised by an encounter that lay in wait for me, as it were, only yards away. And where my relationship with Joyce and Canetti had not produced any revelation, I had witnessed in this other pilgrim's devotion to a Swiss engineer, whose Limmat Foundation supported hundreds of educational and social service initiatives in more than 30 countries on five continents, a connection that was as spiritual as mine was casual. Did I envy this young African his passionate campaign to have Toni Zweifel recognized as a saint or, for that matter, his depth of commitment to Opus Dei, his sense of divine purpose, his cause?

There seemed, when I reflected on it, too much contingency in life to allow for this kind of clarity. And this was brought home to me when I returned to my hotel in Hottingenstrasse and discovered, via the Internet, that Toni Zweifel's parents died within three months of each other in 1985, and that a year later Toni learned that he was suffering from leukemia, for which he underwent chemotherapy. After a temporary return to health, he suffered a first relapse in February 1988 and a second the following November. In June 1989 he was hospitalized for further treatment, but died that November at age 51.

TWENTY-FIVE

Writing about Writers

THE MOMENT I ENTERED MCCLEAN—the immaculate and shrine-like men's room below the main concourse of the Zürich railway station—I thought of Mary Douglas. In its evocation of hygiene, purity, and sanctity, this public urinal, to which you gain access by inserting 1.5 Swiss francs in a turnstile, exemplifies Mary Douglas's thesis that cleanliness is to dirt as order is to disorder. The room was semicircular, with glass partitions separating the stream-lined and undespoiled porcelain urinals. As you piss, soft pastel-colored lights rise and fall behind frosted glass, and when you are done you wash your hands at a porcelain basin on a marble pedestal, with a paper hand towel as soft as premium cotton. Curiously enough, Mary Douglas and her husband James were close friends of the Canettis. Elias refers to Mary's Lele ethnography in *Crowds and Power,* and Mary pays homage to Elias's close friend and fellow émigré Franz Steiner in *Purity and Danger.* Taboos, she observes, help demar-cate boundaries between categories, persons, substances, and species that are thought to be mutually inimical, and whose separation guarantees the preser-vation of social and moral order. The incest taboo prevents sexual intercourse between siblings or between parents and children. Other taboos preserve the health of our environment by keeping fresh water and salt water species apart or preventing blood relationships becoming polluted by monetary transac-tions. But at the same time as the Lele divide the world into opposites,[1] regu-larizing this conceptual order through ritual, and punishing contraventions of it, they seek to cultivate and tap the mysterious power that comes from transgressing the borders between the very things they have so assiduously decided to separate. And so the pangolin, which is anomalous in so many respects (scaly like a fish, it climbs trees; resembling an egg-laying lizard, it suckles its young like a mammal; unlike most mammals, its young are born singly), is made the focus of a cult whose initiates eat the flesh of the pangolin in solemn ceremony in order to draw on its power to render the human world more fecund.

As I left the sanctuary of McClean, I wondered whether there were any Swiss analogues for the Lele pangolin cult—any evidence of a deliberate disordering of the world as a means of gaining creative or divine power. I thought of the kitchenette in my hotel, with its stern instructions to guests on keeping the counters clean and the cupboards tidy. I thought of the city's many clocks, all keeping perfect time as if synchronized by a divine hand. I thought of the great Romanesque Grossmünster Cathedral that zealous reformers stripped bare, in the early sixteenth century, of all ornamentation, opulence, and ostentation, as if access to God could only be gained through austerity, asceticism, and absolute purity. I thought of the referendum in November 2009 in which Swiss voters banned the construction of minarets, and the referendum a year later allowing the "automatic" and immediate deportation of non-citizens to their countries of origin if convicted of certain criminal offences. And I remembered the Swiss People's Party poster of a black sheep being kicked out of the country by three white sheep standing on a Swiss flag.

On the station concourse, I wanted to ask the group of stylishly dressed African women with their beautiful children if they and their Swiss husbands had ever been made to feel that they had crossed a line, betrayed the purity of the race, the order of the state. And I regretted not asking the Italian man I'd met in the breakfast room of my hotel, who had been born and raised in Switzerland but had no claim to Swiss nationality, if he felt stigmatized, like a black sheep.

Like the secretive pangolin cult of the Lele, the shadow world of Switzerland remained as inaccessible to me as the unnumbered accounts in a Swiss bank, and as my train threaded its way south through tunnels, rocky defiles, and glacial valleys, past postcard scenes of chalets and neatly stacked firewood, tiredness crept over me like a cloud shadow or spell, and I woke only as the train pulled into Chiasso and a peremptory announcement directed us to change trains.

As if to signal our transition from the noiseless and orderly ambience of Zürich to the more histrionic and chaotic world of Italy, the train to Milan lurched violently and rumbled loudly, and its diesel motor thudded relentlessly under my seat. A hoar frost covered the landscape. Buildings were suddenly shabbier and more dilapidated. Embankments were littered with trash, graffiti covered every visible wall, and ugly factories stood in their ill-kempt allotments beside pools of polluted water.

Strangely enough, I felt immediately at home in Italy. The Swiss pretension of order gave way to a celebration of sensuality and sociality. Life was allowed to remain rough at the edges. On the train to Venice, I let my imagination drift, making whatever it wished of the frozen fallow fields, the distant smudge of the Alps, the chalky rivers, pollarded trees, and fabulous names like Verona, Padova, Vicenza, and finally Venice. This interplay between what is given historically or contingently and what one's mind makes of what is given, would define my experience of Italy. For seldom had I felt so strongly the *presence* of places and people I had hitherto regarded as dead and gone. Seldom had the gap been art and life been so startlingly closed.

I had long been troubled by the paradoxical relationship of art to reality. Our intellectual or aesthetic responses to life are often mind-boggling in their ingenuity and beauty. But these responses cannot but betray the experiences that inspired them. Though we may justify this betrayal by invoking allegedly higher values like order, spirituality or transcendence, I often mourn the loss of "the real."

> What! Do not yet the red-hot ploughshares burn,/O'er which you stumble in a false ordeal,? And deem this proof of loyalty the *real*.[2]

Venice proved me wrong. Or, rather, it changed my notion of what was real. When I walked out of the railway station and found myself facing not a busy street but a tranquil waterway, Joseph Brodsky's *Watermark* came immediately to mind. "It all felt like arriving in the provinces, in some unknown, insignificant spot—possibly one's own birthplace—after years of absence."[3] Just as I found myself reliving, or resuscitating, the experiences of this Russian poet, born in the same year as myself, so Brodsky had relived, in his first moments in Venice, the opening lines of one of Umberto Saba's poems that he had translated in a "previous incarnation"[4] into Russian. Already I was moving from measuring art against *objective* reality to making *social* reality the measure of its worth—its miraculous ability to mediate connections between disparate individuals, to catalyze overlapping experiences, and to bring the dead to life in the minds of the living.

Fortunately, I could reach my *pensione* on foot, so I quickly checked in, dumped my suitcase in my room, and headed off without breadcrumbs or thread into the labyrinth. More by guess than by guidance I found my way to the Accademia Bridge and straight into a work of art. I mean this literally.

I saw the serene blue of the Grand Canal, the domes of Santa Maria della Salute in the distant haze, the phalanxes of mooring poles in the water, and the mullioned and Palladian windows catching the watery winter light as if I was in a painting by Giovanni Canaletto. I had no sense of being in a real place but rather in a work of the imagination. The distinction I had carried in my head between the real and the ethereal had been instantly abolished, in the same way that Venice blurs the distinction between sea and land. As Brodsky has it, "the overall feeling was mythological."[5] Indeed, the feeling was akin to what the Polish aristocrat Wladyslaw Moes felt when he was twenty-three and read a translation of Thomas Mann's novella, for he suddenly realized that *he* was the boy on whom Mann had modeled Tadzio.[6] Moes had been in Venice in 1905 recuperating from a punctured lung at the time Mann was there. Marveling at how faithfully the German writer had noted his striped linen suit, red tie, and blue jacket with gold buttons, Moes also recalled the "older man" staring intently at him in the hotel elevator.

It was approaching dusk by the time I found my way to the Piazza San Marco. I was already in a daze. Floating more than walking, I was oblivious to the crowds that flowed around me, gathered on the bridges or in the piazzas as if also transfixed, awaiting some revelation. I was vaguely aware of myself standing spellbound in the square, mouth open, lost for words, drinking in the twelfth-century campanile, the basilica, the Ducal Palace, the sea like a divinely sanctioned extension of the city itself, abraded by breeze, reaching toward the Isola di San Giorgio Maggiore, and the sky like mother of pearl. All the clichés rang true—the otherworldly ambience, the aqueous light, the dankness that seeps into one's bones, the dreamlike state of mind that you cannot shake off. You have seen these scenes before—in photographs and in paintings. You have read of them in books by Thomas Mann, Henry James, and Joseph Brodsky. They are, in this sense, familiar. Yet nothing has prepared you for the effect of seeing them yourself, experiencing them on your own skin, through your own senses: the pastel light smeared with pink where the sun is waning in the west, the camponiles and cupolas fading into the atmosphere as stone dissolves in deep water. Like the San Marco tower that has cracked and collapsed only to be rebuilt, the city itself dies, as those who visit or inhabit it will die, only to be reborn in the eyes of each new traveler. So Venice mediates relations between precursors and successors, establishing a genealogy not of kin but of kindred spirits, interweaving their lives. For forty years I had spent my time and resources on ethnographic excursions to West Africa and Aboriginal Australia, postponing for my troisième âge journeys to places that might be regarded as more in keeping with my own cultural heritage. The encounter was uncanny. I could not have anticipated the sense of déjà vu that I felt at every turn, and it occurred to me that this resembled the premonitory experience that ethnographers have documented in nomadic societies, where a person will suddenly feel the presence of an absent kinsman in a part of his or her body conventionally associated with him or her.[7] Among the Warlpiri of Central Australia, for example, a junior sibling is associated with the shoulder (*jija-warnu*—"shoulder-belong"), perhaps because he or she is often carried on an elder sibling's shoulders. To feel a throbbing or twinge in the shoulder muscles may be interpreted as a telepathic sign that a junior sibling is nigh or that something untoward has happened to him or her. This sympathetic relationship between separated *bodies* is reminiscent of the phantom limb phenomenon, in which one's body appears to mourn a lost member, and may be compared with our metaphors of a marriage of *minds,* or an elective affinity, that creates the sense of a "chemical" bond between ourselves and writers from other epochs.

Heading back in the general direction of my pensione, streets aglow with the light from souvenir shops, designer boutiques, Venetian glassware, table lamps and masks, I passed a church where a Vivaldi concert was scheduled for that evening, another where reconstructions of some of Leonardo's machines were on display, and yet another where an exhibition of Morandi's still lifes had recently opened. For a moment I felt overwhelmed, and remembered fragments from Byron's *Ode to Venice,* in which he speaks of how little we learn from "the flow and ebb of each recurring age/The everlasting to be which hath been, as we lean on things that rot beneath our weight, and wear our strength away."[8] As I watched a barge crane upending garbage bins into its hold before setting them back on the quay, I recalled the image of pestilential trash burning in Thomas Mann's *Death in Venice,* and it occurred to me that my situation was not unalike von Aschenbach's—"this longing for the distant and the new, this craving for liberation, relaxation and forgetfulness . . . an urge to escape, to run away from his writing, away from the humdrum scene of his cold, inflexible, passionate duty."[9]

I was again reminded of this search for rejuvenation as I crossed the piazza in the falling darkness and was startled by the unearthly whiteness of a bridal gown as a wedding party assembled for a group photograph against the backdrop of a fountain. For some reason, however, I did not see Venice as a shadow of its former glory, let alone an image of moral corruption. I saw it only as a place to which others had come before me and been changed, a place that gave me a sense of connection with literary precursors and their own fugitive or fictional accounts of what it means to forget, for a moment, the difference between the actuality of a place or event and its imaginative reincarnations. In my writing, I had used the image of the penumbra to describe this shadow line between words and the world, art and reality. Venice was its perfect embodiment.

After a late dinner at a pastaria, I returned home to sleep. But I lay awake from some time, unused to the silence and the unflagging sense of being in a waking dream or embarked, without my will, on a boat journey across an underground lake to a floodlit palace where people danced till dawn, and returned to their real lives only to sleep. How does Brodsky describe it? "The boat's slow progress through the night . . . like the passage of a coherent thought through the subconscious."¹⁰

When I ventured out in the morning, sunlight was glinting on the water and thousands of Saturday strollers and shoppers were thronging the narrow streets or standing in small groups in the squares, wearing scarves, knit hats, and winter jackets. I thought of buying a ticket for a tour of the Doge's Palace, partly to see the Piombi prison where Casanova was incarcerated, but I preferred the fondamenta where I sat for some time, eyes closed, sun on my face, listening to the slap of water against the quay, the whistle of a vaporetto, its engine busily reversing into the steps, the babble of voices, trundle of a suitcase across the stones, and a tourist calling to someone to smile for the camera. As I strolled on past the Bridge of Sighs and its adjacent prison, I was aware that the ghostly enchantment and ethereal light I had experienced yesterday was already fading, the force of first impressions already compromised by the new day. It occurred to me that if we are to be continually renewed, four options are open to us: we can have faith that the initial ecstasy will visit us again, in which case we wait, as mystics wait through the dark night of the soul, for the recurrence of that amazing moment when we first saw God or our beloved; we can have recourse to art as a way of recapturing what we have lost; we can move on, traveling to some new city, as Rilke and D. H. Lawrence did; or we can seek in serial love affairs, like Casanova, a replay of the original experience.

The Eurostar raced and rattled through the darkness. Place names appeared—Bologna, Firenze—only to be instantly erased, so that the fleeting thoughts of what a traveler might have seen, or been, or known, or who he might have met, are snuffed out, and he gazes into the obliterated landscape without a second thought, impassively observing the strings of sodium street lamps and the lit windows of occasional houses. At one point I tried to recover my memory of Carl Sandberg's poem about "riding on a limited express, one of the crack trains of the nation," hurtling across the prairie into blue haze and dark air. The train's fifteen all-steel coaches hold a thousand people. But all the coaches will be reduced to scrap and rust, and all the men and women laughing in the diners and sleepers will pass to ashes. "I ask a man in the smoker where he is going and he answers: 'Omaha.'" And I thought then of W.G. Sebald's *Vertigo,* in which the narrator describes several journeys he took between Vienna, Verona, and Venice in the 1980s, crossing and recrossing the paths of Stendahl, Casanova, and Kafka before revisiting his own childhood village in southeastern Germany. Once again I had the uncanny sensation of being in someone else's fiction, recycling some-one else's experience, though I remained mystified by Sebald's compulsive and solitary wanderings through Europe, staring at his own reflections in a train window or gazing blankly into the impenetrable winter darkness, trying to make something of the same random constellations of light I was observing, listening to the same racket and rumble beneath him, his writing hand jerked about by the lurch and yaw of the coach, and the experience translated, like mine, forty minutes before reaching Rome, into a sense of one's life forever slipping through one's fingers, passing, like the lives of one's forebears, despite one's prayers, petitions, and panaccas, into oblivion while, attending this poignant progress, the angel of history sees fit to accelerate our demise with periodic warfare, plague or punishment.

TWENTY-SIX

Writing in Ruins

THIS TRAIN OF THOUGHT CONTINUED IN ROME, where I followed dutiful tourists around the ruins of the Forum and the Coliseum, casting my cold eye on the pitiful evidence of a once-triumphant, heroic, and hierarchical regime of sacred power. But it was the victims of this regime who were on my mind, the prisoners in bas relief on the monumental arches, and the men and women who died for their faith, in particular Vibia Perpetua, a young married woman from a high-ranking, wealthy Roman family who converted to Christianity and was executed in Carthage on March 7, 203. It is difficult to fully understand what moved this young women to embrace a foreign faith and join a persecuted community, but she was clearly willing to ignore the Emperor's 201 edict against conversion, deny her father's tearful pleading, and die for her beliefs, undergoing what Tertullian called a second baptism in blood in order to enter Paradise.[1]

After a period of house arrest during which Perpetua had her first prophetic dream, she and her baby were thrown into a makeshift underground holding pen. "I was terrified, as I had never before been in such a dark hole. What a difficult time it was! With the crowd the heat was stifling; then there was the extortion of the soldiers; and to crown all, I was tortured with worry for my baby there." One of her greatest anxieties was how she could reconcile her quest for spiritual perfection with her love for her child and her filial duty toward her father, "worn with worry," who visited his twenty-year-old daughter in prison, hopeful yet that he could persuade her from her course. "I tried to comfort him saying: 'It will happen in the prisoner's dock as God wills; for you may be sure that we are not left to ourselves but are in his power.'" On the day of Perpetua's hearing, her father, who had been entrusted with the care of her child, appeared with the baby and appealed to his daughter again. "Have pity on your father's grey head; have pity on your infant son. Offer a sacrifice for the welfare of the emperors." Perpetua refused. I will not, she said. Hilarianus then asked the one question that was pertinent in the hearing, "Are you a Christian?"[2] Perpetua answered, "Yes, I am a Christian." With these words she no longer belonged to Rome.

During her final days, Perpetua recorded in her diary a series of premonitory dreams. Not only do these dreams disclose her fear of what she would face in the arena; they reveal how steeped she was in Roman, Carthaginian, and Christian images of the pain and sacrifice needed to make the journey from this world to the next. In her visions, she saw herself meeting her death with equanimity, her emotions mastered, her worldly qualms allayed. The Carthage amphitheater was second in size only to Rome's Coliseum. Today, nothing remains of its superstructure, the stones having been plundered for other purposes. Perpetua and her companions were sentenced to die in games scheduled to celebrate the birthday of Septimus Severus's son's Geta. In sacrificing enemies of the state, the state would be strengthened. And in the death of those who had defiled Roman religion, the state would be cleansed and order restored.

We cannot know for certain how Perpetua met her death, since her diary was later edited to give her story doctrinal value. But she seems to have walked from the holding cells to the arena with a brave face, "putting down everyone's stare by her own intense gaze," and as she approached the arena she began to sing a psalm.

The men were first to die, gored by the wild boars or bears to which they were tied. However, for Perpetua and her fellow martyr Felicity, a maddened female heifer was used. Stripped naked, the women faced the massive animal. Perpetua was thrown onto her back and went into shock. She was then taken from the arena through the Gate of Life to await her final martyrdom. Several men who had been mauled by a leopard were led ahead of the women to the scaffold. Perpetua was the last to die. Her executioner was inexperienced, and his first sword blow hit her collarbone. According to commentators, she then took the trembling hand of the young gladiator and, despite her pain, guided it to her throat, thus consummating the act of sacrificial suicide.

My morbid ruminations were somewhat relieved when I found my way to the Palatine Hill and could stroll among the pines, olives, cypresses, and Judas trees, but it was not until the day before New Year's Eve, when my family joined me, that I began to feel restored to myself and could enjoy the pleasures of a city that I had for so many years longed to visit. Whether it was drinking a ristretto in a bar on the Campo de' Fiori or eating a focaccia sandwich as I crossed the Ponte Sisto with my wife and children to explore the narrow streets of the Transtevere, I felt as if I had been rescued in some strange way from a Piranesi-like *carceri* of purposeless structures and labyrinthine passages such as Thomas de Quincy recalls in his *Confessions,* quoting Samuel Taylor Coleridge's description of vast Gothic halls, on the floor of which stood all sorts of engines and machinery, wheels, cables, pulleys, levers, catapults, expressive of enormous power put forth and resistance overcome. Creeping along the sides of the walls, you perceived a staircase; and upon it, groping his way upwards, was Piranesi himself: follow the stairs a little further, and you perceive it come to a sudden abrupt termination, without any balustrade, and allowing no step onwards to him who had reached the extremity, except into the depths below. But raise your eyes, and behold a second flight of stairs still higher, on which again Piranesi is perceived, but this time standing on the very brink of the abyss. Again elevate your eye, and a still more aerial flight of stairs is beheld, and again is poor Piranesi busy on his aspiring labors;: and so on, until the unfinished stairs and Piranesi both are lost in the upper gloom of the hall.

I woke that night shivering from cold, clutching my wife for warmth and fearing some impending calamity. By dawn, however, the crisis had passed, and when we set off for our espressos and *cornetti* in the nearby Campo de' Fiori I hugged Francine and assured her that I had never felt better.

That evening we took a taxi to an apartment beyond the Villa Borghese for a New Year's Eve dinner party with friends of our son, Joshua. After artichoke hearts, pomodoro and bacon pasta, and sliced chicory with anchovy dressing, we ate roast lamb and braised carrots, washed down with a sangiovese wine from Tuscany. I had seldom felt so at home among strangers. My son's friendship with Benedetta helped explain our closeness, not to mention the fact that we, like Benedetta's family and the other guests, had all spent several years in Denmark. But conviviality is achieved through a will to find enjoyment in shared food, conversation, and company. And so we played charades, enjoyed more wine, and at midnight went out onto the balcony to see fireworks showering and bursting over the city before we repaired indoors on the stroke of midnight to watch a TV countdown from Rimini. "In Italy you throw everything you don't want into the street," Gianni informed us. It will all be carted away on New Year's day. Old furniture, old clothes.

"Old habits?" I asked.

"Even those."

When Gianni drove us back to our hotel, the downtown streets were packed with revelers. The Piazza Barberini was so crowded that we had to backtrack to the Piazza del Popolo, then across the river and downstream to the Ponte Garibaldi. As we threaded our way through the noisy, smoke-filled streets, I thought of charivari, and asked Gianni if it was an Italian word. He thought it might be cognate with *caribaria,* meaning headache, but didn't really know. But I knew from my ethnographic work that such ritual-ized noise-making and roistering occurs in societies everywhere, marking intervals between different time periods, anachronistic events such as eclipse, or aberrant behaviors like incest, the premature remarriage of widows, or disapproved unions. And so I found it not unreasonable to suppose that my dark moments of a night ago had something to do with the accumulating effects of overly identifying with the past, of losing my way in some of darkest labyrinths of European history.

Though everything depends, as Elias Canetti observed, on "with whom we confuse ourselves,"[3] it remains a mystery why we become enthralled by certain subjects rather than others. As with falling in love, a writer's fixation on his subject can be so absolute that he or she remains partially in eclipse for as long as the infatuation lasts. Consider Marguerite Yourcenar's *Memoirs of Hadrian,* for example. The idea of her book, and the first writing of it, dates from the period between 1924 and 1929. Even in her early twenties, she was aware that "a great part of my life was going to be spent in trying to define, and then to portray, that man existing alone and yet closely bound with all being."[4] The project was begun and abandoned several times. At times, she felt too young to do justice to the work. Or she lost interest in it, feeling shame at ever having ventured upon the undertaking, and suffering that "lapse into despair of a writer who does not write."[5] Then, around 1941, she discovered by chance, in an artist's supply shop in New York, four Piranesi engravings, and bought them. One depicted Hadrian's Villa. Piranesi, she realized, had sensed "the tragic architecture of an inner world."[6] She gazed at this engraving every day, drawing inspiration from thirty years' experience of joy and sorrow, sickness and health, and "the perpetual testing of oneself upon the touchstone of fact."[7] The *Memoirs* were published in 1951, when Yourcenar was forty-eight. "We lose track of everything, and of everyone, even ourselves," she writes.[8] Yet I imagine she might have grudgingly accepted the corollary: that though we disappear into our account of another, we also appear in it in a way we could not have foreseen or ordained. As she describes her habit of writing each night "in almost automatic fashion"[9] before destroying the work each morning, Yourcenar suggests an analogy with how, in each generation, we build our lives from the rubble of our parental or ancestral past, plundering and sundering what others have made in order to give birth to ourselves.

There are, however, precursors who stop us in our tracks, that we cannot get beyond. As the great New Zealander painter, Colin McCahon observed, "Mondrian, it seemed to me, came up in this century as a great barrier—the painting to END all painting. As a painter, how do you get around either a Michelangelo or a Mondrian? It seems that the only way is not more 'masking-tape' but more involvement in the human condition."[10]

We woke before first light, and at 7 a.m. were first in line outside the Vatican Museum, waiting as tour parties with reservations filed into the museum ahead of us, led by guides holding aloft improvised wands with brightly colored taffeta attached, and muttering into microphones attached to their lapels commentaries that their clients listened to on headsets as they moved together, circumspect and on cue, like bemused sheep. It was almost 9 o'clock before our turn came to enter the building, passing from ticket counter to turnstile and on up a flight of stairs and through baroque halls crowded with knots of other visitors, each receiving furtive instructions from a tour guide. Having seen so many hundred tourists enter the museum ahead of us, I expected to find the Sistine Chapel too overcrowded to allow us to contemplate the frescos. But looking up, I was instantly and utterly absorbed, and the people milling around me ceased to exist.[11] I was completely alone, transported, moved to tears.

I could not understand why I was so deeply affected. Was it recognition of images seen in books for so many years, but on a scale and in a setting no book could possibly match? Was it awe at the technical, artistic, and physical achievement of a man in his sixties, working on scaffolding 60 feet above the ground, often alone, day in and day out for more than three years? Or the breathtaking conception of the hand of God reaching out to Adam, the vision of the last judgment, and the biblical narrative, its panels capturing the passion and pity of human existence, striving upward, seeking wild and beautiful beyonds, yet borne downward by blind error, unbridled appetite, indifference to others, or the forces of mortality itself?

As my eyes moved from scene to scene I became dizzy and I felt my way to one of the benches around the chapel walls, where I sat, dwelling on this work the like of which I had never seen, my eyes still stinging from tears.

It was some time before I came back to earth, aware of the people around me, the silence enjoined by the angry shushing of a Vatican usher, and the rapt and marveling responses that the ceiling elicited from almost everyone who entered the chapel. I had scarcely noticed the frescos by Botticelli, Perugino, Ghirlandaio, and other fifteenth-century masters that covered the lower sections of the chapel walls, perhaps because they conjured an uncomfortable sense of crowdedness so that you became conscious not only of how many people had made the pilgrimage to make eye contact with Michelangelo's masterwork but of the overwhelming sight of lost souls rising or falling in the vertiginous vault between heaven and earth. Confronted by this teeming mass of floating, disoriented, contending figures, it is a relief to let one's eyes rest again on the moment of Creation, in which Adam lies languidly on a mountainside, surrounded by a squirming entourage that suggests that the advent of human life on earth is also the beginning of procreative excess and the Malthusian specter of overpopulation. There are also overtones here of Michelangelo's preference for solitude and his aversion to the crowded stream of mundane life. Here was an artist who in an unfinished sonnet from around 1550 imagined himself enclosed in a boulder high in the mountains, then dragged from the mountain to suffer the weight of wagon wheels on the thronged thoroughfares of the human world.

When I saw Michelangelo's *Pietà* in Saint Peter's basilica later that morning, I was again struck by the delicacy and fragility of the figures that animate and transcend the white marble from which they have been fashioned or freed. But if Michelangelo imagined stone as a place of refuge, he also saw it as a living thing from which a self-sufficient, imperishable, and pure ideal could be born.

The history of Rome is the history of a human relationship with stone. The ruins in the Forum testify to a sustained attempt to transmute the ephemeral triumphs of men into something enduring—the mutable made marmoreally permanent, personalities given an adamantine form that would carry them into eternity. Michelangelo subverts this tradition. In his hands, stone is humanized, one might even say feminized. As a baby, he was sent to a wet nurse who was both the daughter and wife of stonemasons and believed this explained his predilection for sculpture. But his natural attraction to stony Madonnas, Dante's stony poems (*rime petrose*), and marble as white as breast milk may have had more to do with the many years he spent in the marble quarries of Carrara.

Michelangelo embraced Petrarch's view that anatomy and quarrying were similar activities. Just as dissecting cadavers helps one understand human anatomy, so exploring the hidden depths of marble enables one to discover the spiritual properties of the human form.

Petrarch and Michelangelo were both echoing what quarry workers had known for centuries. Even today, the Carrara quarry workers speak of the mines as *agri marmiferi* or 'marble fields' that grow and renew themselves like cultivated plots or farms. [12] In his *Natural History,* Pliny made similar observations—of scars on the mountainside that underwent natural healing and of marble that reproduced itself. Anthropomorphic metaphors still permeate the miners' vernacular. "Marble which breaks easily like 'glass' is thought of as being more 'alive' or as having greater *vivezza*. Marble 'sings' and has 'nerves' that make it strong. It 'sleeps' and 'wakes', and is sometimes described as containing an anima or 'soul.'"[13] Mining is also sexualized, so that the rock chisel (*punciotto*) is likened to a penis and drilling to sexual intercourse, while mining itself is a source of masculine pride. Moreover, the mountain is a living body. As one worker observed, "You see the mountain moves. It recreates itself. Some quarries however move while others grow. You can see the way they grow by how much the marble is broken at the bottom. It gets more solid at the top. So it must be growing from the bottom to the top. If you lighten the load at the top some quarries solidify at the bottom."[14] Moreover, it is thought that while quarrymen can to some extent protect themselves from the dangers of using heavy machinery, they can do little to defend themselves from the mountain itself, which is said to be capable of vengeful retaliation for the miners' daily attacks on it. Thus, flaws in a block of marble are known as *peli nemici* or "enemy faults." "The mountain reacts!" said one man. "It makes a noise like a living person. The mountain wants its share." Yet men talk to the mountain, cajoling it, "looking after it," appeasing it, paying it respect, in the hope that the mountain will reciprocate.

There was something else that I found arresting about Michelangelo's work with marble: the frequency with which he left work unfinished. Rather than conclude that he set himself impossibly high standards or was constantly distracted by new commissions, it may be that Michelangelo was simply paying his respects to stone that begrudged him only a glimpse of a human form, holding back what it did not wish to yield. Moreover, might the artist also be mindful of his own uncertain relationship with a world of political intrigue, patronage and religious dogma, and his resolve to withhold that part of himself that he identified as singularly and securely his own. What moved me, I think, about Michelangelo's art is summarized by that space between God's and Adam's fingertips—a gap that Michelangelo refused to close, a circuit between the sacred and the secular, the individual and the crowd, that remains broken. Great art gestures toward an order or purity with one hand, while reminding us with the other of the rough, unready, impure, and incomplete nature of life. Marble's solidity is juxtaposed with the fragility of the figure that has been carved out of it. Wittgenstein asked if one could speak of a stone that causes pain as having "pain patches on it. Michelangelo's unfinished sections represent the rough that always goes with the smooth—the aspects of our life that we cannot wish away with either art or intellect.[15]

TWENTY-SEVEN

Writing as a Way of Life

I HAVE ALWAYS BEEN INTRIGUED by how devious we are in getting around dilemmas we do not know how to address directly. Perhaps all art is an expression of this evasiveness, this cowardly tactic of contriving to have others resolve issues we cannot deal with, or blaming anyone but ourselves for the difficulties we get into. George Johnston grew up in Melbourne, Australia, between the wars.[1] His earliest memories were of walking sticks, wheelchairs, prosthetic limbs, and crutches cluttering up the hallway of his parent's house, and of "a formless shadow of disaster that [he] wanted to shout against or run away from."[2] What oppressed this child was not only the physically disabled and shell-shocked soldiers that his mother brought home in the hopes that they could be nursed back to health, or being dragged around hospital wards every Sunday, ostensibly to bring cheer to the legions of maimed men in their white enameled cots, it was also his growing awareness of the "horrible flatness" of the world in which he was confined, "the unmitigated melancholy"[3] of the suburban streets, and the cynical defeatism of those who had survived the war only to find no future in the peace. After serving an apprenticeship as a lithographer, Johnston worked as a journalist for the Melbourne *Argus,* where he met the woman who, in Johnston's words, decided to make him her husband. He felt less free than he had ever felt. "What I principally remember about [the wedding] is that while waiting for the bride in the church vestry . . . I had the odd wish that something calamitous would happen, like the roof of the church falling in, which might bring to a stop, or at least to a postpone-ment, a series of fantastic processes which quite suddenly seemed to me to be moving me against my will and better judgment towards a suspect destiny."[4] When the newlyweds moved into their double-fronted, red-brick, three-bedroom suburban villa, it was Johnston's wife who "assumed leadership on matters of taste and sophistication,"[5] organizing their social life, shedding unsuitable acquaintances, and acquiring friends more compatible with her idea of their status. Johnston spent more and more time hiding in his study, ignoring his wife's calls to wash the car, fix the TV antenna on the roof, clean his ashtray, or do something about his clutter. One Sunday he drove to a nursery and asked for the fastest-growing tree he could buy. He returned home with a Sugar Gum and despite his wife's protestations planted it in the middle of their front lawn. "I think there are more people than will admit it who are inclined to force their big issues on trivial things, rather than face up to the basic problems full on, and this was the way it worked with me. It was this six-shilling sugar-gum . . . that was to become the bone of contention between [my wife] and me, and ultimately the hammered-in wedge that split us apart."[6]

I thought of George Johnston last summer, when I began work trimming dead branches from the oaks, hickories, and elms around our house. This had nothing to with my marriage, but a lot to do with the artful ways in which we address adversity.

There were obvious limits to what I could safely accomplish with a pruning saw and a twelve-foot ladder, but by the end of a sultry afternoon I began to feel satisfied that I saved myself a considerable amount of money and got rid of most of the dead limbs. But one remained—a single leafy hickory bough overhanging the roof and challenging my ability to reach it. I climbed the ladder, assessed the situation, and made the first cut. My position was precarious, fifteen feet above the ground, one hand holding the tree trunk, the other deploying the pruning saw at an awkward angle. Within minutes the saw got stuck in the green wood and, despite my best efforts, I could not work it free. Exhausted and frustrated, and with the light failing, I climbed down the ladder and went inside to wash up.

That night I could not sleep for thinking of the half-severed branch and my unfinished task. Though I racked my brains for a solution, I could not find one. Had all my work been in vain? Would I have to pay a professional after all? It seemed absurd to hire someone to saw through one small bough. Surely I could manage it after a good night's sleep, by borrowing my neighbor's saw, beginning a new cut at a different angle, or positioning myself differently in the fork of the tree.

But I did not sleep. I went over and over the problem. It was like trying to stop the itching from an insect bite by scratching. You only make matters worse. But gradually my mind turned to the question of why we find it so difficult to rest when a task has not been finished, a problem has not been solved, or what we set out to do has encountered obstacles we can't get around. Why can't we simply walk away with a sigh or a curse, and turn our attention to some other task that we *can* complete? I thought of how uneasy we feel when a quarrel has not been resolved, a question has been left hanging, or more tragically, when we cannot suppress the memory of a traumatic event or perform the work of mourning because the body of a loved one has never been recovered from the place she met her death. There is nothing new in the observation that the incompleteness and imperfectness of our quotidian life is made good in our dreams. In REM sleep, the mind works tirelessly and ingeniously to create patterns from the remains of the day. And the need for closure is a contemporary cliché. Can we say, then, that our minds are continually working—sometimes with and sometimes without our conscious contrivance—to organize our experience into forms that we can live with, so that we no longer have to pick over the past, anxiously trying to put it behind us, or get rid of its ragged edges, fill its holes, plaster over its cracks, round it out? This sense of incompleteness may be banal, like my inability to trim the hickory outside my front door. It may be moral, as when we feel conscience-stricken about something we should have done or not done, said or not said. It may be economic—our books unbalanced, debts unpaid, income in doubt. But in every case, our thoughts oscillate between the task we failed at and imaginary resolutions—the problem taken out of our hands by a supernatural intercessory, or through a lucky break, a stroke of genius, or a fortuitous intervention.

We touch here on the work of art and the religious imagination. Though we struggle to control the course of our lives and our dealings with others, we are constantly coming up against the limits of what we can control, comprehend, cope with, or complete. While practical reason governs much of what we do, art and the imagination are always present, as supplements to what we cannot achieve through care and calculation alone. The essence of art, then, is the creation of a simulacrum of the events or situations that perplexed or thwarted us, supplanting them with an artificial, parsimonious, scaled-down replica of the real that we *can* fashion and refashion to our mind's content. In the work of art and the imagination, we have recourse to simulations of reality that enable us to act in the belief that in working on them we somehow work upon the world. We turn things around, as we say. We call the tune. What was closed to us is now open. What was daunting is now doable. What previously proved impossible now appears possible. What was incomplete or imperfect is now completed or perfected. That so much imaginative energy is poured into these projects of altering the *appearance* of the world is a testimony to the human need to play an active role within it. Art answers an existential need in us, not to be at the center of the world so much as to have a hand in determining how we will conceive it and make it our own.

After several days hard work, the trees were trimmed and the garden weeded. My wife and I stood at the window, surveying our handiwork, deeply satisfied at what we had accomplished. The pruned limbs, tangles of poison ivy, stacks of rotten timber, intrusive creepers, and wild roses were now stacked in piles to be carted away. We had created, at least for a season, a space of domestication in what had been the wilderness of our wooded lot. As garden is to bush as art is to life. And this unending work of bringing artificial order to a world that will inevitably revert to wilderness is the work of ritual, the work of the imagination, the work of art, and arguably, the work of culture. Like many others, I have spent my academic life creating coherent stories and plausible interpretations that purport to reveal the inner workings of the world. But the work of the intellect is as delusional as the work of art. Both enable us to believe that we make and unmake the world that makes and unmakes us, when in truth it is the world that has the edge and calls the final shot.

In "The Idea of Order at Key West" (1934), Wallace Stevens makes the sea suggest all that's "never formed to mind or voice," while a female figure, unidentified except as "she," stands for those prosaic or poetic forms with which we translate the sound of the sea into a language we can live with. When "she" speaks or sings, the world as sea or sky or wind is made over, though never mimetically, to the world of intellectual and aesthetic order. So complete is this transfiguration, mediated by the art and artifice of words, that the world itself is often eclipsed.

> ... when she sang, the sea,
> Whatever self it had, became the self
> That was her song, for she was the maker. Then we,
> As we beheld her striding there alone,
> Knew that there never was a world for her
> Except the one she sang and, singing, made.

But great art never completely closes the gap between the unruliness or refractoriness of life and the order we are so practiced in imposing upon it in the name of art, science, or religion. The singing ends, and as we turn toward the town our "blessed rage for order," "the maker's rage to order words of the sea," gives ground to "ghostlier demarcations, keener sounds." In this view, poetry lies at the limits of language, on the threshold of what is securely in our grasp and all that eludes us—absent loved ones, dead friends, countries from which we have been exiled, youthful ambitions.

No visual artist better captures this inescapable tension between the world as it is and the world that we create in our attempts to mirror, mimic, or master it than Paul Cézanne.

It was during the winter of 1963–64 that I saw my first Cézanne. I was working among the homeless in London at the time, and art galleries were places of warmth where I took refuge from the streets and let my mind wander. The painting is of Montagne Sainte-Victoire (1887), and it hangs in the Courtauld. It was the first painting that moved me to tears. There's a pine tree on the left, leaning away, with a single bough extending across the top of the painting. You can feel it moving in the wind—actually see the effect of the wind on the pine needles—and smell the resin. And then, across this breath-taking plain that reminded me strongly of the Wairarapa, the lilac mountain with its magical presence.

Did I realize, through this painting, the impossibility of ever finding such an idyllic region, of having to accept that the mistral is always buffeting, driving people to distraction or violence, the world a permanently unsettled place in which we struggle for refuge only to find there is no real shelter from the storm? In retrospect, it is easy to read my own cross-purposes into this work, identifying with vagrants even as I searched for home, compelled to go to the ends of the earth in search of a place in which I could be happy, yet nostalgic for the place I had left behind.

For forty-five years now I have returned, time and time again, to the paintings of Paul Cézanne, finding in them analogues of my attempts to artistically assemble the fragments of my experience without reaching for synthesis, closure, or final truth, since the whole, observed Adorno, turning Hegel on his head, is the false.[7]

On the wall in front of me is a framed reproduction of another of Cézanne's landscapes from Aix-en-Provence. Painted between 1890 and 1895, *Large Pine and Red Earth* now hangs in the State Hermitage Museum in St. Petersburg. A distant, arid, and sun-drenched landscape is glimpsed through overlapping pine boughs that extend beyond the frame of the painting. The trunk of the tree establishes a solid vertical to the left of center. In the words of one writer, the work seems to have been conceived as a search for rhythm and perfect composition, a sort of intellectual abstraction.[8] But this is to suggest that Cézanne was looking for a balance he found difficult to achieve, rather than deliberately choosing to convey a tension between order and chaos—the carefully painted planes[9] that hint at houses, the edges of fields and lines of trees juxtaposed with gnarled and entangled branches, blurred patches of undergrowth or scrub, seemingly haphazard brush strokes. Cezanne worked on this painting for almost five years—evidence of the uncertainty and care with which he painted—but his difficulty in completing his work quickly did not reflect his striving for geometrical order, symmetry, or tonal balance but rather a desire to capture the unstable relationship between the solidity of the tree and the wind that bends its branches and sweeps through its leaves, between the order of art and the wildness of the world. With Cézanne, order is provisional and tentative, never certain.

Cézanne gave his all to depicting existence as ambiguous. Our being-in-the-world is neither a stable state nor a completely fluid one. A person can resemble a stone, and the rocks in a quarry can resemble the naked bodies of a group of bathers. For Cézanne, we live betwixt and between consoling illusions of order, provided by our religions or our conventional worldviews and experiences that befall us like bolts from the blue or seismic shocks, reducing our lifeworlds to ruins and leaving us shattered, uncertain, and afraid. Consider Cézanne's masterpiece in the Metropolitan Museum of Art in New York City, entitled *The House with the Cracked Walls* (1892–1894). When I visited the Met in the summer of 2010 and entered the room where the Cézannes are hung, this painting stopped me in my tracks. The wall of the two-story house is painted with the same care with which a plasterer would work, creating an unblemished surface. Blinding sunlight is reflected from the wall, in which is set a pitch black window. From the tiled roof to the rocky ground on which the house stands, a dark gaping crack descends, cleaving the canvas in two. And while the left foreground is composed, in Cézanne's usual manner, of curving planes, it comes up against blocks of granite on the right so that the crack in the wall of the house continues, as it were, into the broken landscape below it. Behind the house there is a line of trees, agitated by the wind. I would later discover that Cézanne often painted abandoned buildings and quarries near his studio outside Aix, though he depicted this house only once. I would also read that this period of the artist's life was marked by a series of crises.

In the spring of 1885, the man who his friend Zola once described as passive in the face of love[10] and not given to amorous conquests, fell head over heels in love. Cézanne was forty-six, with a reputation for being afraid of women, yet he enlists Zola's help in writing love letters to a young woman whose name and situation we may never know.

Here is the draft of one of his love letters[11]:

> I saw you, and you allowed me to kiss you; from that moment, I've been agitated by a profound unrest. You will forgive the liberty of writing you taken by a friend tormented by anxiety: I don't know how to excuse this liberty, which you may consider an enormous one, but could I remain in this depression? Isn't it better to show a feeling than to hide it?
>
> Why, said I to myself, keep silent as to the source of your torment? Isn't it a solace of suffering to allow it to find expression? And since physical pain seems to find some relief in the cries of the victim, is it not natural, Madame, that mental griefs seek some assuagement in confession to an adored being?
>
> I know that this letter, whose foolhardy and premature posting may seem indiscreet, has nothing to recommend me to you save the goodness of. . . .

For six months Cézanne's obsession brought misery to the artist, his common-law wife Hortense Fiquet, and his family, although there is no evidence that Cézanne's love was requited. All we know is that within a year the distraught painter repairs his relationship with Hortense by marrying her, though neither of them would ever find happiness. And after four years of moving from place to place, Cézanne retreats to Aix, where he was born and raised, and absorbs himself in the landscape, as if this is his compromise between the emptiness of his domestic and religious life and the passion he'd felt for this unremembered girl.

The second crisis that year was Cézanne's estrangement from his childhood friend, Émile Zola, following the publication of Zola's novel, *L'Oeuvre*, in 1886. Rightly or wrongly, Cézanne regarded the central character of Claude, a doomed painter, consumed by self-doubt even as he dedicated himself to the creation of a new kind of art, as a mean-spirited commentary on himself. Given the painter's distress and vulnerability at this time, and the domestic tensions of the summer of 1885 when the Cézannes imposed upon the hospitality of the Zolas in Médan, it is easy to see how misunderstandings could arise.

Then the third blow fell. Cézanne's father died in October 1886.

It is striking how often commentators and critics describe Cézanne as an unstable man, racked by self-doubt, who sought to escape the chaos in his personal life by creating monumental and immutable forms with paint.[12] But I see a man living in what John Keats[13] called "negative capability," simultaneously acknowledging the fractured, fragile character of the human world while applying himself to the repair work we may do through art, thought, and faith. If Cézanne became consumed by his art, it was not because he sought perfection or succumbed to despair, but rather because he sought to strike a bearable balance between the disorderly forces of human existence and the ordering powers of art.

But consumed he was—by doubt in his ability to strike that balance. Like the *Seated Peasant* (1892–1896), the portrait of *Mme. Cézanne in a Red Dress* (1888–1890), and the apples rolling off a plate in *Still Life with Ginger Jar and Eggplants* (1893-1894), or the pine boughs stirring in the wind in his numerous depictions of Monte Sainte-Victoire, the painter himself is always caught off balance, upset, destabilized.

In his *Letters on Cézanne*, the poet Rainer Maria Rilke describes the impact of a memorial exhibition of Cézanne's work in the autumn of 1907, a year after the painter's death.[14] Rilke immediately embraced Cézanne as his tutelary spirit, returning to the exhibition day after day and writing to his wife Clara about his reactions. A few years before, Rilke had stood in front of an archaic torso of Apollo and been so moved that he resolved to dedicate his life completely to art. He was convinced that if he expended all his love in his work, he might one day produce something that possessed the purity that Cézanne had achieved in his.

But it was not purity that Cézanne sought, but images that captured the interface between contending impulses, between opposing forces. Ironically and perhaps tragically, to achieve this everything had to go by the board— home comforts, intimate relationships, even physical health. When Merleau-Ponty speaks of how Cézanne struggled to "make visible how the world touches us," it is necessary to remember that the world touches us in contradictory ways. But it was not simply the co-presence of stillness and movement in the world before his eyes that concerned him, but also the division within himself between the demands of life and the demands of his work. Cézanne removed himself from everything that could "hook" him. Often he was so spent at the end of a day's work, so angry, mistrustful, and frustrated at his failure to achieve what he calls *"la réalization,"* that he would take to his bed before six, after a "senselessly ingested meal," seeking oblivion in sleep. He even stayed away from his mother's funeral in order not to lose a day's work—a precursor of Camus's étranger. At the end of his life, he suffered from diabetes, headaches, and bronchitis, yet he painted outdoors every day, relying on his son to take care of Hortense, as well as the day-to-day chores at home. Eight days before his death he collapsed while painting in the rain. He was brought home in a laundry cart. But even at death's door he got out of bed and went to his studio, determined to work.

There's a phrase in one of Rilke's letters to Clara that I find particularly moving. The poet has just returned from another visit to the Cézanne room in the Salon d'Automne, and he's describing how he usually finds the people walking about an art gallery more interesting than the paintings they are looking at. But the Cézanne room is an exception. Here, he says, reality is on his side, and he goes into detail about Cézanne's dense quilted blues, his reds, his shadowless greens, and the reddish black of his wine bottles. The humbleness of the things Cézanne paints: the apples that are cooking apples, the wine bottles that belong to the bulging pockets of an old coat. It's almost as if the painter has become one of the homely, shabby objects in front of him. As if his entire being has gone into his art, leaving only a shell behind. The tragedy was that he gave more life to these things than he gave to his wife and son or to the people he painted. "The landscape thinks itself in me, and I am its consciousness," he once said.[15] And so his landscapes are really abstract portraits—worlds not of rock and pine but of the flesh. Look at Cézanne's portraits of his wife, Hortense Fiquet, and you'll see that the reverse is also true. This man who could not bear to be touched, and whose passion for landforms was stronger than his desire for human company, turned Hortense to stone. He spoke of "nature" almost as if it were a person—a person who was giving him "great difficulties."[16] It wasn't simply that Cézanne treated persons as objects; he treated objects as persons. And all the while he was becoming an object himself, pursued by the local kids each day as he trudged to his studio, stones thrown at him as if he were a stray dog, a butt of jokes, treated like the village idiot.

There is a long-standing romantic view of artists, scholars, and priests as individuals who sacrifice their personal lives in order to create enduring works of art, scholarship, or spiritual perfection. Zola's *L'Oeuvre* belongs to this tradition.

But Claude was not Cézanne, even if Zola drew on Cézanne in creating the storm-tossed obsessional character of Claude Lantier. One can see the similarities—the ambivalence toward women, the perverse conviction that family life is inimical to art, the search for some transcendent object or idea that will outlast the centuries, the notion that art requires absolute devotion, and that a man must, therefore, choose between art and women. Why should Claude distance himself from women, distrust them, feel contempt for them, fear that they will sap his creative power? Why should his mistress have to choose between caring for the child she has borne him and caring for him, "her big child." And this glorious ideal of the masterpiece, the masculine justification for the neglect of children, the sacrifice of our lives! Poor Christine, Claude's mistress and model. She begins to feel trapped in a ménage-à-trois. The painting is her rival. Claude prefers the counterfeit to the real person. Only the masterpiece matters.

When their son dies, he paints the dead child and exhibits the painting in the Salon des Refusés, where it is met with indifference. She implores him: If you can't be a great painter, at least life remains to us. But for Claude, nothing exists beyond art. She makes herself beautiful for him, seduces him, shows that the living flesh is more real than any painted figure. "You've made me pose for you; you wanted to make copies of my body, but why? Surely I'm worth more than all the copies you could ever make! At best they're ugly, besides being cold and stiff as so many corpses. . . . But I love you. I want you. Don't you understand? Why do I have to tell you all the time? Can't you feel it when I'm always near you, when I offer to pose for you, when I'm always wanting to touch you? Do you understand now? I love you. I'm alive and I want you. . . . You can go on living because I love you." But he replies, "Ah, but you'll never love me enough! . . . I know that because I know myself. The only thing that could make life worth living would be something that doesn't exist, the sort of joy that would make me forget everything else. . . . You've already proved you couldn't give me that, and I know you never will."[17]

The difference, as I see it, between Cézanne and Claude is that while Claude sacrifices his well-being (and those he loves) in an impossible attempt to create a perfect work of art, Cézanne ironically loses his grip on reality by attempting to strike a balance between the masterful artifice of art and the turbulent reality of life.

That this motif is often overlooked, both in cursory accounts and in critical commentaries of great art may attest to our all-too-human desire to find in art, the intellect, or religion a means of transcendence so that the world as it rendered in paint, in words, or in ceremony eclipses the world as we know it in our everyday lives. Consider, for example, Pieter Bruegel's Northern Renaissance masterpiece, *The Hunters in the Snow* (1565).

Taking her cue from Eli Siegel's principle of "aesthetic realism" ("All beauty is a making one of opposites"), Nancy Huntting emphasizes the way Bruegel brings near and far, sharpness and softness, stillness and movement, into a single harmonious composition.[18] But does this do justice to the work?

I purchased a fine Austrian reproduction of this painting in Wellington, New Zealand, when I was twenty. It was on display in an art supplies shop in Panama Street and cost me ten pounds—all the money I had in my pocket. I have lived with this painting for fifty years—as I have lived with the landscapes of Paul Cézanne—yet this painting, celebrated for its artful composition and visual power, points to a divided world. The people skating, fishing, or curling on the frozen ponds or stoking an outdoor fire are—like the peasants in *The Fall of Icarus*[19]—oblivious to the tragedy unfurling in the world beyond the mountains or outside the frame of the painting, though it was a tragedy of which the painter himself was all too grimly aware.

The old masters were never wrong about suffering, as W.H. Auden famously observed; "it takes place" as in *The Hunters in Snow*, as children are "skating on a pond at the edge of the wood," or people are "eating or opening a window or just walking dully along." Even as we tend a fire, plough a field, herd animals, hunt game, carry faggots home to a hearth, or feast at a table, a tragedy is unfolding somewhere for someone. How do we know we are not skating on thin ice?

Is Bruegel intending to communicate this paradox to us? Is it not only Auden who sees the poignant co-presence in our lives of events occurring outside our comprehension or control and pedestrian events that so absorb us that we are blind to all else?

Some scholars have argued that, for Bruegel, the events occurring outside our comprehension and control belong to a realm beyond the senses, beyond the reach of rational thought, and outside our ordinary comprehension of space and time.[20] This interpretation rests on evidence of Bruegel's close association with a "heretical" Flemish school known as the Family of Love that repudiated the religious rivalries among Catholics, Lutherans, and Calvinists in favor of a humanist and mystical vision of an "invisible church" unfettered by rites and doctrines. But when Bruegel's friend, the cartographer Abraham Ortelius, expressed the view that Bruegel painted many things that cannot be painted,[21] was he alluding not only to a shared commitment to Perennial Philosophy but also to the difficulty of holding in tension two perspectives on the world in the same frame? The tower of Babel aspires to join earthly and heavenly realms, but the tower is always unfinished, falling short of its goal. In the same way, the order we create in art is countermanded by our worldly limitations, our unbridled appetites, our foolish ambitions, our stupidity, intolerance, and short-sightedness.

Look closely, and even *The Hunters in the Snow* betrays these disruptive forces. The sign outside the inn hangs from a single hinge, angled so that it leads one's eye down the snowy slope into the frozen valley. But the sign's placement is not determined solely by compositional requirements, for it depicts Hubertus, patron saint of hunters, standing before a stag or hart that holds a crucifix between its antlers. Not only does the image recall Saint Hubert's conversion in the Ardennes Forest in the late seventh century; it suggests that God may have withdrawn His blessings from the hunters in Bruegel's painting. The unhinged sign is thus an oblique reference to the religious turmoil of the late sixteenth century on which Pieter Bruegel's God must surely have looked askance—the excesses of the Protestant Reformation inspiring violent countermeasures by the Catholic Church, repressing heresies and reestablishing papal authority. At the same time, a Little Ice Age had descended over Europe. Glaciers expanded, warm summers were few and far between, winters were long and harsh, harvests were poor (1565, the year Bruegel painted *The Hunters in the Snow,* was particularly bad), and epidemics swept the land. Bruegel's vivid depictions of death and of hell must surely have come from direct personal knowledge of the rape, killing, and pillaging that swept the Flemish countryside during this period. People are playing on the frozen rivers and lakes, but hunger and death stalks the land. Crows fly overhead as if waiting for carrion. Hunters return from the wintry woods, their dogs' morose expressions and exhausted demeanor giving us a glimpse of what their masters were feeling as they trudged home with only the emaciated corpse of a fox to show for their labors. These ciphers of an unsaid[22] suggest that hell is on earth and heaven unattainable unless it is through the lens of art, which creates the appearance of a well-tempered geometry[23] in a world where death and disorder are, nonetheless, always present and impinging. Michel de Certeau's analysis of Hieronymous Bosch's *The Garden of Earthly Delights* holds true for the work of Pieter Bruegel, who, as a young man, was hailed as a new Hieronymous Bosch.[24] The strictly ordered mise-en-scène[25] coexists with an elsewhere comprising pathways of nonmeaning, disorderly combinations and space without beginning or end, exits, or entrances. If there is mystery about the work of these sixteenth-century Flemish masters, it is in the negative dialectic that obtains between the order humanity brings to the world through language, geometry, or art and the world's complexity, contradictoriness, changeability, and confusion that subvert that order. One hand gestures toward an idea of design—geometrical, theological, cultural—while the other hand stays the first, pointing to all that prevents the completion or consummation of the initial impulse.

In W.H. Auden's poem, "The Shield of Achilles," an idealistic young woman looks over the shoulder of the Greek hero, expecting to see on his shining metal shield vistas of vines and olive trees, marble, well-governed cities, and ships upon untamed seas. She finds instead an artificial wilderness, a sky like lead, and a weed-choked field where unspeakable scenes of violence and depravity unfold.

The genius of artists like Paul Cézanne, Wallace Stevens, Wystan Hugh Auden, and Pieter Bruegel lies in their capacity to create a space where opposites can be held or contained, to show all sides of the human condition without attempting to resolve the quandary of how we can accept the blind forces of history and circumstance even as we search for certainty and control in our lives. How, to quote Keats, we can "live in uncertainties, Mysteries, doubts, without any irritable reaching after fact & reason."[26]

I left the Metropolitan Museum and strolled up 5th Avenue toward the Guggenheim. The day was hot, and tourists were milling around the gallery entrance, some eating snacks, others examining the postcards they had bought in the gallery shop or staring up at the façade of the building. A young woman asked me if I wouldn't mind taking a photograph of her and her friend. They were anxious that the photo should have the Guggenheim in the background, proof, perhaps, that they had been there.

A friend of mine, Tyler Zoanni, knowing of my interest in Cézanne, had recently sent me a postcard from the Guggenheim—a reproduction of Cézanne's *Still Life, Flask, Glass, and Jug* (1877). Tyler suggested that if I was ever in New York City I should make sure I saw this painting, and he mentioned a mysterious female figure reflected in the jug. My first thought was that Cézanne might have smuggled a miniature portrait of his lover into the still life, but the dates were wrong and the surmise implausible. Nonetheless, I was eager to get a closer look at the image on the jug, which in the postcard reproduction was too ambiguous to decipher.

The jug is a Provençal olive jar, half-covered in a viridian glaze, and it appears in several of Cézanne's still lives. Within this dark-green glaze is a rough square of reflected light, and on this light blue ground a small silhouetted figure appears to be wading through waist-deep water, his or her reflection streaking the water in the foreground. The figure is exquisitely painted, left arm and hand outstretched as if pulling the body forward against the weight of the water, right hand trailing behind. And yet, one cannot be convinced that Cézanne intended to paint this miniature, but simply daubed some cobalt on the light blue ground just as he smudged the reflection on the flask to add to its verisimilitude.

After leaving the Guggenheim, I found a place on Lexington and 88th Street where I ordered lentil soup, organic bread, and espresso. I ate in silence at a communal table not unlike the one in Bruegel's *Village Wedding Feast*. I was thinking of how the carefully prepared food in front of me carried no evidence of the place where the wheat was harvested, the environment in which the vegetables were grown, or the people who made their living from growing them. Culture belies its origins in cultivation. Domestication denies the wildness of the world. Art abstracts itself from life. And even the food on our plate bears few traces of the fields and gardens from whence it came. Yet every day nature resurfaces, reminding us in the form of flood, drought, hurricane, or earthquake that it coexists with what we call culture and cannot be quelled.

At that moment my thoughts returned to the paintings I had seen that morning, particularly the blue figure in the Cézanne still life that appeared to be wading through water. This minor ambiguity—a random brush stroke giving the impression of a carefully painted figure leaning into a body of water—captured my wider theme, of how we live betwixt and between opposing moods, moments, and emotions, always in two minds, aware that there are always two sides to every story, the order we bring to the world confounded by the world's invasions of our most carefully cultivated spaces, not to mention to perennial oscillation between our sense of being a part of and being apart from the landscapes, the lives of others, the still lives, that encompass us—abandoned quarries, cracked walls, unfinished towers, broken hinges, ghostlier demarcations, keener sounds.

NOTES

PREFACE

1. I draw on Bernard Stiegler's extensive discussions of technics in theorizing writing less in terms of what is communicated than as a technology for creating webs of intersubjective connectedness (Bernard Stiegler, *Technics and Time,* trans. Richard Beardsworth and George Collins. Stanford, CA: Stanford University Press, 1998/2009). Svetlana Boym argues that technologies of communication might be compared with nostalgic longings for lost times, far-flung places, or absent loved ones. Both are modes of "mediation." Indeed, *techné* and *art* share the same etymology. "Technology is not a goal in itself but an enabling medium. While nostalgia mourns distances and disjunctures between times and spaces, never bridging them, technology offers solutions and builds bridges, saving the time that nostalgia loves to waste (*The Future of Nostalgia.* New York: Basic Books, 2002, p. 347).

2. For a sustained and detailed account of this point of view, see Michael Jackson, *The Palm at the End of the Mind: Relatedness, Religiosity, and the Real.* Durham, NC: Duke University Press, 2009, pp. xii–xv, 5–8.

3. Michael Jackson, *Latitudes of Exile.* Dunedin, New Zealand: McIndoe, 1976.

4. For example, my own recent book, *Road Markings: An Anthropologist in the Antipodes.* Dunedin, New Zealand: Rosa Mira Books, 2012, www.rosamirabooks .com

5. Gerard MacDonald and David Hursh, *Twenty-First Century Schools: Knowledge, Networks and New Economies.* Rotterdam: Sense Publishers, 2006, pp. 139–142, 185.

6. Rudolf Otto, *The Idea of the Holy.* London: Oxford University Press, 1923.

7. Electronic document, available at http://joi.ito.com/may8,2011

8. Frank Moss, *The Sorcerers and Their Apprentices: How the Digital Magicians of the MIT Media Lab Are Creating the Innovative Technologies That Will Transform Our Lives.* New York: Crown Business, 2011, p. 10.

9. David Howes speaks of this as "a crisis of intonation," and describes the "dwindling power" of traditional songs in the Trobriand Islands, where older people

lament the passing of a "golden age of orality," when the measure of human greatness was the resounding quality of one's vocal presence. (*Sensual Relations: Engaging the Senses in Culture and Social Theory*. Ann Arbor: University of Michigan Press, 2003, pp. 64–67.)

10. J.C. Carothers, "Culture, Psychiatry and the Written Word," *Psychiatry* 22, 307–320, 1959; Jack Goody, ed. *Literacy in Traditional Societies*. Cambridge, United Kingdom: Cambridge University Press, 1968; Marshall McLuhan, *The Gutenberg Galaxy*. London: Routledge and Kegan Paul, 1962; Walter J. Ong, *Orality and Literacy: The Technologizing of the Word*. London: Methuen, 1982; David Riesman, "The Oral and Written Traditions." In: Edmund Carpenter and Marshall McLuhan, eds., *Explorations in Communications*. Boston: Beacon Press, 1960.

11. Walter Benjamin, "The Storyteller." In: *Illuminations,* trans. Harry Zohn. New York: Schocken Books, 1968.

12. Plato's *Phaedrus,* trans. Christopher Rowe. Harmondsworth, United Kingdom: Penguin, 2005, pp. 61–64. See also, Jacques Derrida, "Plato's Pharmacy" In: *Dissemination,* trans. Barbara Johnson. London: Athlone, 1981, pp. 66–94.

CHAPTER ONE

1. My chapter title is from Octavio Paz's *The Bow and the Lyre*. Paz argues that writing is a way we seek to conjoin ourselves with someone we love but cannot reach or possess, or with another existence or self that might complete us, another time or place in which we might find fulfillment. "Man is that which is incomplete, although he may be complete in his very incompletion; and therefore he makes poems, images in which he realizes and completes himself without ever completing himself completely" (*The Bow and the Lyre,* trans. Ruth L.C. Simms. Austin: University of Texas Press, 1973, p. 247). Variations on this theme may also be found in Ernst Bloch's work on hope and utopian longing and in my own recent ethnographic explorations of the nature of existential dissatisfaction and existential incompleteness. (See Ernst Bloch, *The Spirit of Utopia,* trans. Anthony A. Nassar. Stanford, CA: Stanford University Press, 2000; Ernst Bloch, *The Principle of Hope,* trans. Neville Plaice, Stephen Plaic, and Paul Knight. Cambridge, MA: MIT Press, 1986; Michael Jackson, *Life within Limits: Well-Being in a World of Want*. Durham, NC: Duke University Press, 2011.

2. Walter Benjamin, "On the Mimetic Faculty." In: *Reflections: Essays, Aphorisms, Autobiographical Writings,* trans. Edmund Jephcott. New York: Schocken Books, 1986, p. 333.

3. J.M. Coetzee, *Elizabeth Costello: Eight Lessons*. Milsons Point, NSW, Australia: Vintage, 2004, p. 228. The line is from a letter purporting to be from Elizabeth, Lady Chandos, to Francis Bacon.

4. In this phrase, the English writer Hilary Mantel sums up her sense that being a writer is like being a Catholic, because "Catholicism tells you at a very early age the

world is not what you see; that beyond everything you see, and the appearance . . . there is another reality, and it is a far more important reality." Electronic document, http://www.guardian.co.uk/books/2011/mar/26/authors-secrets-writing

5. As Theodor Adorno observed, "Artworks detach themselves from the empirical world and bring forth another world, one opposed to the empirical world as if this other world too were an autonomous entity." *Aesthetic Theory,* trans. Robert Hullot-Kentor. Minneapolis: University of Minnesota Press, 1997, p. 1. Elsewhere (p. 335), he aphoristically notes that "art is an entity that is not identical with its empiria. What is essential to art is that which in it is not the case, that which is incommensurable with the empirical measure of all things."

6. *The Man Died: Prison Notes of Wole Soyinka.* Harmondsworth, United Kingdom: Penguin, 1975, p. 9.

7. Gabriel Garcia Márquez, *The Fragrance of Guava.* London: Faber and Faber, 1998.

8. Gabriel Garcia Márquez, *One Hundred Years of Solitude.* London: Picador, 1978, p. 27.

9. Jorges Luis Borges, "The Circular Ruins." In: *Labyrinths: Selected Stories and Other Writings,* trans. James E. Irby. Harmondsworth, United Kingdom: Penguin, 1970, pp. 72–77.

10. Paz, p. 117.

11. Paz, p. 247.

12. Maurice Blanchot, *The Space of Literature,* trans. Ann Smock. Lincoln: University of Nebraska Press, 1989.

13. Walter J. Ong, "The Writer's Audience Is Always a Fiction." *Publications of the Modern Languages Association* 90 (1), Jan. 1975, 9–21.

14. William Faulkner once ranked Thomas Wolfe ahead of his contemporaries because he had tried the hardest to do what Cervantes and Dostoevsky had done, "to put inside the covers of a book the complete turmoil and experience and insight of the human heart . . . to try to put all the experience of the human heart on the head of a pin." He loved best his own masterpiece, *The Sound and the Fury,* for the same reason, "that it was the most splendid failure." Interview with Frederick Gwynn, February 15, 1957. Electronic document: http://faulkner.lib.virginia.edu/display/wfaudio001_1. Hurt by Faulkner's remarks, Ernest Hemingway, nonetheless echoed them in his 1954 Nobel Prize Acceptance Speech: "For a true writer each book should be a new beginning where he tries again for something that is beyond attainment. He should always try for something that has never been done or that others have tried and failed."

15. Orhan Pamuk, Nobel Lecture, December 7, 2006. http://nobelprize.org/nobel_prizes/literature/laureates/2006/pamuk-lecture_en.html

16. Paul Auster, "Interview with Larry McCaffery and Sinda Gregory." In: *The Red Notebook and Other Writings.* London: Faber and Faber, 1995, pp. 116–154, 144.

17. George J. Zytaruk and James T. Boulton, eds. *The Letters of D.H. Lawrence,* Vol. II. Cambridge, United Kingdom: Cambridge University Press, 1982, p. 302.

18. "Were anthropologists to draw up a complete list of all known types of cultural behavior, this list would overlap, point by point, with a similarly complete list of impulses, wishes, fantasies, etc. obtained by psychoanalysis in a clinical setting, thus demonstrating, by identical means and simultaneously, the psychic unity of mankind. . . ." George Devereux, *Ethnopsychoanalysis: Psychoanalysis and Anthropology as Complementary Frames of Reference.* Berkeley: University of California Press, 1978, pp. 63–64.

19. T.S. Eliot, *East Coker,* lines 85–89.

CHAPTER TWO

1. "Il a peut-être des secrets pour *changer la vie?* Non, il ne fait qu'en chercher, me répliquais-je." *Season in Hell,* trans. Louise Varèse. New York: New Directions, 1961, p. 40.

2. "Départ dans l'affection et le bruit neufs." Arthur Rimbaud, "Departure." In: *Illuminations,* trans. Louise Varèse. New York: New Directions, 1957, pp. 34–35.

3. *Cælum non animum mutant qui trans mare currunt.* Horace, Epistle 1.11, v. 27.

4. Charles Nicholl, *Somebody Else: Arthur Rimbaud in Africa 1880–1891.* Chicago: University of Chicago Press, 1997, p. 84.

5. Joseph Conrad, *Youth, Heart of Darkness, The End of the Tether: Three Stories.* London: J.M. Dent, 1961, p. 65.

6. ONUC was the acronym for the Organisation des Nations Unies au Congo, established shortly after Congo's independence in June 1960 to keep the peace, prevent secessionist moves by the mineral-rich provinces of Kasai and Katanga, and supervise aid and development projects. I worked as a volunteer for ONUC and the Congolese Ministry of Youth and Sports.

7. "On suit la route rouge pour arriver à l'auberge vide." "Enfance." In: *Illuminations,* p. 8.

8. Nicholl, p. 148.

CHAPTER THREE

1. I had, of course, been reading Joseph Conrad's author's note to *Heart of Darkness*—a story he describes as "the spoil I brought out from Africa, where, really, I had no sort of business."

2. This line, that passed through my mind at that moment, was from Blaise Cendrars' epic poem, *La Prose de Transsibérien et de la Petite Jehanne de France.* Paris: Éditions des Hommes Nouveaux, 1913.

3. George Orwell, "Reflections on Gandhi." *Partisan Review,* 1949.

CHAPTER FOUR

1. Italo Calvino, *If on a Winter's Night a Traveller,* trans. William Weaver. London: Picador, 1982, p. 61.

2. Jay Bochner, *Blaise Cendrars: Discovery and Re-Creation.* Toronto, ON: University of Toronto Press, 1978, pp. 27–28.

3. "Modern man has discovered modes of thinking and feeling that are not far from what we call the nocturnal part of our being." Octavio Paz, *The Bow and the Lyre,* trans. Ruth L.C. Simms. Austin: University of Texas Press, 1973, p. 102.

CHAPTER FIVE

1. "Art Market: Leopoldville" and "Le Royal," *Landfall* 19(3), 231–232, 1965. "Execution" and "The Red Road," *Landfall* 20(4), 312–314, 1966.

2. "Rhodesia and Survival," *New Zealand Monthly Review* 6(63), 10–11, 1965–1966. Blaise Cendrars, "Noël en Nouvelle-Zélande," In: *Trop c'est Trop.* Paris: Denoël, 1957, pp. 109–112, trans. Michael Jackson, *Comment* 25, 35–36, 1965.

3. "East Coker," lines 70–71.

4. "East Coker," line 207.

5. Charles Baudelaire, "Au Lecteur."

6. Cendrars in Aix-en-Provence. Louis Parrot, *Blaise Cendrars, Poètes d'Aujourd'hui.* Paris: Editions Pierre Seghers, 1948, p. 7.

7. Blaise Cendrars, *L'Homme Foudroyé.* Paris. Denoël, 1945, pp. 265–266; "La Carissima est le roman de sainte Marie-Madeleine, la plus belle histoire d'amour, du grand amour qui ait jamais été vécu sur terre." "Blaise Cendrars Vous Parle," Entretien Premier, and Entretien Cinquième. In *Oeuvres Complètes,* vol. 8. Paris: Denoël, 1964, pp. 547 and 599.

8. Miriam Cendrars, Interview with Frédéric Ferney, Boulogne-sur-Seine, December 21, 1992. In: Frédéric Ferney, *Blaise Cendrars.* Paris: Éditions François Bourin, 1993, p. 134.

9. Ludwig Wittgenstein, *Tractatus Logico-Philosophicus.* eds. B. F. McGuiness, T. Nyberg, and G.H. Wright. London: Routledge and Kegan Paul, 1922. Last sentence.

10. Blaise Cendrars, L'Homme Foudroyé, Paris: Denoël, 1945.

CHAPTER SIX

1. Nicolas Tomalin, *The Strange Last Voyage of Donald Crowhurst.* London: Stein and Day, 1970.

2. Malcolm Lowry, *Hear Us O Lord From Heaven Thy Dwelling Place* and *Lunar Caustic*. Harmondsworth, United Kingdom: Penguin, 1969, pp. 26–98 (27–28).

CHAPTER SEVEN

1. M. Meggitt, "Uses of Literacy in New Guinea and Melanesia." In: *Literacy in Traditional Societies,* ed. Jack Goody. Cambridge, United Kingdom: University of Cambridge Press, 1968, pp. 300–309 (302).

2. Max Weber, "Science as a Vocation." In: *Sociological Writings,* ed. Wolf Heydebrand. New York: Continuum, 1994, p. 20.

CHAPTER EIGHT

1. Antoine de Saint-Exupéry, *Wartime Writings 1939–1944,* trans. Norah Purcell. San Diego: Harcourt Brace Jovanovich, 1986; Joy D. Robinson, *Antoine de Saint-Exupéry.* Boston: Twayne, 1984; Stuart Gilbert, "Introduction." *The Wisdom of the Sands,* trans. Stuart Gilbert. New York: Harcourt Brace, 1950.

CHAPTER NINE

1. My first published collection of poetry, *Latitudes of Exile,* won the Commonwealth Poetry Prize in 1976, and my second collection, *Wall,* was awarded the New Zealand Book Award for Poetry in 1981. In the same year that my monograph on the Kuranko was published in London (1977), I won the Curl Essay Prize (Royal Anthropological Institute of Great Britain and Ireland).

2. R.B. Foster, *W.B. Yeats: A Life II: The Arch Poet 1915–1939.* Oxford, United Kingdom: Oxford University Press, 2003.

3. Lawrence Durrell, *Justine.* London: Faber and Faber, 1957, p. 17.

4. Virginia Woolf, *Moments of Being: Unpublished Autobiographical Writings.* London: Triad Grafton Books, 1978, p. 81.

5. This and the following quotations concerning Norman Lewis, appear in a review of a Lewis biography by novelist and essayist Andrew O'Hagen, "Candle Moments." *London Review of Books,* 25, 30(18), 2008, p. 23.

6. Cited in Brian Boyd, *Vladimir Nabokov: The Russian Years.* Princeton, NJ: Princeton University Press, 1990, pp. 486, 488.

7. Lyndall Gordon, *A Private Life of Henry James: Two Women and His Art.* London: Chatto & Windus, 1998.

8. Letter of Henry James to Grace Norton (1880). Cited by Colm Tóibín, "A Man with My Trouble," *London Review of Books,* January 3, 2008, 15–18.

9. This and the following quotations are from Joseph Conrad's "Author's Note" to *Victory*. London: J.M. Dent & Sons, 1962, pp. ix–xvii.

CHAPTER TEN

1. Michael Jackson, *Rainshadow*. Dunedin: John McIndoe, 1988, p. 191.
2. Jean-Luc Godard, Screenplay for *Alphaville,* trans. Peter Whitehead. London: Immediate Publishing, 1966, p. 43.
3. Joyce Johnson, *Minor Characters: A Beat Memoir*. London: Virago, 1983, p. 237.

CHAPTER ELEVEN

1. "Song of a Man Who Has Come Through." In: *The Complete Poems of D.H. Lawrence*. Ware, Hertfordshire, United Kingdom: Wordsworth Editions, 1994, p. 195.
2. Robert Graves, "The White Goddess." In: *Collected Poems 1965*. London: Cassell, 1965, p. 201.
3. Robert Graves, *The White Goddess: A Historical Grammar of Poetic Myth*. New York: Farrar, Straus and Giroux, 1966, p. 406.
4. Mirka Zemanová, *Janáček: A Composer's Life*. London: John Murray, 2002, p. 67.
5. John Tyrrell, *Janáček: Years of a Life, Volume I (1854–1914): The Lonely Blackbird* (London: Faber and Faber, 2006), 336.
6. John Tyrrell, *Janáček: Years of a Life, Volume II (1914–28): Tsar of the Forests* (London: Faber and Faber, 2007), 844.
7. Zemanová, p. 174.
8. Zemanová, p. 182.
9. Zemanová, p. 195.
10. Zemanová, p. 220
11. Zemanová, pp. 237–238.
12. Graves, op. cit.
13. Karen Horney, *Feminine Psychology*. New York: W.W. Norton, 1967.
14. Bruno Bettelheim, *Symbolic Wounds: Puberty Rites and the Envious Male*. New York: Collier Books, 1962, p. 45.

CHAPTER TWELVE

1. Edouard Peisson, "Blaise Cendrars à Aix-en-Provence." In: *Blaise Cendrars 1887–1961*. Paris: Mercure de France, 1962, pp. 131–139. Cf. Blaise Cendrars'

"Dedication" to his sons, Odilon and Rémy in *La Main Coupée*. Paris: Denoël, 1946, p. 7: "Mon fils repose, au milieu de ses comrades tombés comme lui, dans ce petit carré de sable du cimitière de Meknès réservé aux aviateurs et déjà surpeuplé, chacun plié dans son parachute, comme des momies ou des larves qui attendent chez les infidèles, pauvres gosses, le soleil de la résurrection."

2. Meyer Fortes, *The Web of Kinship among the Tallensi*. London: Oxford University Press, 1949, p. 163.

3. Margaret Trawick, *Notes on Love in a Tamil Family*. Berkley: University of California Press, 1990, p. 159.

4. Agehananda Bharati, *The Light at the Center: Context and Pretext of Modern Mysticism*. Santa Barbara, CA: Ross-Erikson, 1976, p. 161.

5. *The Diaries of Franz Kafka 1910–1923*. Harmondsworth, United Kingdom: Penguin, 1964, p. 207.

6. The character, Georg, has the same number of letters as Franz," Kafka wrote, and "Frieda has as many letters as F. and the same initial." *The Diaries*, p. 215. "In one of his first letters to Bauer, Kafka wrote that his thinking about her was connected to his writing." Klaus Wagenbach, *Kafka,* trans. Ewald Owen. Cambridge, MA: Harvard University Press, 2003, p. 92.

7. *Diaries,* p. 163.

8. Letter to Max Brod, July 1922, cited in Wagenbach, pp. 82–83.

9. Wagenbach, p. 79.

10. *Diaries,* p. 220.

11. *Diaries,* p. 225.

12. *Diaries,* p. 225.

13. Franz Kafka, *Wedding Preparations in the Country and Other Stories,* trans. Ernst Kaiser and Eithnew Wilkins. Harmondsworth, United Kingdom: Penguin, 1978, p. 8.

14. *Wedding Preparations,* p. 8.

CHAPTER THIRTEEN

1. George Easton, "Being Christopher Hitchens." *New Statesman,* July 12. 2010.

2. Christopher Hitchens died on December 15, 2011, at age 62.

3. Joseph Conrad, "Preface to *The Nigger of the Narcissus,*" Harmondsworth, United Kingdom: Penguin, 1963, pp. 11–12.

4. Aleksandar Hemon, "The Aquarium: A Child's Isolating Illness." *The New Yorker,* June 13 & 20, 2011, pp. 50–62 (passim 60).

5. I have used the version of this story published in N.J. Dawood's translation of *The Tales from the Thousand and One Nights*. Harmondsworth, United Kingdom: Penguin, 1973, pp. 15–23. Apart from changing the spelling of Shahrazad to the more familiar Scheherazade, I have retained Dawood's spellings of the names of the characters in the story.

6. Martin Heidegger, "...Poetically Man Dwells..." *Poetry, Language, Thought,* trans. Albert Hofstadter. New York: Harper & Row, 1975, p. 215.

7. Heidegger, p. 226.

CHAPTER FOURTEEN

1. Czesław Miłosz, *History of Polish Literature,* 2nd ed. Berkeley: University of California Press, 1983, p. 193.

2. Ian MacLean, "Introduction." Jan Potocki, *The Manuscript Found in Saragossa,* trans. Ian MacLean. New York: Viking, 1995, pp. xi–xviii (xii). In 1905, a twenty-one-year-old Polish philosophy student, Bronisław Malinowski, was awarded the Potocki Foundation stipend for Polish Noblemen, though the funds were insufficient to pay his way to England, where he embarked on his career in anthropology in 1910.

3. Frank Bren, *World Cinema 1: Poland.* London: Flicks Books, 1986, p. 68.

4. Theodor Adorno, "On Subject and Object." *Critical Models: Interventions and Catchwords,* trans. Henry W. Pickford. New York: Columbia University Press, 1998, pp. 245–248 (245).

CHAPTER FIFTEEN

1. Orhan Pamuk, "My Father's Suitcase: The Nobel Lecture, 2006," *New Yorker,* December 25, 2006, and January 1, 2007, pp. 82–96, 90.

2. Orhan Pamuk, interview with Neghar Azimi, "The Objects of the Exercise," *New York Times Magazine,* October 29, 2009.

3. Allen Feldman, *Formations of Violence: The Narrative of the Body and Political Terror in Northern Ireland.* Chicago: University of Chicago Press, 1991, p. 250.

4. Oscar Wilde, *De Profundis.* New York: Modern Library, 2000.

5. Wilde, p. 116.

6. Etty Hillesum, *Letters from Westbork,* trans. Arnold J. Pomerans. London: Grafton Books, 1988, p. 132.

7. Hillesum, p. 124.

8. Hillesum, p. 146.

9. Joan Didion, *The White Album.* New York: Farrar, Straus and Giroux, 1990, p. 11.

10. The period in question was 1966–1971. Didion, p. 11.

11. Didion, pp. 12–13.

12. Samuel Beckett, *Proust. Three Dialogues: Samuel Beckett and Georges Duthuit.* London: John Calder, 1987, p. 103.

13. Dan P. McAdams, *The Stories We Live by: Personal Myths and the Making of the Self.* New York: Guilford Press, 1993, p. 5.

14. John Berger, *About Looking*. London: Writers and Readers Cooperative, 1984, p. 30.

15. Alasdair McIntyre, *After Virtue: A Study in Moral Theory*, 2nd ed. Notre Dame: Indiana: University of Notre Dame Press, 1984, p. 212.

16. "My life is a hesitation before birth," noted Kafka in January 1922. *Diaries,* ed. Max Brod. Harmondsworth, United Kingdom: Penguin, 1972, p. 405. "I have always sensed that there was within me an assassinated being," Beckett said in an interview with Charles Juliet. "Assassinated before my birth. I needed to find this assassinated person again. And try to give him new life. I once attended a lecture by Jung in which he spoke about one of his patients, a very young girl. After the lecture, as everyone was leaving, Jung stood by silently. And then, as if speaking to himself, astonished by the discovery that he was making, he added: "In the most fundamental way, she had never really been born. I, too, have always had the sense of never having been born." Cited by James Olney, *Memory and Narrative: The Weave of Life-Writing*. Chicago: University of Chicago Press, 1998, p. 325. This same theme recurs in the last lines of Beckett's *The Unnameable*. "Perhaps it's done already, perhaps they have said me already, perhaps they have carried me to the threshold of my story, before the door that opens on my story, that would surprise me, if it opens, it will be I, it will be the silence, where I am, I don't know, I'll never know, in the silence you don't know, you must go on, I can't go on, I'll go on."

17. Frank Kermode, *The Sense of an Ending: Studies in the Theory of Fiction*. New York: Oxford University Press, 1967, p. 127.

18. Tobias Wolff, "Introduction." *Matters of Life and Death: New American Stories,* ed. Tobias Wolff. Green Harbor, MA: Wampeter Press, 1983, p. x.

19. Lorrie Moore, *Birds of America*. New York: Knopf, 1998, p. 222.

20. Moore, p. 237.

21. In her essay on Isak Dinesen (Karen Blixen), Hannah Arendt makes a similar point: "If it is true, as her 'philosophy' suggests, that no one has life worth thinking about whose story cannot be told, does it not follow that life could be, even ought to be, lived as a story, that what one has to do in life is to make the story come true?" Hannah Arendt, *Men in Dark Times*. Harmondsworth, United Kingdom: Penguin, 1973, p. 107.

22. Martin Amis, *Experience*. London: Vintage, 2001, p. 11.

23. Jean-Dominique Bauby, *The Diving Bell and the Butterfly,* trans. Jeremy Leggat. New York: Knopf.

24. A.R. Luria, *The Man with a Shattered World: The History of a Brain Wound,* trans. Lynn Solotaroff. Cambridge, MA: Harvard University Press, 1987, p. xx.

25. Luria, p. 86.

26. Luria, p. 84.

27. João Biehl, *Vita: Life in a Zone of Social Abandonment*. Berkeley: University of California Press, 2005, pp. 1–2.

28. Biehl, p. 1.

29. Biehl, pp. 2–3.

30. Biehl, p. 11.

31. Biehl, p. 82.

32. Biehl, pp. 72–73.

33. Biehl, p. 359.

CHAPTER SIXTEEN

1. Dannie Abse, "Not Adlestrop." *Penguin Modern Poets 26,* ed. Anthony Thwaite. Harmondsworth, United Kingdom: Penguin, 1975, p. 33.

2. R.S. Thomas, "In Church." In: *Pieta.* London: Rupert Hart-Davis, 1967, p. 44.

3. Sylvia Plath, "The Arrival of the Bee Box." *The Collected Poems: Sylvia Plath,* ed. Ted Hughes. New York: HarperPerennial, 1992, pp. 212–213.

4. Seamus Heaney, "Punishment." In: *North.* London: Faber and Faber, 1975, pp. 37–38.

5. William Blake, "Auguries of Innocence." *The Penguin Book of English Verse,* ed. John Hayward. Harmondsworth: Penguin, 1956, pp. 243–246.

6. Gerard Manley Hopkins, "The Wreck of the Deutschland." *Gerard Manley Hopkins: Poetry and Prose,* ed. W. H. Gardner. Harmondsworth, United Kingdom: Penguin, 1953, pp. 12–24.

7. Anna Akhmatova, "Requiem." *Poems of Akhmatova,* trans. Stanley Kunitz, with Max Hayward. London: Collins and Harvill Press, 1974, pp. 99–117.

8. Jorge Luis Borges, "The Dream of Coleridge." *Other Inquisitions 1937–1952.* New York: Simon & Schuster, 1964, pp. 14–17.

9. Gerard Manley Hopkins, "The Windhover," op. cit., p. 30.

10. Carol Ann Duffy, "Prayer." *New British Poetry,* ed. Don Paterson and Charles Simic. Saint Paul, MN: Graywolf Press, 2004, p. 51.

11. Philip Larkin, "The Whitsun Weddings." *Collected Poems: Philip Larkin,* ed. Anthony Thwaite. London: Marvell Press and Faber and Faber, 1988, pp. 114–116.

12. Arthur Rimbaud, Letter to Paul Demeny, Charleville, May 15, 1871. In: *Illuminations,* trans. Louise Varèse. New York: New Directions, 1946, p. xxix.

13. In his masterful study of Bahian Candomblé, Mattijs van der Port observes that yielding to the world—as in spirit possession and mysticism—is one manifestation of a search for "the-rest-of-what-is: the 'surplus' of our reality definitions, the 'beyond' of our horizons of meaning, that [gets] excluded as 'impossible,' 'unknown,' 'mere fantasy,' or 'absurd' for our worldview to make sense." He adds, "Academia has long kept its doors locked [against] such forms of inquiry." Van der Port, *Ecstatic Encounters: Bahian Candomblé and the Quest for the Really Real.* Amsterdam: Amsterdam University Press, 2011, pp. 18–19.

14. Eugen Herrigel, *Zen in the Art of Archery,* trans. R.F.C. Hull. London: Routledge and Kegan Paul, 1953, pp. 85–86.

15. Vladimir Nabokov, "The Art of Literature and Commonsense." *Lectures on Literature,* ed. Fredson Bowers. New York: Harvest, 1982, pp. 371–380 (379).

16. Italo Calvino, *If on a Winter's Night a Traveler,* trans. William Weaver. London: Picador, 1982, p. 139.

17. Rainer Maria Rilke, *Letters to a Young Poet,* trans. Stephen Mitchell. New York: Vintage Books, 1986, p. 4.

18. Rilke, *Letters,* p. 6.

19. T.S. Eliot, "East Coker." In: *Four Quartets.* London: Faber and Faber, 1959, p. 31.

20. Rilke, *Letters,* p. 4

21. Rilke, *Letters,* p. 14.

22. Rilke, *Breifen das Ehepaar S. Fischer, p. 66.* Cited by Wolfgang Leppmann, *Rilke: a Life,* trans. Russell M. Stockman. New York: Fromm International, 1984, p. 259.

23. Rilke, *Letters,* p. 13.

24. Cited by Leppmann, *Rilke: A Life,* pp. 287–288. Rilke would say that the monologues in the *Elegies* came to him naturally in rhymeless verses. "They were as though 'dictated' to him, he always averred. To say the god had spoken is one way of putting it: more realistically, we can regard this sudden inspiration as the result of his instinctive determination, after the long preoccupation with his troubles, to heal himself." Donald Prater, *A Ringing Glass: The Life of Rainer Maria Rilke.* Oxford, United Kingdom: Clarendon Press, 1986, p. 206.

25. J.F. Hendry, *The Sacred Threshold: A Life of Rainer Maria Rilke.* Manchester, United Kingdom: Carcanet, 1983, pp. 81–82.

CHAPTER SEVENTEEN

1. Dylan Thomas, "Poem on his Birthday." *Collected Poems 1934–1952.* London: J.M. Dent & Sons, 1952, p. 170.

2. Rainer Maria Rilke, *Letters to a Young Poet,* trans. Stephen Mitchell. New York: Vintage Books, 1986, p. 9.

3. Andrey Tarkovsky, *Sculpting in Time: Reflections on the Cinema,* trans. Kitty Hunter-Blair. New York: Knopf, 1987, p. 168.

4. Eugenio Montale, *The Second Life of Art: Selected Essays,* trans. Jonathan Galassi. New York: Ecco Press, 1982, pp. 20–24 (24).

CHAPTER EIGHTEEN

1. Michel de Montaigne, *The Essays: A Selection,* trans. M.A. Screech. Harmondsworth, United Kingdom: Penguin, 2004, p. 3.

2. Walter Benjamin, "The Storyteller: Reflections on the Works of Nikolai Leskov." In: *Illuminations,* trans. Harry Zohn. New York: Schocken Books, 1969, pp. 83–109 (94).

3. Benjamin, "The Storyteller," p. 98.

4. Thomas W. Knox, *The Underground World: A Mirror of Life below the Surface*. San Francisco: J.M. Rising, 1878, p. 934.

5. Knox, p. 943.

6. Enrique Rodríguez Larreta, *"Gold Is Illusion": The Garimpeiros of the Tapajos Valley in the Brazilian Amazonia*. Stockholm: Almqvist & Wiksell, 2002, p. 4.

7. Theodor Adorno, *Negative Dialectics*, trans. E.B. Ashton. New York: Continuum, 1973, p. 365.

8. Judith Sherman, *Say the Name: A Survivor's Tale in Prose and Poetry*. Albuquerque: University of New Mexico Press, 2005, p. 151.

9. Hélène Cixous, *Coming to Writing and Other Essays*, trans. Sarah Cornell, Deborah Jenson, Ann Liddle, and Susan Sellers. Cambridge, MA: Harvard University Press, 1991, p. 3.

10. Theodor Adorno, "Cultural Criticism and Society." In: *Prisms*, trans. Samuel and Shierry Weber. Cambridge, MA: MIT Press, 1983, p. 34.

CHAPTER NINETEEN

1. W.G. Sebald, *The Emigrants*. London: Harvill Press, 1997, p. 230.

2. Scott M. Foran, "The Benefits of a Writing Habit," *Writers Studio* 2(3) 2007, pp. 1–2, (1).

3. Elias Bredsdorff, *Hans Christian Andersen: The Story of His Life and Work*. London: Phaidon, 1975, p. 124.

4. Oscar Nyaungwa, "Folktale Influence on the Shona Novel," M.A. thesis, University of South Africa, Nov. 2008.

5. Bredsdorff, p. 79.

6. Hans Andersen, letter to Caroline Amalie, Queen Dowager of Denmark, July 14, 1857. In: Elias Bredsdorff, *Hans Andersen and Charles Dickens: A Friendship and its Dissolution*. Copenhagen: Rosenkilde and Bagger, 1956, p. 104.

7. Bredsdorff, *Hans Andersen and Charles Dickens*, p. 115.

8. Hannah Arendt, *The Human Condition*. Chicago: University of Chicago Press, 1958, pp. 95, 169.

9. Bredsdorff, p. 182.

10. John Forster, *The Life of Charles Dickens*. London: Chapman and Hall, 1929.

11. Elie Wiesel, *Night*, trans. Marion Wiesel. New York: Hill and Wang, 2006, p. vii.

CHAPTER TWENTY

1. Gaston Bachelard, *The Poetics of Space*, trans. Maria Jolas. Boston: Beacon Press, 1969, p. xvii.

2. Bachelard, pp. xxviii–xxix.

3. Journals, October 16, 1859.

4. Martin Heidegger, *Being and Time,* trans. J. Macquarrie and E. Robinson. San Francisco: Harper, 1962, p. 58.

5. Seamus Heaney, "The Harvest Bow." In: *Field Work.* London: Faber and Faber, 1979, p. 58.

6. Cited by Jane Reichhold in *Bashō: The Complete Haiku,* trans. Jane Reichhold. Tokyo: Kodansha International, 2008, p. 72.

7. *The Collected Letters of Katherine Mansfield,* vol. 1, ed. Vincent O'Sullivan and Margaret Scott. Oxford, United Kingdom: Clarendon, 1984, p. 330.

8. Gary Snyder, "On the Road with D.T. Suzuki." In: *A Zen Life Remembered,* ed. Masao Abe. New York: John Weatherill, 1986, p. 207.

9. Nobuyuki Yuasa, "Introduction." *Bashō: The Narrow Road to the North and Other Travel Sketches,* trans. Nobuyuki Yuasa. Harmondsworth, United Kingdom: Penguin, 1966, pp. 9–49 (25–26).

10. Bashō, "The Records of a Weather-Exposed Skeleton." In: *The Narrow Road to the Deep North and Other Travel Sketches,* trans. Nobuyuki Yuasa. Harmondsworth, United Kingdom: Penguin, 1966, p. 51.

CHAPTER TWENTY-ONE

1. Jane Bennett, *The Enchantment of Modern Life: Attachments, Crossings, and Ethics.* Princeton, NJ: Princeton University Press, 2001, ch. 1.

2. Julian Barnes, *Flaubert's Parrot.* London: Pan Books, 1985, p. 74.

3. Barnes, p. 80

4. Roger Colet, "Introduction" to Guy De Maupassant, *Selected Short Stories,* trans. R. Colet. Harmondsworth, United Kingdom: Penguin, 1971, p. 10.

5. Elias Canetti, *Kafka's Other Trial: The Letters to Felice,* trans. Christopher Middleton. New York: Schocken Books, 1974, pp. 6–7.

6. Cited by Canetti, p. 7.

7. It is possible that this conclusion is a Eurocentric misunderstanding of what is more possibly a lack of familiarity with, and knowledge of what to expect from, images on a two-dimensional surface. Of the Abelam of the Sepik (New Guinea), Anthony Forge observes, "their vision has been socialized in a way that makes photographs especially incomprehensible, just as ours is socialized to see photographs and indeed to regard them as in some sense more truthful than what the eye sees." Abelam could hardly fear the photographic theft of their images if they could not actually recognize their features in a photo. Anthony Forge, "Learning to See in New Guinea." In: *Socialization: The Approach from Social Anthropology,* ed. Philip Meyer, London: Tavistock, 1970, pp. 269–291 (287).

8. *Poems of Akhmatova,* trans. Stanley Kunitz and Max Hayward. London: Collins and Harvill Press, 1974, p. 67.

9. Vladimir Nabokov, *Speak Memory: An Autobiography Revisited*. Harmondsworth, United Kingdom: Penguin, 1969), 18.

10. Max Hayward, "Introduction." *Poems of Akhmatova*, trans. Stanley Kunitz and Max Hayward. London: Collins and Harvill Press, 1974, p. 15.

11. Hayward, pp. 3–26 (23).

12. W.G. Sebald, *Austerlitz,* trans. Anthea Bell. London: Hamish Hamilton 2001, p. 175.

13. Jessica Coulson, "Translator's Preface." F.M. Dostoevsky, *Memoirs from the House of the Dead*. London: Oxford University Press, 1956, p. vii.

14. Coulson, p. ix.

CHAPTER TWENTY-TWO

1. Henry Miller, *The Books in My Life*. New York: New Directions, 1969.

2. Miller, pp. 22–39.

3. Albert Camus, "The Enigma." In: *Lyrical and Critical Essays,* ed. Philip Thody, trans. Ellen Conroy Kennedy (New York: Vintage, 1967), 156.

4. Benjamin, op. cit., p. 336.

5. Bruce Chatwin, "A Lament for Afghanistan." In: *What Am I Doing Here?* London: Picador, 1990, pp. 286–293 (286–287).

6. Anthony Kerrigan, "Editor's Epilogue." In: *Jorge Luis Borges, A Personal Anthology,* trans. Anthony Kerrigan, Alistair Reid, and others. London: Jonathan Cape, 1968, p. 209.

7. Jorges Luis Borges, "The Enigma of Edward Fitzgerald." In" *Other Inquisitions 1937–1952,* trans. Ruth L.C. Simms. New York: Simon & Schuster, 1960,pp. 75–78 (77–78).

8. W.G. Sebald, *The Rings of Saturn,* trans. Michael Hulse. London: Harvill Press, 1999, p. 200.

9. Sebald, p. 200.

10. Miller, p. 12.

CHAPTER TWENTY-THREE

1. This was the title of the book Jack London published in 1903, based on his experiences of living rough among the slum dwellers of East London. George Orwell's *Down and Out in Paris in London* (1933) is clearly indebted to Jack London's pioneering ethnography of the streets.

2. Elias Canetti, *Party in the Blitz: The English Years,* trans. Michael Hofmann. London: Harvill Press, 2005, p. 230.

3. Michael Jackson, *Life within Limits: Well-Being in a World of Want*. Durham, NC: Duke University Press, 2011.

4. Ernst Bloch, *The Principle of Hope,* Vol. 1, trans. Neville Plaice, Stephen Plaice, and Paul Knight. Cambridge, MA: MIT Press, 1986, p. 21.

5. Bloch, pp. 353, 371.

6. Will and Ariel Durant, "Rousseau and Revolution: A History of Civilization in France, England, and Germany from 1756, and in the Remainder of Europe from 1715, to 1789." In: *The Story of Civilization: Part X.* New York: Simon & Schuster, 1967, p. 3.

7. Jean-Jacques Rousseau, *The Confessions,* trans. J.M. Cohen. Harmondsworth, United Kingdom: Penguin Books, 1953, p. 19.

8. Elias Canetti, *The Memoirs of Elias Canetti.* New York: Farrar, Straus and Giroux, 1999, p. 285.

9. Geoff Dyer, *Out of Sheer Rage: Wrestling with D.H. Lawrence.* New York: Picador, 2009, pp. 126–127.

10. Anne Whitehead, *Paradise Mislaid: In Search of the Australian Tribe of Paraguay.* St. Lucia: University of Queensland Press, 1997.

11. Robin Dunbar, "You've Got to Have (150) Friends." *International Herald Tribune,* Dec. 27, 2010, p. 8.

12. Elias Canetti, *Memoirs,* pp. 161–162.

CHAPTER TWENTY-FOUR

1. Louis MacNeice, cited by Jeremy Adler, "Introduction." Elias Canetti, *Party in the Blitz: The English Years,* trans. Michael Hofmann. London: Harvill Press, 2005, p. 13.

2. Adler, "Introduction." Canetti, *Party in the Blitz,* p. 15.

3. Elias Canetti, *Crowds and Power,* trans. Carol Stewart. New York: Farrar, Straus and Giroux, 1984, p. 275.

4. Canetti, *Party in the Blitz,* pp. 196–197.

CHAPTER TWENTY-FIVE

1. Mary Douglas, *Purity and Danger: An Analysis of Concepts of Pollution and Taboo.* Harmondsworth, United Kingdom: Pelican Books, 1970, pp. 197–204.

2. Lord Byron, *Ode to Venice,* lines 71–73.

3. Joseph Brodsky, *Watermark.* New York: Farrar, Straus and Giroux, 1992, p. 8.

4. Brodsky, p. 8.

5. Brodsky, p. 13.

6. Naomi Ritter, ed., *Death in Venice: Complete, Authoritative Text with Biographical and Historical Contexts, Critical History, and Essays from Five Contemporary Critical Perspectives.* Boston: Bedford Books, 1998, p. 9.

7. I am thinking of Elias Canetti's commentary on W.H.J. Bleek's and L.C. Lloyd's *Specimens of Bush Folklore*. London: Allen and Unwin, 1911; in *Crowds and Power*, pp. 337–342; and Adam Kendon's *Sign Languages of Aboriginal Australia: Cultural, Semiotic and Communicative Perspectives*. Cambridge, United Kingdom: Cambridge University Press, 1988, pp. 352–353.

8. Byron, lines 58–61.

9. Thomas Mann, *Death in Venice*, ed. Naomi Ritter. Boston: Bedford Books, 1998, p. 26.

10. Brodsky, p. 12.

CHAPTER TWENTY-SIX

1. Joyce E. Salisbury, *Perpetua's Passion: The Death and Memory of a Young Roman Woman*. New York: Routledge, 1997, p. 83.

2. Salisbury, pp. 90–91.

3. Elias Canetti, *Notes from Hampstead: The Writer's Notes: 1954–1971*, trans. John Hargraves. New York: Farrar, Straus and Giroux, 1998, p. 13.

4. Marguerite Yourcenar, *Reflections on the Composition of Memoirs of Hadrian*. New York: Farrar, Strauss and Giroux, 2005, p. 320.

5. Yourcenar, p. 323.

6. Yourcenar, p. 324.

7. Yourcenar, p. 325.

8. Yourcenar, p. 330.

9. Yourcenar, p. 340.

10. Colin McCahon, *Survey Exhibition* 1972, p. 28. Cited in *Colin McCahon: Gates and Journeys*. Auckland, New Zealand: Auckland City Art Gallery, 1988, p. 78.

11. Though many would agree that the art of Michelangelo Buonarroti "tends to obliterate everything in its vicinity," Pope Paul IV threatened to destroy the *Last Judgment* in the Sistine Chapel because it was indecent, and for much of the seventeenth and eighteenth centuries Michelangelo's work was criticized for its coarseness and incompleteness. James Hall. *Michelangelo and the Invention of the Human Body*. New York: Farrar, Straus and Giroux, 2005, p. xv.

12. Alison Leitch, "The Life of Marble: The Experience and Meaning of Work in the Marble Quarries of Carrara," *Australian Journal of Anthropology* 7(3), 235–257, 1996.

13. Leitch, p. 242.

14. Leitch, p. 242.

15. Hall, p. 233. Henry Moore makes a similar point, speaking of a contrast between opposites—"like the rough and the smooth, the old and the new, the spiritual and the anatomical." Cited in Hall, p. 232.

CHAPTER TWENTY-SEVEN

1. I have drawn details about George Johnston's childhood, youth, and early married life from his autobiographical novel, *My Brother Jack,* though corroborated many of these details by consulting Garry Kinnane's *George Johnston: A Biography.* Harmondsworth, United Kingdom: Penguin, 1989.

2. George Johnston, *My Brother Jack.* North Ryde, Sydney: Collins Angus and Robertson, 1990, p. 9.

3. Johnston, pp. 29–30.

4. Johnston, p. 233.

5. Johnston, p. 239. It should be noted that in these details Johnston's real life and the life of his fictional alter ego diverge radically. "While there was certainly a contrast in personality between George and Elsie [his first wife], there was at this stage no great conflict of values between them of a kind that would foreshadow a breakdown in the marriage." Johnston did plant sugar-gums in front of the house he and Elsie rented, but Elsie was pleased, not outraged. Kinnane, p. 33.

6. Johnston, p. 278.

7. Theodor Adorno, *Minima Moralia: Reflections from Damaged Life,* trans. E.F.N. Jephcott. London: Verso, 1974, p. 50.

8. Philip Conisbee and Denis Coutagne, *Cézanne in Provence.* Washington, DC: National Gallery of Art, in association with Yale University Press, New Haven, CT, 2006, p. 159.

9. *Plans,* or "animated planes" was Rodin's expression, adopted by Cézanne.

10. Zola's exact description: he had "un comportement amoureux plûtot passif que conquérant." Cited in Ruth Butler, *Hidden in the Shadow of the Master: The Model-Wives of Cézanne, Monet, and Rodin.* New Haven, CT: Yale University Press, 2008, p. 56.

11. Paul Cézanne, *Letters,* ed. John Rewald, trans. Seymour Hacker. New York: Hacker Art Books, 1984), 215. Cited in Butler, p. 56.

12. Conisbee and Coutagne, p. 150.

13. John Keats, *The Letters of John Keats 1814–1821, vol. 1,* ed. H.E. Rollins. Cambridge, United Kingdom: Cambridge University Press, 1958, p. 193.

14. Rainer Maria Rilke, *Letters on Cézanne,* ed. Clara Rilke. New York: Fromm International, 1985.

15. Maurice Merleau-Ponty, "Le Doute de Cézanne," *Fontaine,* 47, December 1945. Cited in *Sense and Non-Sense,* trans. Hubert L. Dreyfus and Patricia Allen Dreyfus. Evanston, IL: Northwestern University Press, 1964, p. 17.

16. Butler, p. 53.

17. Émile Zola, *The Masterpiece,* trans. Thomas Walton. New York: Macmillan, 1959, pp. 350–352.

18. Nancy Huntting, "How Can We Be Composed? Bruegel's *Hunters in the Snow.*" Available at http://www.nancyhuntting.net/Bruegel-Talk.html

19. Long attributed to Pieter Bruegel, *The Fall of Icarus* is probably a copy of a lost original.

20. R.C.C. Temple, "Pieter Bruegel the Elder and Esoteric Tradition," Ph.D. thesis. The Prince's School of Traditional Arts, University of Wales, 2006, p. 22.

21. (*Multa pinxit quae pingi non possunt.*) Cited in Temple, p. 263.

22. Michel de Certeau, *The Mystic Fable, vol. 1 The Sixteenth and Seventeenth Centuries,* trans. M.B. Smith. Chicago: University of Chicago Press, 1992, p. 51.

de Certeau, p. 65.

23. Temple, p. 243.

24. de Certeau, pp. 50–51, 66, 67, 69.

25. Keats, op. cit, p. 193.

ACKNOWLEDGMENTS

Sincere thanks are due to Barbara Larson, commissioning editor, Longacre Press, Dunedin, New Zealand, for permission to reprint excerpts from *The Accidental Anthropologist* (Longacre Press, 2006), pages 129–139, 155–160, 200–208, and to *Common Knowledge* 19.1 (Winter 2013) where sections of chapter 27 first appeared.